# Canada Among Nations 2013

· · · · · · · · · · · · · · · · · · · · · · · · · · · · · · ·

# Canada Among Nations 2013

## CANADA-AFRICA RELATIONS
Looking Back, Looking Ahead

Edited by Rohinton Medhora and Yiagadeesen Samy

Published by The Centre for International Governance Innovation
in partnership with the Norman Paterson School of International Affairs,
Carleton University.

ISBN 978-0-9867077-4-2 (paper)
ISBN 978-0-9867077-5-9 (ebook)

The Centre for International Governance Innovation and Carleton University gratefully acknowledge and thank the International Development Research Centre for its financial support of this publication.

Published by The Centre for International Governance Innovation in partnership with the Norman Paterson School of International Affairs, Carleton University.

Printed and bound in Canada.

Cover and page design by Steve Cross.

The Centre for International Governance Innovation
57 Erb Street West
Waterloo, ON Canada N2L 6C2

www.cigionline.org

# Contents

• • • • • • • • • • • • • • • • • • • • • • • • •

# Preface

## Rohinton Medhora and Dane Rowlands

• • • • • • • • • • • • • • • • • • •

This is the 27th edition of the Canada Among Nations series. While the series was conceived and developed at the Norman Paterson School of International Affairs (NPSIA) at Carleton University, it has, over the years, been produced in partnership with other Canadian institutions. This year sees the revival of the partnership between NPSIA and The Centre for International Governance innovation (CIGI), which was first forged for the 2005 edition. This partnership has been enhanced with the generous support of the International Development Research Centre (IDRC). This will be the first of three years in which NPSIA, CIGI and IDRC will work together on the series, and we all look forward to a productive and innovative collaboration.

Given the participating members of the consortium, it is not surprising that the topic for this edition focusses on a region where their mutual interests clearly intersect: Africa. But there is a deeper reason for this choice. The Foreword by the Right Honourable Paul Martin and the Introduction by the editors (Rohinton Medhora and Yiagadeesen Samy) highlight the timeliness (if not tardiness) of taking a closer look at Africa by Canadian researchers and policy makers. These chapters, and the Conclusion by Gerald Helleiner, describe the intersection of African and Canadian affairs and relations, and consider the future directions these relations may take. What emerges is the story of a continent where many (but not all) of its countries are poised to emerge from decades of frequent disappointment and neglect, with a new optimism that is creeping (sometimes even sweeping) across it. This nascent renaissance needs to be nurtured and accommodated. To maximize the benefits for Africans, and indeed for Canadians, our foreign policy must engage with Africa's states and citizens in more imaginative and sustained ways. The task for the authors in this year's volume of Canada Among Nations is to define what this new engagement should look like. Africa is not likely to become a Canadian foreign policy priority; few would argue that it should be. But the opposite of *priority* should not be *neglect*, benign or otherwise. A balanced and mutually beneficial partnership can be constructed with Africa just as Canada has done elsewhere, which we hope this volume demonstrates.

Canada Among Nations was established to explore different topics in order to shed light on how Canada's foreign policies are formed, to provide the analysis by which those policies can be improved and to strengthen Canada's research community around a particular theme. We at NPSIA and CIGI, with IDRC's generous support, look forward to working together in coming years to continue this tradition.

# Foreword

## The Right Honourable Paul Martin

• • • • • • • • • • • • • • • • • • • •

The global significance of Africa's growth over the past decade cannot be over estimated. As such, the 27th volume of Canada Among Nations explores our relationship with Sub-Saharan Africa at a pivotal time for the continent and for Canada. As Gerald Helleiner says in his concluding essay, "there is indeed a new Africa emerging, and Canada will have to respond to it." This volume, with both retrospective and prospective prisms, provides a stimulating discussion on the need for Canada to strengthen its historic and, unfortunately, now waning relationship with the continent whose track is increasingly one of progress.

Africa currently has a population of just under one billion. In 2030, it will have a population of 1.5 billion, equal to or more than the anticipated populations of China or India. Of even greater significance, at that time, Africa will also have the largest population of young people anywhere on the planet. Coupled with the entrepreneurial instincts easily witnessed in its rapidly growing cities, a growing technology revolution and significant advances in health, Africa has the potential to become tomorrow's engine of global growth, comparable to what China is today.

Although Canada is a wealthy country, our domestic market is simply too small to support our standard of living. If we are going to penetrate the new markets of the world, then we must do so when they need us, not just when we need them.

That said, age-old problems do not vanish because we wish them to. Economic growth does not necessarily lead to poverty alleviation. The struggle for human rights and good governance remains a struggle. It is here that the moral and economic reasons for reviewing the declining interest in Africa by some of Canada's "officialdom" become so urgent.

Canada's long history in Africa is peopled by many, such as Father Georges-Henri Lévesque, whose devotion to human development led the way for the countless Canadian non-governmental organizations now working throughout the continent. Our bilingual nature gives us a distinct advantage over other international actors in that we are deeply involved with both Anglophone and Francophone Africa. Our mining companies are there, as are the African graduates of Canadian universities. We must not throw all of this away.

The rise of Sub-Saharan Africa has been led by the expertise and confidence of its own people. Although often referred to as a single narrative, individual countries have taken their own unique paths at addressing their challenges. For example, Nigeria has empowered the private sector creating economic growth that will build upon itself; Ghana has overcome the "resource curse" by reinvesting oil revenues to improve its schools and hospitals; Senegal's civil society formed a coalition to help build a peaceful democratic transition in 2012; and Botswana is the textbook case for all developing countries.

Yet much remains to be done.

Five years ago, I co-chaired a High Level Panel responsible for submitting a report on a new strategic vision for the African Development Bank, the continent's most important financial institution. One of the conclusions we drew was the need, building on the base of its many regional groupings, to build an African common market and the infrastructure required to make it possible.

The issue is quite straightforward. Africa's small, fragmented and shallow markets offer no economies of scale and represent one of the most devastating consequences of colonialism. For example, although Rwanda and Saskatchewan are roughly equidistant from the ocean, Rwanda is landlocked while Saskatchewan has access to three oceans. The inability of so many African countries to achieve their export potential is surely an issue to be addressed. An even greater obstacle, however, is the inability of African countries to trade between themselves due to the lack of adequate rail and road infrastructure. Linking Africa's distant home markets to each other may not be a sufficient condition for economic growth, but it certainly is a necessary condition, as those of us who live in Canada's vast geography can testify.

Similarly, Africa needs a common energy policy. While the world remains focussed on its potential for oil exports, should domestic Africa not seek to develop its potential for hydroelectric power? The Congo River's partially developed Inga Dam is in a lamentable state due to civil conflict. If it were to be completed, it could electrify all of Sub-Saharan Africa and, surely if the will was there, the local benefits could go a long way towards bringing peace to the region. Hydroelectric power is an area where Canadians have unparalleled engineering and financial expertise. Eventually someone will take the lead. The question is will Canada be there?

The collection of essays contained in this volume provides the basis for an up-to-date and dispassionate analysis, with sections on the themes of foreign policy and diplomacy, security and conflict management, trade, investment and governance as well as development and health. The candid views found herein will, without doubt, further our understanding of the challenges and opportunities ahead — hopefully contributing to a long-term framework for a fruitful partnership between Africa and Canada.

Quite simply, Canada's relationship with Africa is too strong to let it wither. That is why this edition of Canada Among Nations is so timely. Its critical review of past, present and future policy should be read by all those who are interested in what Canada's world and Africa's world will look like 10 years from now.

# Acronyms

• • • • • • • • • • • • • • • • • • • • • • •

| | |
|---|---|
| ABC | Brazilian Cooperation Agency |
| ACBF | African Capacity Building Foundation |
| ADB | Asian Development Bank |
| AERC | African Economic Research Consortium |
| AfDB | African Development Bank |
| AfDF | African Development Fund |
| AGOA | African Growth and Opportunity Act |
| AHSI | Africa Health Systems Initiative |
| AIR | African Institute for Remittances |
| AMCOST | African Ministerial Council on Science and Technology |
| AMIS | AU Mission in Sudan |
| ANC | African National Congress |
| APCE | African Peacekeeping Centers of Excellence |
| APSA | African Peace and Security Architecture |
| ASF | African Standby Force |
| AU | African Union |
| AUC | African Union Commission |
| BRICS | Brazil, Russia, India, China and South Africa |
| CAHS | Canadian Academy of Health Sciences |
| CANADEM | Canada's Civilian Reserve |
| CCAfrica | Canadian Council on Africa |
| CCGHR | Canadian Coalition for Global Health Research |
| CCIC | Canadian Council for International Cooperation |
| CCSRC | Canadian Centre for the Study of Resource Conflict |
| CEWS | Continental Early Warning System |
| CF | Canadian Forces |
| CFA | Canada Fund for Africa |
| CFSP | Canadian Francophonie Scholarship Program |

| | |
|---|---|
| CGD | Center for Global Development |
| CHET | Centre for Higher Education Transformation |
| CIDA | Canadian International Development Agency |
| CIDP | Canadian International Development Platform |
| CIGI | The Centre for International Governance Innovation |
| CIHR | Canadian Institutes of Health Research |
| CIIED | Canadian International Institute for Extractives and Development |
| COHRED | Council on Health Research for Development |
| CPA | Comprehensive Peace Agreement |
| CSO | civil society organizations |
| CSR | corporate social responsibility |
| DDI | Diamond Development Initiative |
| DFAIT | Department of Foreign Affairs and International Trade |
| DFATD | Department of Foreign Affairs, Trade and Development |
| DFI | Development Finance Institution |
| DFID | Department for International Development (United Kingdom) |
| DRC | Democratic Republic of the Congo |
| ECOWAS | Economic Community of West African States |
| ED | executive director |
| EDC | Export Development Canada |
| EITI | Extractive Industries Transparency Initiative |
| ENHR | essential national health research |
| EVIPNet | Evidence-Informed Policy Network (WHO) |
| FDI | foreign direct investment |
| FIPA | Foreign Investment Protection Agreement |
| FIPPA | Foreign Investment Promotion and Protection Agreement |
| FOCAC | Forum on Africa-China Cooperation |
| G8 | Group of Eight |
| GBS | general budgetary support |
| GCC | Grand Challenges Canada |
| GHRI | Global Health Research Initiative |
| GPSF | Global Peace and Security Fund |
| HDI | Human Development Index |
| IADB | Inter-American Development Bank |
| ICMM | International Council on Mining and Metals |
| IDA | International Development Association |
| IDRC | International Development Research Centre |
| IFC | International Finance Corporation |
| IFIs | international financial institutions |
| IIAG | Ibrahim Index of African Governance |

| | |
|---|---|
| IMF | International Monetary Fund |
| INC | Industrial Cooperation Program |
| INGO | international non-governmental organization |
| IPEA | Institute of Applied Economic Research |
| KP | Kimberley Process |
| KPCS | Kimberley Process Certification Scheme |
| KT | knowledge translation |
| LDCs | least developed countries |
| LMICs | low- and middle-income countries |
| MAI | Market Access Initiative for Least Developed Countries |
| MDB | multilateral development bank |
| MDGs | Millennium Development Goals |
| MI | Muskoka Initiative |
| MIMAP | Micro Impacts of Macro and Adjustment Policies |
| MNCH | Maternal, Newborn and Child Health |
| MP | Member of Parliament |
| NATO | North Atlantic Treaty Organization |
| NEPAD | New Partnership for Africa's Development |
| NGO | non-governmental organization |
| NPSIA | Norman Paterson School of International Affairs |
| NPTCI | Nouveau PTCI |
| N-S | North-South |
| NTPs | non-traditional providers |
| OAU | Organisation of African Unity |
| ODA | official development assistance |
| ODI | Overseas Development Institute |
| OECD | Organisation for Economic Co-operation and Development |
| OECD DAC | OECD Development Assistance Committee |
| PAC | Partnership Africa Canada |
| PEP | Partnership for Economic Policy |
| PERPA | Political Economic Relations and Public Affairs |
| PSUs | Program Support Units |
| PTCI | Programme de troisième cycle interuniversitaire |
| R2P | Responsibility to Protect |
| RCMP | Royal Canadian Mounted Police |
| RDB | regional development bank |
| RMC | regional member countries |
| RPI | Réseau de recherche sur les politiques industrielles |
| RUF | Revolutionary United Front |
| SADC | South African Development Community |
| SAPs | Structural Adjustment Programs |

| | |
|---|---|
| SMEs | small- and medium-sized enterprises |
| SPLA | Southern People's Liberation Army |
| SSC | South-South cooperation |
| SSDC | South-South development cooperation |
| START | Stabilization and Reconstruction Task Force |
| TEHIP | Tanzania Essential Health Intervention Project |
| UNAMID | AU/UN hybrid operation in Darfur |
| UNCTAD | United Nations Conference on Trade and Development |
| UNECA | United Nations Economic Commission for Africa |
| UNDP | United Nations Development Programme |
| UNICEF | United Nations Children's Fund |
| UNITA | União Nacional para a Independência Total de Angola |
| UNMISS | UN Mission in the Republic of South Sudan |
| UPeace | University for Peace |
| WEF | World Economic Forum |
| WHO | World Health Organization |

# Introduction

## Rohinton Medhora and Yiagadeesen Samy

● ● ● ● ● ● ● ● ● ● ● ● ● ● ● ● ● ●

This, the 2013 edition of Canada Among Nations, is about Canada's relations with Sub-Saharan Africa, or Canada-Africa relations for short. It is a book that is untimely, but only in the sense that it is long overdue. It is timely because a new Africa (a narrative qualified further below) has emerged in the last decade. It is long overdue because Canada has never had a clear, coherent and overarching Africa policy. Writing about Canada's relations with Africa almost four decades ago, Robert O. Matthews (1975: 568) concludes his article by saying: "Canada's relations with Africa are thus neither wholly altruistic nor entirely self-seeking, though certain dimensions of these relations may approximate one end of the spectrum more closely than the other. For the most part, Canadian policies towards Africa reflect the ambivalent and often contradictory nature of Canadian interests." To be sure, "coherence" is seldom a feature of any country's relations with any other country, and scholars routinely decry its absence, while also recognizing that international relations are driven as much by long-term interests as they are by short-term exigencies. But Africa's marginal status in Canadian foreign policy is a fact, as is the paucity of systematic analyses of the range of Canada-Africa relations.

This lack of a coherent policy may have been true in the past, and it is perhaps not surprising given that Canada has been largely preoccupied with managing its relations with its largest trading partner, the United States, as a cornerstone of its foreign policy. But times have changed; both the United

States and several European economies have been struggling in the last few years, while emerging markets are likely to drive global growth once again this year. Geoffrey York (2012), in the first of a six-part series on Africa in *The Globe and Mail,* has recently argued that the rise of Africa will have important implications for Canada's aid policy, Canadian mining and energy companies, and Canadian manufacturers looking for future destinations for their goods. Many countries, most notably China, have already responded to the trend of "Africa rising" by increasing their presence in the region. In response to these trends, Canada needs clear guidance about its policy towards Africa and a thought-provoking discussion on what should define Canada-Africa relations in the coming years. The need to engage a rising Africa in an increasingly competitive environment is one of several themes that is discussed in this volume and was candidly debated during the authors' meeting in Waterloo, Ontario. Additionally, despite the dramatic political changes that have swept across North Africa and the Middle East in the last two years, including Canada's recent role in Libya, a conscious decision was made early on in the project to not include North African countries in the various chapters of this collection in order to strike the right balance between depth and breadth of analysis.

The objective of this current volume was thus to analyze the ebb and flow of Canada's engagement with Sub-Saharan Africa through different lenses over the past several decades by looking back and looking forward. The goal of the chapters in this book is to highlight both the opportunities and the difficulties that exist for Canada and Sub-Saharan Africa at a crucial moment in the latter's development, and at a time when the current Government of Canada is sometimes slowly, but always surely, reshaping many elements of Canada's foreign policy. To be fair, despite the lack of a comprehensive policy, Canada's relations with the countries of Sub-Saharan Africa have a long history, which was initially driven mostly by humanitarian and development assistance that aimed to help the newly independent countries of Africa. Even if very ad hoc and reactive, Canada's engagement, whether it was for developmental reasons, peacekeeping, nation building, democracy promotion or human rights, reflected familiar Canadian values. Commercial interests, although present, have never been a defining feature of that relationship. The influence that Canadian domestic politics, especially as it relates to Quebec and national identity questions, has had on Canada's engagement with both francophone and anglophone countries in Africa cannot be discounted. The collection of papers in this volume — written by academics, former government officials, as well as people from the non-governmental organization (NGO) and private sectors — cover a range of issues that have defined Canada-Africa relations under the following broad areas: security, peacekeeping, diplomacy and nation building; trade and investment (with special emphasis on the natural resource sector where Canadian firms are heavily invested, as well as corporate social responsibility); and development, health and research capacity. In the tradition of good academic scholarship, authors were encouraged to formulate their arguments clearly at the beginning of each chapter, to be critical and analytical, to take stock of what had been accomplished to date, and to offer their thoughts and recommendations going forward — no small feat given the severe time and space constraints that they faced.

## "AFRICA RISING" AND CANADA-AFRICA RELATIONS

The narrative about Africa has become more optimistic in recent years. Whereas famine, conflict, disease and poverty made headlines in the 1980s and 1990s, as well as in the early post-colonial years, the recent discourse (for example, in articles in both *The Economist* [2011a; 2011b] and by Alex Perry in *Time Magazine* [2012]) have been about "Africa rising" as a result of several factors. First, and foremost, is Africa's growth performance. Despite the 2007-2008 food crisis and the global financial crisis, a diverse group of countries that includes Angola, Chad, Ethiopia, Mozambique, Nigeria and Rwanda, have been among the fastest-growing economies in the world over the 2001–2010 period, and several African countries are projected to grow at more than six percent over the next few years. Due to deficiencies in standard household surveys of wealth, income and consumption, the accompanying increase in living standards might have been systematically and significantly understated (Young, 2012). Still, in spite of this impressive growth and living standards performance, the number of poor people in Sub-Saharan Africa — defined as those living on less than $1.25 day — has increased in absolute terms from 1999 to 2008; however, because the population of many African countries also increased, the head-count ratio (the number of poor people relative to population) fell by more than 10 percentage points (see Table 1).[1]

While the role of natural resources in fuelling the African boom is still much debated, according to a report by the McKinsey Global Institute, a decomposition of Africa's GDP growth from 2000 to 2008 shows that one-third was from the natural resources sector (due to the boom in commodity prices), while the rest came mostly from the manufacturing and service sectors; the main explanations for this growth acceleration "were improved political and macroeconomic stability and microeconomic reforms" (2010: 2).

### Table 1: Selected Indicators for Sub-Saharan Africa

| | 1960-69 | 1970-79 | 1980-89 | 1990-99 | 2000-09 | 2011 |
|---|---|---|---|---|---|---|
| GDP growth (%) | 4.65 | 4.07 | 2.14 | 2.10 | 4.59 | 4.72 |
| GDP per capita growth (%) | 2.11 | 1.29 | -0.69 | -0.56 | 2.02 | 2.13 |
| Exports of goods and services (% of GDP) | 24.48 | 25.82 | 26.92 | 27.20 | 32.70 | 33.57 |
| FDI, net inflows (% of GDP) | na | 0.90 | 0.51 | 1.40 | 3.16 | 3.19 |
| Infant mortality rate (per 1,000 live births) | 142.30 | 125.86 | 110.20 | 102.20 | 83.35 | 69.30 |
| | **1960** | **1970** | **1980** | **1990** | **2000** | **2010** |
| Life expectancy at birth (years) | 40.49 | 44.46 | 48.04 | 49.52 | 49.73 | 54.16 |
| Adult literacy rate (% of people ages 15 and above) | na | na | na | 53.23 | 57.41 | 62.59 |
| Human Development Index | na | na | 0.365 | 0.383 | 0.401 | 0.460 |
| | | | **1981** | **1990** | **1999** | **2008** |
| Head count (%), 2005 PPP* and $1.25/day PL* | na | na | 51.45 | 56.53 | 57.89 | 47.51 |

Note: Data from World Development Indicators (World Bank), except for Human Development Index (UN Development Programme) and Headcount (PovcalNet). *PPP indicates purchasing power parity; PL indicates the poverty line.

*The Economist* identified several promising signs for the "Africa rising" narrative: the emergence of a middle class; improvements in labour productivity; increases in trade and foreign direct investment (FDI) flows; declines in inflation, foreign debt and budget deficits; and a possible demographic dividend in the future (2011b). For example, FDI inflows to Sub-Saharan Africa increased from US$1.2 billion in 1990 to reach US$40.9 billion in 2011, representing a more than 33-fold increase (Figure 1). Over the same period, exports of goods and services as a percentage of GDP has increased by seven percentage points, and both exports and imports of goods and services have more than quadrupled since 2000.[2] Although there has been a slight improvement in recent years, Sub-Saharan Africa's share of world trade is very small,[3] and the same is true of FDI (discussed below). However, there has been a diversification of trade towards emerging markets and an increase in intra-regional trade in recent years (Sundaram, Schwank and van Arnim, 2011). We note in passing that although concerns about the quality and intent of foreign aid persist, per capita aid to Sub-Saharan Africa by the Organisation for Economic Co-operation and Development's Development Assistance Committee (OECD DAC) donors more than doubled from 2000 to 2010; net aid received by the region has been on an upward trend since 2000 and exceeded US$40 billion in the past few years.

In addition to the drivers of growth identified by the McKinsey Global Institute report, *The Economist* also considered the application of technology (such as increased cell phone use, and improved health care as a result of more and better bed nets to fight malaria and reduced HIV-infection rates) as an important factor (2011b). And who can fault them for being so optimistic when per capita income shrank in Sub-Saharan Africa from 1980 to 2000, and when the number of civil wars was at its highest in the early 1990s.[4] A lot of progress has taken place on the political front as well. The wave of democratization that began in the mid-1980s has clearly transformed the continent in the last two decades. Governance has improved since 2000, according to the 2012 Ibrahim Index of African Governance (IIAG)[5] (Mo Ibrahim Foundation, 2012) and almost 60 percent of countries in Sub-Saharan Africa are now ranked as "free" or "partly free" by Freedom House (2013).

**Figure 1: Foreign Direct Investment in Sub-Saharan Africa, 1990–2011**

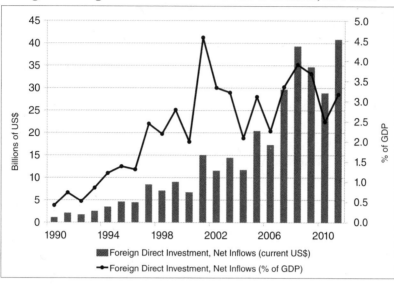

Source: World Development Indicators, World Bank.

Once one gets past the headlines, however, cautious optimism seems to be more appropriate. Simply put, much of the discourse and the numbers that are presented are about Africa in the aggregate and on average. As such, the aggregate numbers do not reflect the trajectory of every particular African country. Indeed, when one examines country-level data, a different picture emerges because of the considerable variation in performance across countries. Given the volatility in Africa's growth performance historically (Arbache and Page, 2007), it remains to be seen whether the kind of growth that has been observed in the last few years is sustainable over the long term. Achieving sustainable growth in Africa is important because prolonged economic expansion is necessary in order to achieve meaningful poverty reduction, as has been the case in East Asia (and China specifically).

The increase in FDI (Figure 1) is another example of how overall numbers can be misleading. In the African (and Sub-Saharan African) case, the share of world FDI when compared to other developing regions is very small and highly concentrated in the mining and extractive industries; its impact on broad-based development is highly questionable, to the extent that it does not lead to significant job creation, export diversification or even the transfer of technology (Sundaram, Schwank and van Arnim, 2011). More broadly, the question of the dominance of the raw materials sector in contemporary African development and policy remains a live one. The McKinsey results cited above thus sit at odds with the findings of other studies. There is a quite serious concern that the "renaissance" has not been accompanied by economic diversification or a significant strengthening of economic and political institutions (Ajakaiye and Afeikhena, forthcoming 2013); at the very least, the opportunities for exploiting the commodities boom to broaden and deepen development outcomes have not yet been adequately seized (Morris, Kaplinsky and Kaplan, 2012). The question of the sources and sustainability of Africa's growth remains an open one, for scholarship and for policy. It is worth noting that in the past few years, much of the discussion has focussed on the new phenomenon of South-South FDI, especially from China and India, in resource extraction as well as other sectors such as infrastructure and telecommunications.

When we examine data from the UN Development Programme's (UNDP) 2013 *Human Development Report*, we find that even though the average Human Development Index (HDI) score for the region has improved over time, the gap with other regions has also widened since the 1980s; the 10 worst performers on the HDI are all from Africa (UNDP, 2013: 151). The demographic dividend which the continent is expected to benefit from is not guaranteed unless economies are democratized to allow greater participation of citizens, and unless people are educated and jobs created for them. Concerning political stability and overall security, the current situation in Mali is a reminder of how quickly things can change. More generally, although the number of civil wars has declined to about half of what it was in the early 1990s, several countries remain in a precarious position. The top five countries[6] on the 2012 Failed States Index, which is an annual ranking of countries based on their levels of stability and capacity published by the Fund for Peace, are all from Sub-Saharan Africa (Fund for Peace, 2012). Several other Sub-Saharan African countries are in the top 20 and all of these fragile states will not meet most of the UN Millennium Development Goals. When one examines Freedom House data more carefully, the peak in the percentage of countries ranked "free" or "partly free" was reached in 2005, and since then has dropped by about 10 percentage points (Freedom House, 2013). According to the IIAG, countries such as Kenya, Nigeria and South

Africa have seen deteriorations in safety and rule of law, and participation and human rights, in the last six years (Mo Ibrahim Foundation, 2012).

In light of the above, the narrative of "Africa rising" or an "African renaissance" is one that deserves qualification, and we hope we have made a case for being more cautious when examining the evidence. But more importantly, how do Canada-Africa relations fit into all this? "Inconsistent," "episodic," "narrow," "disconnected" and "difficult" are some of the qualifiers used by the authors of this volume to describe Canada-Africa relations as it relates to development, trade and investment, nation building, post-conflict reconstruction and relationships with South Africa. A Canadian presence on the continent through trade and investment remains very limited today, even if there is a feeling that our initial engagement in Africa, which had to do with our "humane internationalism" as reflected in development, poverty reduction and promotion of human rights, has given way to a more commercial relationship. Less than one percent of Canada's exports go to Africa, while Canadian imports from Africa were about three percent in 2011, according to data from Industry Canada (Industry Canada, 2011). Likewise, Canadian direct investment to Africa was 0.5 percent of the total stock of investments abroad (Government of Canada, 2011). But, as suggested in the chapter by Schorr and Hitschfeld in this volume, this is perhaps an opportunity for the Canadian government to be more proactive and help the private sector develop more trade and investment relationships. The mining sector is an important part of Canada's investment abroad, and, after Latin America and the Caribbean, Africa was the second destination of Canadian mining assets abroad in 2009 and 2010. Canadian aid, which has been the subject of much criticism in recent years, is still an important component of Canada-Africa relations. Although eight African countries were dropped from the Canadian International Development Agency's (CIDA's) list of countries of focus in 2009 and seven African countries remained, Canadian aid to Sub-Saharan Africa continued to increase and was US$1.3 billion in 2011 after reaching an all-time high of US$1.4 billion in 2010 (OECD DAC, 2011). To the extent that aid is a proxy for our "humane internationalism," the data thus does not fully support the view that the latter is declining, notwithstanding the fact that our relationship with Africa seems to be more on a commercial basis as highlighted above. The trend going forward, and the nature of Canada's assistance to the continent, remains open to conjecture, and forms an abiding preoccupation in many of the chapters in this volume.

These elements — of change on the continent, change in the Canada-Africa relationship, tension in the Canadian response, and the need to forge a clearer sense of why we deal with Africa and how we do so — run throughout the chapters in this volume, and are reprised by Gerald Helleiner in the concluding essay.

We provide an overview of the different chapters in the next section.

## THE CHAPTERS

The chapters of this book on Canada-Africa relations are organized according to the following five broad themes: diplomacy and foreign policy; security and conflict management; trade, investment and governance; development and health; and research capacity.

In the first section on diplomacy and foreign policy, **David C. Elder** takes us through a rich tour of Canada's diplomatic engagement in Africa over the past century, focussing on how relations were established with countries of the Commonwealth as they became independent, as well as the establishment of relations with countries of French-speaking Africa and other countries, arguing that the latter was part of a less-structured process. Rather than an expression of the overarching conception of the role Canada should play in international affairs or based on an assessment of Canada-Africa relations, Elder argues that it was a combination of factors such as the geopolitical and security situation and relations with its allies, humanitarian factors, concerns for equity and social justice, development imperatives, and economic and commercial interests, that have shaped Canada's foreign policy towards Africa. Over time, other factors such as immigration to Canada and increased mobility of Canadians have become more important; however, as trade and investment promotion were prioritized, reporting on political matters declined and resources have been cut, especially on relations with Canada in countries of secondary accreditation. **David J. Hornsby** examines Canadian engagement with South Africa and argues that this relationship has declined in recent years, even if historically the two countries were quite close — for example, each country seems to be less important to one another when one examines aid and trade flows. However, given South Africa's regional importance, Hornsby argues that this relationship should be important to Canada as it attempts to engage with the region, because South Africa is still comparatively well-governed and democratic, an economic powerhouse on the subcontinent and a leader in many regional forums. According to Hornsby, this engagement could take place via areas of mutual interest that include a focus on regional economic development, international agricultural liberalization, regional security issues and democracy development. **David Carment, Milana Nikolko and Dacia Douhaibi** make the case for Canada to develop a diaspora policy that will both shield diaspora groups from being used instrumentally by the state and prevent the state from being captured by diaspora interests. Drawing on an analysis of two African diaspora communities (Sudan/South Sudan and Somalia) within Canada, they point out how these diaspora communities currently interact with their home countries, how they might affect policy in the future and how Canada could potentially leverage these communities to aid in its foreign policy and help stabilize and develop each respective diasporas' home country. In their view, Canada currently lacks a coherent diaspora policy, which is problematic because diaspora groups in Canada are rapidly growing and because such groups can have a large influence on Canada's foreign policy. In an examination of Canadian nation building in Africa, **Chris Brown** concludes this first section by arguing that the history of Canada's official engagement has been "episodic" and "inconsistent" over time and across countries. The episodic nature of Canada's foreign policy in Africa results from the fact that Canada lacks any core national interests in the subcontinent. After parsing the concept of nation building and reviewing 50 years of Canada's diplomatic engagement in Africa, Brown identifies a single consistent and common thread throughout Canada's decades of engagement — namely, that when and where Canada has engaged Africa, it has done so with an eye toward building the Canadian nation, with all the ambiguity that that concept might imply.

Under the second theme of security and conflict management, **Robert I. Rotberg's** chapter on state fragility in Africa compares and contrasts the features of strong and fragile African states and argues that poor governance, and poor leadership in particular, are the primary causes of state fragility in Africa. In his view, donors such as Canada should focus their efforts on building the leadership capacity of future African leaders, by, for example, holding leadership workshops that bring together carefully selected groups of likely persons of future influence, similar to the African Leadership Council in 2004. The next two chapters, by **Evan Hoffman** and **Edward Ansah Akuffo,** examine the issue of peace building. Hoffman argues that there are number of problems with the way that Canada currently approaches peace building. In particular, he criticizes Canada for spending too much on responding to humanitarian issues and not enough on peace building, shifting away from its traditional image as a mediator nation, and for focussing too selectively on individual countries when many issues are regional in nature. Hoffman makes this argument by looking at the peace-building opportunities Canada has taken and missed in recent years, which he then uses to suggest ways in which Canada can chart a way forward. He concludes by suggesting that Canada should become more transparent about its interests and goals, recognize the interdependence between peace building and economic growth, and spend more resources on peace-building activities. Using a constructivist framework, Akuffo argues that Canada's peace and security efforts in Africa have been primarily driven by efforts to maintain its identity as moral actor, which has prevented it from developing a long-term strategy to promote Canada's national interests. Such an approach is not sufficient to ensure its continued importance in Africa during the current period of dynamic African growth, and Canada will need to back its moral identity with substantial, long-term support of the African Union's efforts to promote peace, stability and development.

**Victoria Schorr and Paul Hitschfeld** open the section on trade, investment and governance by arguing that the attention of Canadian businesses has not kept pace with the growth rates of a "rising Africa," which in their view might increase even further if Africa can harness its demographic dividend. However, they also recognize that Canada-Africa trade numbers are relatively very low for the following two reasons: first, government programs such as foreign investment and protection agreements and Market Access Initiatives for Least Developed Countries have not gotten a lot of traction in African markets; and second, Canada and Africa have a lot of commonality in some export lines, such as natural resources, so trade between Canada and Africa in these areas is unlikely. The authors conclude by considering what can be done to increase trade and economic interaction between Canada and Africa. They argue that Canada should engage more with African countries, and it also needs to address the erroneous perception among Canadian business and investors that Africa does not present a wealth of opportunities for Canadian companies. In the following chapter on mining codes in Africa, **Hany Besada and Philip Martin** focus on four stages or "generations" of regulation and deregulation. In particular, they highlight that an initial period of liberalization and deregulation has, over the past decade or so, given way to an increase in self-regulation via the emergence of corporate social responsibility principles that now guide the extractive industries. The authors highlight that while there are some good things to come from the newest round of "industry self-regulation," it is not as effective because host states lack the capacity to enforce standards onto companies. They then describe some of the activity of Canadian mining companies in Africa and point out that Canada's current approach to the extractive industry sector is a combination of public and private collaboration, which aims to allow the extractive sector to operate while also ensuring that the economic activity of the miners contributes to economic growth in the host country. Lastly, and echoing the previous chapter, they describe the growing importance of the BRICS (Brazil, Russia, India, China and South Africa) countries in the extractive industry in Africa. They note that more mining companies results in more competition for contracts, which can provide African states with more leverage to get development enhancing deals. However, they also note that much of the involvement of BRICS companies in African countries takes the form of "land grabs" or is perceived as unaccountable by locals. The authors conclude that Canada needs to focus on promoting transparent and accountable mining contracts, and call for a "re-imaging" of current legal codes and "refocussing" of efforts for promoting broad-based economic development through natural resources.

 **Ian Smillie's** chapter focusses on the specific case of global governance of conflict diamonds through the Kimberley Process. After reviewing the history of diamonds and their connection to conflict in Angola, Sierra Leone and Liberia, and pointing out how the brutal conflicts in these countries were exacerbated by the presence of alluvial diamonds, he outlines the positive role that Canada has played, both via non-governmental organizations (NGOs) such as the Partnership Africa Canada and at the United Nations, in identifying the link between conflict and diamonds. Smillie also outlines the positive role that Canada played in the Kimberley Process, which restricted reconstruction and peace building, relative to shorter-term humanitarian assistance. The authors lament the fact that a once "collaborative, responsive and flexible" relationship has been damaged by the current government, and conclude that it is high time that Canadian and African CSOs meet and discuss how best to respond to the shifting environment in which CSOs now operate. **Bruce Montador** examines Canada's relationship with the African Development Bank (AfDB), arguing that it played an important role through its above-average contributions, especially during the recent financial crisis, and its role as an "honest broker." He points out that the AfDB is in turn an important multilateral partner for Canada, because the bank's continent-wide coverage allows Canada to demonstrate its continued commitment to all of Africa, despite the increasingly focussed nature of its bilateral aid. Montador concludes by highlighting a number of areas in which Canada could continue to advance its role on the AfDB, such as encouraging more participation from emerging donors, stressing the need for regional integration, and helping countries develop the regulatory framework to deal with resource boom-and-bust cycles. In the view of the author, Canada could do more by building on past contributions and current common interests, and such a re-engagement would be timely given a renewed interest in Africa's economic prospects. This would make up for the political engagement that several contributors to this volume have noted as lacking. **David R. Black** examines the Muskoka Initiative (MI), which focussed on promoting maternal, newborn and child health, with most of the funding designated for Africa. Black argues that the MI "needs to be understood, in part, as an effort to refresh and recast the ethical identity of the (Conservative-led) Canadian state, and that it was indeed a 'good initiative.'" However, despite being an admirable undertaking, it was compromised by the secretive and controversial process by which it was implemented, by the government's inability to clearly articulate and analyze the gender dimensions of the initiative, and by the disconnect between its goals and the way in which Canada has actually focussed its aid. In Black's view, such weaknesses echo the ongoing failure of Canadian policies in Africa, in particular, as they relate to global health. This finding provides a nice segue to the next chapter by **Dr. Victor Neufeld**, whose central argument is that, despite modest improvements, Canada's efforts to promote health research in Africa are still hindered by a number of problems, such as fragmented investments, imbalanced research partnerships and the need for better knowledge translation. Dr. Neufeld reviews several Canadian health research initiatives since 2000, and argues that Canada's footprint is very small when compared to other high-income countries. He concludes that Canada needs to better align its health research investments with the priorities of its African partners, ensure that asymmetries between nations do not become barriers to collaboration, and work to translate discoveries into practical outcomes. He specifically makes a case for the continuing support of the International Development Research Centre (IDRC) and the Canadian francophone health research community.

In the final section on research capacity, **John Cockburn and Diéry Seck** argue that past engagement between Canada and francophone countries has led to an increase in human capacity in many African countries, but that recent cuts endanger the gains that have been made. Focussing on the efforts of the IDRC, they describe how Canada's assistance has helped develop capacity in francophone countries through grant funding, an emphasis on socio-economic elements of development, graduate training and a pooling or networking of research talent. Their conclusion is that Canadian efforts have been too diffuse and should thus be more focussed in order to be effective. They propose that Canada renew its commitment to research focussed on socio-economic policy in francophone Africa, focus on tertiary school and graduate training, and more thoroughly incorporate local expertise into development initiatives. **Jeffrey C. Fine and Peter Szyszlo** review three elements of academic links between Canada and Africa, namely doctoral education, research and institutional capacity building. Focussing on the first two elements exclusively, they note that there is a rapidly growing demand for post-secondary education in Africa, but that resources and capacity to meet that demand are lacking. Furthermore, although collaborations with Africa used to play a larger relative role, they argue that there is now more interest to establish partnerships with China, India and even Latin America. They suggest by way of recommendations that the linkages between Africa and Canada should be recast as something other than development assistance and that the engagements should be done as equals. Additionally, Canadian funding institutions should provide "global bonus" grants to help maintain and develop more linkages between Africa and Canada.

In the concluding chapter of this book, **Gerald Helleiner** notes that more than ever there is a need for policy-relevant research by Africans and Canadians on Canada-Africa relationships and that "open criticism be encouraged and welcomed." Recognizing the "enormous diversity of African experience," Helleiner outlines four major themes from the above chapters. First, Africa is changing, and while problems persist, there is a considerable amount of evidence to suggest that there is a "new Africa" emerging, one that will be richer and more assertive than before. Second, Canada-Africa relations are also changing and, increasingly, Africa has become assertive and vocal about what it wants from this relationship. Given the changing nature of the relationship from one that was traditionally dominated by development imperatives to the now growing role of commercial opportunities and the private sector, new policy and institutional instruments will be required. Third, Helleiner points out that there are tensions in how Canada is responding to a "new Africa," especially as they relate to policies of CIDA; in particular, when the interests of African states and Canada conflict, whose interests are to be prioritized? Existing policies are "inconsistent and confused" and more clarity of where we stand is needed. Fourth, and more generally, Helleiner summarizes that Canada needs a coherent strategy towards Africa. The incoherent nature of Canada's foreign policy towards Africa has limited its influence and effectiveness in African countries and Canada-Africa relations would benefit from a "transparent and predictable road map."

Just as the manuscript for this volume was being finalized, the Government of Canada announced in its annual budget the amalgamation of CIDA into the now renamed Department of Foreign Affairs, Trade and Development (DFATD). Several of the chapters in this volume assess the implications of this move on specific aspects of the Canada-Africa relationship. By definition, it is early days to do anything but speculate. We are clear, as are many of the authors in this volume, that Canada's engagement with Africa goes well beyond aid, and that a policy that strikes a balance between the various imperatives — poverty alleviation, trade, security, democratization — while recognizing changes on the continent itself, is in order. At the broadest possible level, the amalgamation appears to point in the same direction. But whether policy "coherence" follows the organizational change, and indeed whether it is a "coherence" wherein the aid/poverty agenda is entirely subsumed in an economic or ideological imperative is unknown.

Lost in the multitude of analyses of the disappearance of CIDA into DFATD is the wider question of how Canada engages with the developing and formerly developing world. This world, Africa very much included, still contains multitudes of poor, is making advances on the democracy and good governance fronts, and increasingly has the means, financial and intellectual, to address its own challenges. We trust this volume accurately portrays the profound transition underway in Africa currently, and provides the basis for a sound discussion on policy and scholarship on how best the Canada-Africa relationship might evolve.

## Acknowledgements

We would like to thank Kevin Arthur for managing this project, Lauren Amundsen for organizing the authors' meeting in Waterloo and Carol Bonnett for ensuring the design and production of this book in a timely manner. We also thank Aaron Aitken and Eric Jardine, both graduate students at the Norman Paterson School of International Affairs, and Sharon Kennedy, a graduate student at the University of Waterloo, for their excellent research assistance. We are grateful for the financial support of Carleton University, The Centre for International Governance Innovation and IDRC. Last, but certainly not least, we thank all the contributors to this volume, and the external reviewers, for all their hard work in meeting our tight deadlines, and ensuring the delivery of manuscripts of high quality.

## ENDNOTES

[1]   Using data on PovcalNet, the World Bank's online poverty analysis tool.

[2]   Using data from the World Development Indicators, World Bank.

[3]   It is 2.4 percent of world merchandise exports in 2011, according to the UN Conference on Trade and Development statistics database, available at www.unctad.org.

[4]   This is based on the Armed Conflict Database from the Uppsala Conflict Data Program and the Peace Research Institute of Oslo. Armed conflicts are coded using a low threshold of 25 battle-related deaths per year.

[5]   For more information, please see IIAG (2012), *Ibrahim Index of African Governance: Data Report,* Mo Ibrahim Foundation, available at: www.moibrahimfoundation.org/downloads/2012-IIAG-data-report.pdf.

[6] They are Somalia, the Democratic Republic of the Congo, Sudan, Chad (a high-growth performer) and Zimbabwe, respectively. Although South Sudan was not ranked because of incomplete data, it would have ranked in the fourth position.

## WORKS CITED

Ajakaiye, Olu and Jerome Afeikhena (forthcoming 2013). "Economic Development — the Experience of Sub-Saharan Africa." In *International Development: Ideas, Experience and Prospects,* edited by Bruce Currie-Alder et al. Oxford: Oxford University Press.

Arbache, Jorge and John Page (2007). "More Growth or Fewer Collapses? A New Look at Long-Run Growth in Sub-Saharan Africa." Policy Research Working Paper 4384. Washington, DC: World Bank.

Freedom House (2013). *Freedom in the World 2013: Democratic Breakthroughs in the Balance.*

Fund for Peace (2012). "The Failed States Index." Available at: http://ffp. statesindex.org/rankings-2012-sortable.

Government of Canada (2011). "Overview of Canada's Investment Performance." In *Canada's State of Trade: Trade and Investment Update 2012.*

Industry Canada (2011). "Trade Data Online (TDO)." Available at: www.ic.gc.ca/eic/site/tdo-dcd.nsf/eng/Home?OpenDocument#tag.

Matthews, Robert O. (1975). "Canada's Relations with Africa." *International Journal* 30, no. 3: 536–568.

McKinsey Global Institute (2010). "Lions on the Move: The Progress and Potential of African Economies." June.

Mo Ibrahim Foundation (2012). "2012 Ibrahim Index of African Governance." October.

Morris, Mike, Raphael Kaplinsky and David Kaplan (2012). *One Thing Leads to Another: Promoting Industrialisation by Making the Most of the Commodities Boom in Sub-Saharan Africa.* Available at: http://tinyurl.com/CommoditiesBook.

OECD DAC (2011). *Statistics on Resource Flows to Developing Countries: Development Co-operation Directorate: February 2011.* OECD DAC. Available at: www.oecd.org/investment/stats/47137659.pdf.

Perry, Alex (2012). "Africa Rising." *Time Magazine* 180, no. 23.

Sundaram, Jomo Kwame, Oliver Schwank and Rudiger van Arnim (2011). "Globalization and Development in Sub-Saharan Africa." DESA Working Paper No. 102, February.

The Economist (2011a). "The Hopeful Continent: Africa Rising." December 3.

——— (2011b). "Africa's Hopeful Economies: The Sun Shines Bright." December 3.

UNDP (2013). "Summary: Human Development Report 2013: The Rise of the South: Human Progress in a Diverse World." New York: UNDP. Available at: http://hdr.undp.org/en/media/HDR2013_EN_Summary.pdf.

York, Geoffrey (2012). "Africa Next: With Investment Outpacing Aid, Is this a New Golden Age for the Poorest Continent?" *The Globe and Mail,* September 22.

Young, Alwyn (2012). "The African Growth Miracle." *Journal of Political Economy* 120, no. 4: 696–739.

# Part One:
# Diplomacy and Foreign Policy

· · · · · · · · · · · · · · · · · · · · · · · ·

# Canada's Diplomacy in Africa

David C. Elder

● ● ● ● ● ● ● ● ● ● ● ● ● ● ● ● ● ● ●

## INTRODUCTION

Canada now has diplomatic missions in 15 countries in Sub-Saharan Africa, with resident embassies in eight countries and high commissions in seven Commonwealth countries. Canada therefore relies on non-resident accreditation for its day-to-day relations with the 30 other countries in the region and has to depend on sporadic coverage through visits from the principal mission and contacts from a distance. While it has developed other forms of representation to deliver some government programs, including subordinate offices of its missions, program support units to assist with the development assistance programs, and honorary consulates to provide consular services, it has difficulty ensuring adequate presence and representation. The relatively small number of Canada's diplomatic missions in Africa,[1] with the consequent reliance on non-resident accreditation, and the limited financial and human resources devoted to its diplomatic representation hinder Canada's effectiveness in the traditional promotion and cultivation of Canada's political interests and its ability to pursue new priorities and interests in developing trade and investment, promoting security and stability and in advancing democratic governance. The emphasis on development assistance has meant that Canada is perceived as a donor country more than a political player or a commercial and financial partner. The amalgamation of the Department of Foreign Affairs and International Trade and the Canadian International Development Agency (CIDA), announced in the March 2013 Budget, will bring together under one institutional roof responsibility for most of the Canadian government policies and programs involving and affecting Africa. While it is not yet clear what internal structure the new department will have, the co-locating of units responsible for developing policy and delivering programs and services across Canada's diplomatic, security and consular relations, its trade and investment promotion activities, and its development assistance programs has the potential for attaining greater knowledge and understanding of Sub-Saharan Africa and the countries in it, for achieving greater coherence in Canada's policy approach and for providing for a coordinated and country-focussed approach to issues of diplomacy, development, defence and security, and trade and investment, thereby giving better guidance and direction to the missions in the region.

This chapter analyzes the evolution of Canada's representation in Africa, and how Canada organizes and mobilizes its limited resources to reflect political and policy choices regarding the priorities and the means to advance its interests, to respond to the imperative of development assistance, and to deliver on broad governmental objectives. For the purpose of its analysis, this chapter considers "diplomacy" in terms of this official engagement and governmental mobilization.


## THE FOUNDATIONS: COMMONWEALTH AFRICA

Canada's first official governmental representation on the African continent predates the establishment of the Department of External Affairs in 1909; the Department of Trade and Commerce set up, in 1902, the office of a full-time trade commissioner in Cape Town, then the capital of the Cape Colony. The office was established because Canada wanted to take advantage of the boom in gold and diamond mining. The first agent appointed to the office investigated the potential for an "increase of trade between the Dominion of Canada and South Africa" and, after visiting "all the principal places from Cape Town to Zanzibar," concluded that "nothing will succeed like a personal visit of principals or representatives of Canadian firms" (Hill, 1977: 52-53).

This was, perhaps, the first time a Canadian representative articulated the need for Canadians to become active in Africa.

South Africa was also the first country in Africa with which Canada established diplomatic relations; in 1939, following the declaration of World War II, Canada established a high commissioner's office in the Union of South Africa, which at that time, like Canada, was a self-governing dominion within the British Empire. The high commission, building on the existing trade office, reflected Canada's relations within the Commonwealth, as Canada also set up offices in the other dominions — Australia, New Zealand and Ireland (Hilliker, 1990: 220). Thus, the "Commonwealth connection produced the first direct diplomatic contact with Africa as an incidental result" (Stigger, 1971: 245).

As the territories in Sub-Saharan Africa moved in the mid-1950s from the status of colonies or protectorates to independence, Canada's membership in the Commonwealth provided a structure in which Canada decided on its relations with, and representation in, the newly independent countries.

The first of the countries to come to independence was Ghana. Canada agreed, on the proposal of the United Kingdom, that Ghana should be admitted to the Commonwealth and, as it had done up to then in all Commonwealth countries, opened a high commission in Accra in October 1957. Commonwealth membership gave a structure and a process for Canada's relations, but it did not provide a policy rationale for the decisions of the Canadian government to establish diplomatic representation in Africa.

One of the few articulations of the reasons behind Canada's establishment of a diplomatic presence in Sub-Saharan Africa is a memorandum to the Minister of External Affairs, "Canadian Relations with an Awakening Africa," dated December 9, 1955, prepared in response to the announcement by the United Kingdom earlier that year on the independence of colonies in Africa (Donaghy, 1999: 747). The memorandum sets out the broad geopolitical considerations leading to the recommendation that Canada establish a mission in the independent Gold Coast, expressing concern that the Union of Soviet Socialist Republics would use decolonization as the opportunity to "propagandize, meddle and generally make trouble in the African area" (ibid.). On the basis of the geopolitical argument, the Department stresses the "necessity for the West to put forward some imaginative plan of aid and welfare for an emergent Africa, which may have the effect both of holding the line against Communism in Africa and removing from the West the taint of colonialism" (ibid.). It points out that "the symbolic importance of the Gold Coast as the first all-African negro independent nation to emerge from colonial status will not be lost on the rest of Africa, nor on the anti-colonial nations or the Soviet Union," and it will show that Canada supports "accepting Africans as full and equal members of the Commonwealth" (ibid.).

Very soon after the establishment of Canada's diplomatic representation, the Government of Ghana raised the issue of Canadian development assistance. The Canadian government responded positively to the request from Ghana, at least in part for the same political, strategic and developmental reasons that underlay the Colombo Plan[2] for assistance to Commonwealth South and South-East Asia, but with the realization that new models of cooperation would have to be developed for Africa. The evident link between diplomatic presence and development assistance would structure Canada's relations with virtually all of the countries of Africa.

The Secretary of State for External Affairs proposed to Cabinet on July 30, 1959, the opening of high commissions in Nigeria and the Federation of Rhodesia and Nyasaland, the next countries to become independent in the Commonwealth, because of "the growing importance of Africa and the Canadian interest in Commonwealth territories in the Continent" (Government of Canada, 1959). Cabinet agreed to send officers to Lagos ahead of independence to "lay the foundation for future operations" (ibid.); the Department[3] assigned a resident commissioner, who became high commissioner on Nigeria's independence in 1960. When Sierra Leone became independent within the Commonwealth in 1961, Canada did not open a resident high commission for the first time in a Commonwealth member country in Africa. The government accredited the high commissioner in Lagos on a non-resident basis. Henceforth, Canada would use multiple accreditation for its representation in Africa: Accra and Lagos became centres for Canadian representation in West Africa, being accredited on a non-resident basis to both Commonwealth and French-speaking countries.

In establishing high commissions in Commonwealth countries in East Africa, Canada followed a similar approach to that taken in West Africa. The Minister recommended to Cabinet in November 1961 that Canada establish an office of high commissioner in Dar-es-Salaam, Tanganyika (later Tanzania), pointing out, perhaps disingenuously, that "it had been the practice to establish missions in all new Commonwealth countries"; Cabinet agreed with the proposal (Government of Canada, 1961) and a high commission was established in Dar-es-Salaam in 1962, which became responsible on a non-resident basis for Uganda (Hilliker and Barry, 1995: 177).

Finally, in 1965, External Affairs brought forward, in consultation with the Department of Trade and Commerce and the External Aid Office, responsible for the delivery of Canada's official development assistance program, a comprehensive plan "to extend and strengthen" Canadian diplomatic representation in Africa over the next three years (Government of Canada, 1965). The document acknowledges that while "the continent was still undergoing rapid political change," Canada could not have missions in every country, but must make choices based on its interests (ibid.). Without defining the interests, Cabinet approved the plan and agreed to establish an Embassy in Addis Ababa, Ethiopia (opened in 1966) and the following year a mission in Nairobi, Kenya (ibid.). Kenya, which had become independent in 1964, had initially been covered from Dar-es-Salaam; the justification for opening a high commissioner's office in Nairobi in 1967 was the administration of Canada's aid program (Hilliker and Barry, 1995: 319-320).

The breakup of the Federation of Rhodesia and Nyasaland in 1963, and the Unilateral Declaration of Independence by the white minority government in Southern Rhodesia led to the decision to close the office of the trade commissioner in Salisbury (now Harare), opened in 1955, and put in place sanctions against Rhodesia. It was only in 1973 that Canada finally opened a resident high commission in Zambia, formerly Northern Rhodesia.

As other countries in Commonwealth Southern Africa came to independence, Canada used non-resident accreditation from South Africa, with the mission in Pretoria covering Botswana and Lesotho, which gained independence in 1966, and Swaziland, which became independent in 1968.

## THE FOUNDATIONS: FRENCH-SPEAKING COUNTRIES

Canada's diplomatic presence in Commonwealth Africa raised the question of diplomatic relations with other countries in Africa; the memorandum "Canadian Relations with an Awakening Africa" recognized that Canada should consider representation in French-speaking countries and would face pressures, both internationally and from within Canada, to extend similar status in Canada's representation and assistance to non-Commonwealth countries, and the arguments in geopolitical terms, in a Cold War context, were as valid. There was, however, no structure or process that guided Canada's policy with French-speaking Africa, which the Commonwealth connection provided.

In 1960, France granted independence en bloc to its African colonies, but Canada moved slowly to enter into diplomatic relations with the former French colonies.

Circumstances dictated that the first French-speaking country in which Canada established diplomatic representation was the Republic of the Congo, a former Belgian colony. It became independent on June 30, 1960, but fell into chaos. To bring the situation under control and oversee the withdrawal of the Belgian forces, the United Nations Security Council authorized military assistance through the Opération des Nations unies au Congo peacekeeping operation. Canada, having participated in every UN peacekeeping mission, agreed to send a large contingent of Canadian troops as part of the operation. The Congo became the country with the "most urgent need for representation" in Africa (Hilliker and Barry, 1995: 176). A trade office, established by the Department of Trade and Commerce in 1948, was converted by External Affairs to a Consulate General in August 1960, and then became an embassy in 1962, with responsibility for Rwanda from 1962 and for Burundi from 1969. A resident ambassador took office in 1965 (Hilliker and Barry, 1995: 320).

In 1962, the Department established an embassy in Yaoundé, Cameroon; the Minster had overruled the Department's recommendation to establish an embassy in Côte-d'Ivoire, preferring Cameroon, a bilingual country. The new embassy covered, on a non-resident basis, Gabon, Chad, the Central African Republic and the Republic of Congo (Congo-Brazzaville).

The other former French colonies were covered on a non-resident basis: the high commission in Nigeria received responsibility for Sénégal, Niger, and Dahomey (later Bénin), and the high commission in Ghana was assigned responsibility for Guinea and Upper Volta (later Burkina-Faso) in 1963, and later Côte d'Ivoire and Togo.

Finally, in 1966, Canada established a mission in French West Africa, opening an embassy in Dakar, Sénégal, which assumed responsibility for Guinea from Accra, as well as being accredited for the first time to Mali, which had become separate from Sénégal in 1960, and to Mauritania, independent the following year, and to The Gambia, which had become independent in the Commonwealth in 1965. It took a further three years before the Department established another resident mission in French-speaking Africa; in 1969, it opened an embassy in Abidjan, Côte-d'Ivoire, which immediately took up responsibility for Niger and Burkina-Faso, and in 1971, for Liberia.

## NEW FACTORS IN DEVELOPING DIPLOMATIC RELATIONS

By 1967, Canada's diplomatic representation in Sub-Saharan Africa had resident missions in Commonwealth capitals: Accra, Lagos, Dar-es-Salaam and Nairobi; as well as some in French-speaking capitals: Kinshasa (formerly Léopoldville), Yaoundé and Dakar; and in Addis Ababa, Ethiopia, as well as Pretoria, South Africa.

The Canadian government gave little attention to an overall policy toward Africa, but clearly the drivers of Canada's official representation were changing. The political situation in Canada, with Québec's greater interest in international affairs, influenced the federal government's participation in la Francophonie and the consequent articulation of foreign policy as "the extension abroad of national policies." The priority to the struggle for "social justice" against the white minority regimes, announced in *Foreign Policy for Canadians* "United Nations" booklet (Government of Canada, 1970a: 20), confirmed the role Canada would take in the Commonwealth and the United Nations in supporting the transition to majority rule in Zimbabwe, Namibia and South Africa. The need to manage increasing development assistance programs brought about changes in aid administration across Africa and led to regional programming to deal with the drought in large parts of Africa and particularly the Sahel region. With changes in Canada's immigration policy, Africa increasingly became a source of immigrants, and the government assigned additional official resources to deal with the flow. The government also enhanced its support for trade and investment as Africa's role in the world economy became more promising.

## FRANCOPHONIE

Canada's steps to develop a diplomatic presence in French-speaking Africa were, essentially, politically motivated. The government, faced by Québec's challenge to the federal pre-eminence in international affairs, strengthened its bilateral relations with individual countries and its role in multilateral cooperation, particularly within la Francophonie, to "improve its capacity to project a bilingual and bicultural foreign policy" (Donaghy, 2006:135).

The review of Canada's foreign policy, commissioned by Prime Minister Trudeau and published in 1970 as *Foreign Policy for Canadians* "International Defence" booklet (Government of Canada, 1970b), did not define a Canadian policy for Africa, but it reinforced the principle that foreign policy must be the "extension abroad of national policies" (ibid.). The principle applied to the "special sense of concern and responsibility in Canada for particular countries or areas of the developing world such as...the francophone countries of Africa, or the Commonwealth countries of...Africa" (ibid.: 18).

Canada made development assistance "the primary vehicle for enhancing official Canadian presence in the region. It proved to be an effective way of ensuring that francophone African governments understood Ottawa's position on external relations" (Morrison, 1998: 78). As Douglas Anglin said, Ottawa set out to "buy African goodwill with aid offers"; for him, this political choice represented "perhaps the most dramatic new direction in foreign policy ever undertaken by a Canadian government" (1983: 178).

Canada also worked to bring about the institutionalization of la Francophonie in Canadian foreign policy as an organization like the Commonwealth, in which it could engage with countries in Africa on international issues as well as those related to development.

## SOUTHERN AFRICA

The Canadian position opposing the white minority regimes in Southern Africa had a major effect on Canadian diplomacy. Prime Minister Diefenbaker had led the effort in 1961, at the Commonwealth Prime Ministers' Conference, in forcing South Africa out of the Commonwealth following its becoming a republic. Pursuant to Commonwealth and United Nations actions, Canada implemented sanctions against the white minority regime in Rhodesia.

Canada continued to take a lead role in international efforts in the 1970s to isolate South Africa and to pressure it to dismantle its apartheid system and promote the establishment of a multi-ethnic, multi-racial, democratic society. In December 1977, Canada decided to "phase out all government-sponsored, commercial-support activities in South Africa," and particularly to withdraw Canada's trade commissioners and close the trade offices in Johannesburg and Cape Town (Freeman, 1985). In 1980, the government abrogated the Commonwealth preferential trade treatment that South Africa had been benefitting from (ibid.: 122-123).

The government established a resident high commission in Zimbabwe as soon as it came to independence, following the process launched at the Lusaka Commonwealth Heads of Government Meeting in 1979.

Canada had also worked for Namibia's transition to independence, as a member of the Western Contact Group, formed in 1977, of foreign ministers who were then members of the United Nations Security Council (the United States, the United Kingdom, Canada, France and West Germany). Finally, with the agreement to implement the transition plan in 1989, Canada provided a Canadian Forces logistics unit and Royal Canadian Mounted Police (RCMP) officers to oversee the police operation during the election. On independence, Namibia joined the Commonwealth. Canada had little subsequent ongoing involvement; shortly after independence Canada closed the diplomatic mission it had opened in Windhoek.

Canada's diplomatic presence in Southern Africa changed after Nelson Mandela was elected by the National Assembly as South Africa's first black president, and a government of national unity was installed. When South Africa rejoined the Commonwealth in 1994, Canada's representation changed back to a high commission.

The role contemplated for the high commission in Harare, Zimbabwe, as the regional mission for Southern Africa, with responsibilities for Mozambique and Botswana, and later Angola, was compromised by Zimbabwe's political and economic instability. Pretoria consolidated activities such as the Citizenship and Immigration program and the trade development programs for Southern Africa, reopening the trade office in Johannesburg, closed since 1977. In addition, the government had opened an office in Maputo, Mozambique, in the late 1980s, to strengthen ties with the Frontline States[4]; in 1995, Mozambique joined the Commonwealth and, in 2004, the office was upgraded to a full high commission, which became responsible for relations with Malawi in 2008 and Swaziland in 2010.

## COOPERATION AND RESPONDING TO THE DROUGHT IN SAHEL

In the early 1970s, the severe drought in the Sahel brought about extreme famine and social dislocation. To manage Canada's response and to direct the enhanced development assistance effort, the Canadian government had to reorganize its representation. The embassies in Dakar, Sénégal, through its non-resident responsibility for Mali, and Abidjan, Côte-d'Ivoire, through its non-resident accreditation to Upper Volta (now Burkina Faso) and Niger, shared responsibility for the Sahel area.

The government decided, in 1972, to open offices of the embassy in Bamako, Mali, and in Ouagadougou and Niamey, Niger, and to consolidate in the embassy in Abidjan the oversight of the government's actions toward the Sahel. The offices of the embassy were headed by a senior Canadian International Development Agency (CIDA) officer, and their activities were restricted to the administration of Canada's aid programs and to liaison with officials of the host country on cooperation. The office heads became de facto the senior resident representatives of Canada in the country; host governments sought their views on the whole range of issues in the relationship, and visiting Canadians sought their consular assistance. With the pressure to provide more services, Bamako and Ouagadougou became full embassies in 1995, while Niamey remained an office of the embassy until 2012, when it was closed and Bamako was given responsibility.

## THE PRESENT SITUATION

Canada now has resident diplomatic missions in 15 of the 45 countries of Sub-Saharan Africa; there are resident embassies in Burkina Faso, Democratic Republic of Congo (Kinshasa), Côte d'Ivoire, Ethiopia, Mali, Sénégal, Sudan, Zimbabwe and resident high commissions in Cameroon, Ghana, Kenya, Mozambique, Nigeria, South Africa, Tanzania. All have multiple non-resident accreditations. Within constrained resources, Canada now interacts with the countries of Africa through a network of official representation ranging from full resident missions to non-resident accreditation, including offices particularly to support the delivery of official development assistance, trade offices and honorary consulates.

With many of the countries in Africa classified among low-income countries, Canada's relations have a very strong development assistance/cooperation dimension. Increasingly, other drivers — including economic development and promotion of trade and investment, considerations of security and defence, the increased mobility and travel of Canadians, and immigration to Canada — have become important, and the government functions that support these drivers have also found their expression in Canada's diplomatic representation.

The high commissions in Nairobi and Pretoria, and the embassy in Dakar are the largest Canadian missions in Sub-Saharan Africa and have strong regional roles; all three have the Department's programs of Political Economic Relations and Public Affairs (PERPA), Trade and Investment/Commercial Economic, consular services and the management of common services, and they deliver the development assistance program, and Citizenship and Immigration programs in the visa section, and serve as the base for the Canadian Forces Attachés of the Department of National Defence.

In addition, the mission in Nairobi provides a platform for several other government departments and agencies that deliver regional programs and services, including Public Safety and the Canada Border Services Agency. All three have multiple accreditation: the high commission in Nairobi is accredited to Kenya, Rwanda, Uganda, Burundi, Eritrea and Somalia, and serves as the Permanent Delegation of Canada to UN Environment Program and the UN Habitat Program and UN offices in Nairobi; the high commission in Pretoria covers South Africa, Lesotho, Namibia, Madagascar and Mauritius; and the embassy in Dakar is responsible for Senegal, Guinea, Guinea Bissau, The Gambia and Cape Verde.

The Canadian government has developed other forms of representation in countries where there is no resident Canadian mission, including offices of the embassy or, in Commonwealth countries, offices of the high commission, in four countries: Burundi, Rwanda, South Sudan and Zambia (there had formerly been a full diplomatic mission in Zambia). Often, in addition to the development assistance personnel supporting the aid program, an officer from the Department oversees other functions including political reporting and consular work.

The Department has developed a network of honorary consuls, who are local residents, often Canadians, or persons with ties to Canada, appointed by the Department in places where there is no resident mission. The mandate is limited to providing consular services, especially to travelling Canadians requiring assistance or needing emergency passport services; the honourary consul does not represent the Canadian government, but may support other government programs if authorized by the responsible mission.

Development assistance and cooperation have dominated Canada's relations with individual African countries, particularly those that are designated by CIDA as countries of focus. The dominant attention to aid in Canada's relations particularly with CIDA's countries of focus is magnified by the resources that Canada has on the ground; in addition to the development or technical cooperation sections, staffed with CIDA personnel, in Canada's diplomatic missions, CIDA has also established decentralized Program Support Units (PSUs), with locally engaged contract employees, to provide administrative and logistic support to the delivery of development programs, to improve management, control and accountability of its programming and to bring about enhanced local ownership. There are now 21 PSUs in Sub-Saharan Africa; they were established following the conclusion, in 1987, that a "significant transfer of planning and programming to the field would lead to a much more relevant assistance" (Morrison, 1998: 252-253).

The PSUs are managed under the development assistance budget as a bilateral project reporting to the head of the development assistance program and consist mainly of locally engaged personnel; the contracted providers vary from international organizations to private, commercial organizations and local individual consultants. While very important in their responsibilities providing administrative and logistical support to the development assistance program, the PSUs lead to an erroneous perception of official Canadian presence, confuse the responsibility of the head of mission for all Canadian government programs and contribute to a silo effect in Canadian representation.

The PSUs have a status and functions that are ambiguous.[5] They are not subject to Canadian government practices and rules, and they make clear in their public websites that they are not official agencies of the Canadian government. Yet, especially in countries where there is no official Canadian presence, they are easily taken for official representatives of the Canadian government. Although a memorandum of understanding between CIDA and Foreign Affairs and International Affairs had provided that heads of mission have authority for all mission operations, including development assistance, the PSUs with the large number of staff and often separate offices are perceived as having a separate and independent existence and as constituting an official presence, detracting from that of the diplomatic mission; the amalgamation will clarify the functions and the reporting relationship of the PSUs.

A major development over the past 15 years has been the significant increase in the support Canadian missions in Africa give to trade and investment promotion. Sub-Saharan Africa is one of the few regions of the world to have positive economic growth with 5.2 percent real GDP growth in 2011 and expectations of 5.3 percent in both 2012 and 2013, according to the International Monetary Fund (IMF) (2012: 2), and is increasingly seen as promising in terms of Canadian trade and investment partnership. The economies of Sub-Saharan Africa still represent a small percentage of total Canadian exports, but they have "posted strong growth in value of Canadian exports," increasing from $600 million in 2002 to $1.9 billion (Government of Canada, 2012b: 67).

Canadian firms have increased their investment in Sub-Saharan Africa, particularly in mining and extractive industries, where Canada is among the top countries of foreign investors.

Canada now has nine missions in Sub-Saharan Africa that have full-time, Canada-based trade commissioners to promote Canadian trade and investment: Yaoundé, Kinshasa, Abidjan, Addis Ababa, Accra, Nairobi, Dakar, Johannesburg (Canadian high commission trade office in South Africa), Lagos (deputy high commission in Nigeria), and full-time locally engaged trade officers in Ouagadougou, Bamako, Lusaka (office of the high commission) and Harare.

The delivery of programs for the Department of Citizenship and Immigration has also changed considerably. Africa has increasingly become a source of permanent resident immigrants. According to Statistics Canada, there were 29,000 immigrants from the continent of Africa in 2008 (11.7 percent of all immigrants to Canada), increasing to 33,400 in 2009 (13.2 percent). While many of these immigrants were not from Sub-Saharan Africa, there were increasing numbers of immigrants to Canada from Nigeria, Cameroon and the Demographic Republic of the Congo in recent years (Statistics Canada, 2011).

The citizens of all countries in Sub-Saharan Africa are subject to the visitor/ temporary resident visa regime. The visa sections in the Canadian missions in Pretoria, South Africa; Nairobi, Kenya; Dakar, Sénégal; and Accra, Ghana are responsible for delivering visa and immigration services on behalf of Citizenship and Immigration Canada. The present system has a particularly negative effect on residents of Africa; the complex approval process, combined with the limited geographic coverage of Canadian missions, makes very difficult travel from Africa to Canada for business or non-governmental purposes.

## CONCLUSION

Canada's diplomatic representation in Africa is characterized by a presence that is broad, but not deep. It has a limited number of diplomatic missions delivering a range of government programs in which development assistance predominates and often overshadows other programs and interests.

The Department has indicated in its 2011-2012 *Report on Plans and Priorities* (Government of Canada, 2011b: 19) that it is developing a "whole-of-government engagement strategy with Africa" directed toward "strengthening key bilateral and continental/regional relationships." This strategy provides an occasion to articulate an approach to Canada's relations with Sub-Saharan Africa based on an assessment of the full range of Canada's interests.

In recent reviews of its international activities and posts, such as the "Transformation Agenda,"[6] Sub-Saharan Africa has mainly seen reductions in Canadian diplomatic representation. The Department closed embassies in Guinea in 2005 and in Gabon in 2006, downgraded its high commission in Zambia to an office of the high commission, closed its offices in Malawi and Niger, and in September 2009, the consulate general in Cape Town, South Africa, the last vestige of Canada's first official presence on the continent.

Government program activities in diplomatic missions are under strain. The coverage of multiple countries presents problems particularly for political reporting under PERPA activity and for trade and investment development under the Commercial/Economic program. The non-resident status does not allow for in-depth country knowledge and relevant reporting. Both human and financial resources have been cut. Most posts have only one PERPA officer assigned to political relations, besides the Head of Mission, and there are insufficient funds for travel to countries of secondary accreditation. The trade and investment presence is limited to only nine countries.

A promising development, given the pressures on the resources allocated to diplomacy in Africa, is the opening, in 2011, in Juba, South Sudan, of the office of the Canadian embassy (Nairobi, Kenya), which complements the embassy in Khartoum, Sudan (opened in 2000); the office in South Sudan and the embassy in Sudan represent, on the ground, a coordinated approach and an effort to bring coherence to Canada's contribution to the international effort to bring a just and lasting peace to two countries, based on three pillars of activity — aid, diplomacy and security, and involving CIDA, the RCMP and National Defence under the Department's leadership.

The government's announcement in the March 2013 Budget of the amalgamation of Foreign Affairs and International Trade and CIDA will have significant consequences for Canada's relations with Africa and its diplomatic presence there. Given the economic status of the countries in the region, development assistance programs will remain a strong focus for Canada. However, the amalgamation provides an opportunity to integrate foreign policy, trade and development objectives, to reassess Canada's diplomatic missions and their operations, and to review how CIDA does business abroad, with a view to bringing about what the Budget calls an "enhanced alignment of our foreign, development, trade and commercial policies and programs (which) will allow the Government to have greater policy coherence on priority issues and will result in greater overall impact of our efforts."

While it is not yet clear what internal structure the new Department will have, the co-locating, within a single Department, of units responsible for developing policy and delivering programs and services across Canada's diplomatic, security and consular relations, its trade and investment promotion activities, and its development assistance programs will bring together all of the officials responsible for relations with the region. Such co-location has the potential for attaining greater knowledge and understanding of Sub-Saharan Africa and the countries in it, for achieving greater coherence in Canada's policy approach and for providing for a coordinated and country-focussed approach to issues of diplomacy, development, defence and security, and trade and investment, and thereby for giving better guidance and direction to the missions in the region. It will also provide the base for the new Department to reallocate the financial and human resources in various programs and units in the missions abroad, to support the coordinated approach.

The Organisation for Economic Co-operation and Development (OECD) has challenged Canada to consider how its development assistance contributes to other foreign policy goals: "While aid is recognised as an aspect of Canada's foreign policy, it has yet to be developed as an enabler to achieve long-term objectives, such as international security, stability and global prosperity." (OECD Development Assistance Committee [DAC], 2012: 23). The amalgamation has the potential for Canada to have a coordinated official presence in Sub-Saharan Africa that is able to build stronger relations with the countries of the region, taking advantage of aid as an enabler as the OECD recommends, and bringing to bear non-aid interventions and contributions to support their development.

## Author's Note

All views expressed in this chapter are my own, based on the sources cited and other public information; they do not reflect the views of the Government of Canada or any of its departments. I am grateful to my colleague, John Schram, for the comments he provided.

## ENDNOTES

[1]  By comparison (according to the websites of ministries of foreign affairs), the number of diplomatic missions in Sub-Saharan Africa is as follows: Germany 36; Italy 31; Brazil 29; Japan 25; Netherlands 18; Belgium and Korea 17; Sweden 16; Norway 15; Finland 8; and Australia 7 (with another embassy, its first in francophone Africa, planned in Dakar, Sénégal).

[2]  The Colombo Plan, instituted by seven Commonwealth nations — Australia, Britain, Canada, Ceylon, India, New Zealand and Pakistan — in 1950 as the Colombo Plan for Cooperative Economic Development in South and Southeast Asia, provided a regional framework in which

the developed members provided technical assistance to the developing countries in the region to support their economic and social development; Canada's participation in the Colombo Plan was justified initially by considerations of "Cold War security and support for the American-led Western alliance" and later by the conviction that "economic and social progress was essential to a durable peace" (Morrison, 1998: 12).

[3] This chapter uses the word "Department" to designate the Department of External Affairs or its successor Departments, the Department of External Affairs and International Trade, from 1982 to 1993, and after, the Department of Foreign Affairs and International Trade.

[4] "Frontline States" are countries bordering on, or in close proximity to, South Africa, including Angola, Botswana, Lesotho, Malawi, Mozambique, Swaziland, Tanzania, Zambia and from 1980, Zimbabwe. From the 1970s they formed a loose coalition coordinating their responses to apartheid and to its political, economic and social effects on them and their approaches to the liberation movements in Southern Africa.

[5] The 2012 OECD DAC review of Canada notes that CIDA is dealing with the administrative and legal issues of the status of the PSUs as the current "arrangement carries with it significant financial and legal risks as it is not fully compliant with the Government of Canada's Financial Administration Act and CIDA may be viewed as exceeding its authorities by creating perceived Government of Canada entities abroad" (OECD DAC, 2012: 16).

[6] The Department's Transformation Agenda, begun in 2008, was an initiative to review and "improve DFAIT operations through enhanced policy capacities, a reinforced network of missions abroad, improved financial management and accountability, and renewed human resources" (Government of Canada, 2011a: 6). See also Government of Canada, 2012a.

## WORKS CITED

Anglin, Douglas G. (1983). "Canada and Africa: The Trudeau Years." *Africa Contemporary Record (1983-84)*.

Donaghy, Greg (ed.) (1999). *Documents on Canadian External Relations Volume 22 1956-57.* Minister of Public Works and Government Services Canada. Available at: www.international.gc.ca/department/history-histoire/dcer/browse-en.asp.

Donaghy, Greg (2006). "There Are No Half-Countries: Canada, La Francophonie, and the Projection of Canadian Biculturalism, 1960–2002." In *Handbook of Canadian Foreign Policy,* edited by Patrick James, Nelson Michaud and Marc J. O'Reilly. Lexington.

Freeman, Linda (1985). "The Effect of the World Crisis on Canada's Involvement in Africa." *Studies in Political Economy* 17.

Government of Canada (1959). "Cabinet Conclusions (Summaries of discussions at the meetings of the Federal Cabinet — 'Cabinet Minutes')." July 30. Ottawa: Privy Council Office. Available at: www.collectionscanada.gc.ca/databases/conclusions/index-e.html.

——— (1961). "Cabinet Conclusions (Summaries of discussions at the meetings of the Federal Cabinet — 'Cabinet Minutes')." November 20. Ottawa: Privy Council Office. Available at: www.collectionscanada.gc.ca/databases/conclusions/index-e.html.

——— (1965). "Cabinet Conclusions (Summaries of discussions at the meetings of the Federal Cabinet — 'Cabinet Minutes')." August 18. Ottawa: Privy Council Office. Available at: www.collectionscanada.gc.ca/databases/conclusions/index-e.html.

——— (1970a). *Foreign Policy for Canadians.* United Nations booklet. Ottawa: Department of External Affairs.

——— (1970b). *Foreign Policy for Canadians.* International Development booklet. Ottawa: Department of External Affairs.

——— (2011a). *Foreign Affairs and International Trade Canada: Departmental Performance Report 2010-11.* Ottawa: Treasury Board. Available at: www.tbs-sct.gc.ca/dpr-rmr/2010-2011/inst/ext/ext-eng.pdf.

——— (2011b). *Foreign Affairs and International Trade Canada: Report on Plans and Priorities 2011-2012.* Ottawa: Treasury Board. Available at: www.tbs-sct.gc.ca/rpp/2011-2012/inst/ext/ext-eng.pdf.

———— (2012a). *Evaluation of the Transformation Agenda: Final Report.* Ottawa: Foreign Affairs and International Trade Canada.

———— (2012b). "Canada's State of Trade: Trade and Investment Update — 2012." Ottawa: Foreign Affairs and International Trade Canada.

Hill, O. Mary (1977). "Trade and Commerce Weekly Report." August 22, 1904, quoted in *Canada's Salesman to the World: The Department of Trade and Commerce.* Montreal: McGill-Queen's University Press.

Hilliker, John F. (1990). *Canada's Department of External Affairs: The Early Years, 1909–1946, Volume 1.* Montreal: McGill-Queen's University Press.

Hilliker, John F. and Donald D. Barry (1995). *Canada's Department of External Affairs: Coming of Age, 1946–1968, Volume 2.* Montreal: McGill-Queen's University Press.

IMF (2012). *Regional Economic Outlook: Sub-Saharan Africa — Sustaining Growth Amid Global Uncertainty.* Washington, DC: IMF.

Morrison, David R. (1998). *Aid and Ebb Tide: A History of CIDA and Canadian Development Assistance.* Waterloo: Wilfrid Laurier University Press.

OECD DAC (2012). *Canada — Peer Review.* Report by the OECD. Paris: OECD.

Statistics Canada (2011). *Report on the Demographic Situation in Canada Migration: International, 2009.*

Stigger, Philip (1971). "Canadian Diplomatic Service." In "A Study in Confusion: Canadian Diplomatic Staffing Practices in Africa and the Middle East." *Canadian Journal of African Studies* 5, no. 3: 241–262.

# Canada's (Dis)Engagement with South Africa

David J. Hornsby

● ● ● ● ● ● ● ● ● ● ● ● ● ● ● ● ● ● ●

## INTRODUCTION

The role of South Africa on the African continent cannot be ignored. South Africa wields substantial influence in Africa, often representing it in international settings and playing a direct role in building managerial and technical capacity for the continent's economic expansion. Indeed, there is a remarkable story of growth in Africa since 2000, which has excited the international community and changed attitudes towards the viability of doing business on the continent. With the exception of niche sectors such as the mining industry, this growth has escaped Canadian attention.

South Africa is an integral part of Africa's renaissance and, despite many critical reports focussing on its internal challenges or slowing growth rate, its economy is still the largest on the continent, the most diversified and stable, and likely to remain so for the foreseeable future. South Africa often adopts a leadership position within regional and international institutions, and is the only African country that is a member of the BRICS (Brazil, Russia, India, China, South Africa) group, the largest and most influential of the emerging economies. Given its status both globally and on the continent, Canada's engagement with Africa therefore requires a consideration of its relationship with South Africa.

On the surface, Canada and South Africa appear to be the closest of allies. In the immediate post-apartheid context, Canada has been an important bilateral and regional partner providing much needed developmental assistance and investment. The Constitution of South Africa was developed using the Canadian Charter of Human Rights and Freedoms as a template. In 2001, Canada bestowed honorary citizenship on Nelson Mandela — an honour given to only four other people in Canadian history. In 2003, President Thabo Mbeki signed a Joint Declaration of Intent in Ottawa, aimed at strengthening bilateral relations and cooperation. And in 2006, Canada's then-Governor General Michäelle Jean made a state visit to the "Rainbow Nation" to reaffirm ties.

Behind all of these displays of goodwill, however, these two countries often find each other on opposing sides of important international issues. The conflicts in Côte d'Ivoire, Libya, Sudan (and the International Criminal Court arrest warrant for Sudan's President Omar al-Bashir) and Syria, the political crisis in Zimbabwe and international efforts to achieve multilateral agreements on climate change are all indicative of the differing positions that each country appears to be taking. The story detailed here speaks of a relationship that once appeared to be strong, but is now disconnected and difficult.

In this chapter, I argue that the traditional mechanisms of Canadian foreign policy used to build strong bilateral relations, aid and trade are declining in relevance and no longer facilitating close bonds with South Africa. Allowing this relationship to continue to weaken threatens Canada's interests on the continent as a whole, given that South Africa is a critical actor in the region. Integral to Canada's engagement with South Africa is viewing it as an important partner for Canada, especially with respect to the themes covered in other parts of this volume.

## CANADA-SOUTH AFRICA RELATIONS: A STORY OF DECLINE

It is curious that Canada-South Africa relations are currently in a moment of unease, as many believe that both countries maintain close ties. Certainly, it would seem seared into the consciousness of both countries that Canada was a staunch supporter of the anti-apartheid movement and in the immediate post-1994 context following the elections and the return to democracy. Even if Canada's claim to the former is contested, and scholars have argued that Canada was late in the application of sanctions and maintained an active trade and investment relationship with the apartheid government (Keenleyside, 1983; Freeman, 1997; Fairweather, 2008), it is undeniable that the Mulroney government and Canadian civil society provided important support for the anti-apartheid movement. This was evident by the support given to anti-apartheid organizations, civil society and the alternative media inside South Africa, and exiled African National Congress (ANC) activists in neighbouring countries, through raising global awareness of the horrors of apartheid, not least through leadership in the Commonwealth, and by encouraging disinvestment campaigns. In addition, the Canadian government was a constructive partner throughout much of the 1990s. Canada is, therefore, still perceived positively by many in the region. Hornsby and Van Heerden (2013) argue that the present relationship has cooled largely because the traditional structures — development assistance and trade — on which the relationship was based, are no longer proving effective at bringing these two middle powers together. Such a context supports the idea that Canada needs to be focussing its Africa engagement strategy on long-term results, as discussed in Part Three: Trade, Investment and Governance.

## Development Assistance

With the return to democratic rule in South Africa, Canada was an important development partner, contributing over CDN$300 million in assistance that touched on a broad range of programs from constitutional development to gender equality initiatives to addressing HIV/AIDS (Government of Canada, 2012). In 2006, Canada and South Africa signed a General Agreement on Development Cooperation, which would focus Canada's contributions to areas identified by the South African government (Republic of South Africa, 2006). This mean that programming for HIV/AIDs, improving accountability among public institutions and funding for the African Development Bank (AfDB) all shared the just over CDN$11 million that Canada contributed in 2011.

Canada's development assistance to South Africa has, however, been on the decline as a proportion of its Sub-Saharan Africa official development assistance (ODA) since the early 2000s. Figure 1 compares Canadian ODA to South Africa as a percentage of Canadian contributions to Sub-Saharan Africa since 1993, which was just prior to the lifting of sanctions on South Africa. It can be seen that in 1994, Canadian ODA to South Africa rose dramatically as a proportion of the aid given to Sub-Saharan Africa, and even outpaced it. This situation underpins why there was such a close relationship during this period, as South Africa was a real focus for Canada. But since then, the trend suggests that the focus on South Africa has been steadily declining. In fact, 2004 marks a sharp decline in Canadian ODA to South Africa. The trend lines are telling, suggesting that as Canada has increased its assistance to Sub-Saharan Africa the share normally apportioned to South Africa decreased time and again.

**Figure 1: Canada ODA to South Africa as Percentage of ODA to Sub-Saharan Africa since 1993 (derived from constant US dollar)**

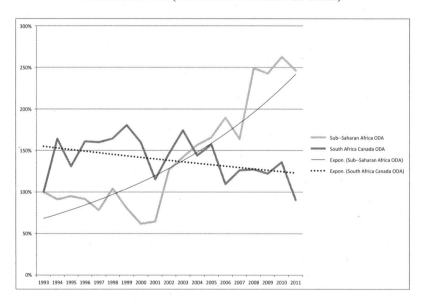

Source: Author, based on Organisation for Economic Co-operation and Development (OECD), 2012 data. Available at: http://stats.oecd.org/qwids/.

Additionally, the percentage of Canadian contributions to South Africa as a portion of global ODA into South Africa suggests a story of decline. During the 1990s, Canada's portion of ODA kept pace with percentage increases provided by other donors, but as Figure 2 highlights, in 2004 Canadian contributions diverged. It should be recognized that Canada has always been a small contributor to South Africa in real dollar terms, providing just over CDN$11 million of the approximate US$1.2 billion in ODA in 2011, but it maintained a targeted and impactful set of programs in the country throughout the 1990s and early 2000s. Canada's contribution to South Africa now pales in comparison to the assistance given by other middle-power states such as the Netherlands, Sweden and Norway (OECD, 2012; Black, 2012). In a sense, as the world increased its percentage contributions since 1993 to South Africa, Canada's ODA contribution has declined, as Figure 2 shows. This presents challenges for Canada's influence in South Africa and the region as a whole.

**Figure 2: Percent Changes in South African ODA Received in Total and from Canada since 1993 (derived from constant US dollar)**

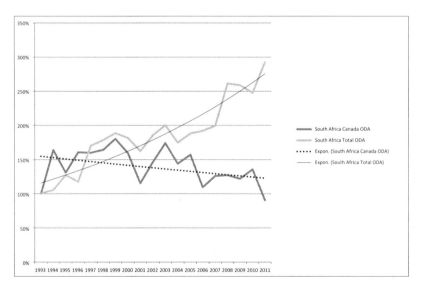

Source: Author, based on OECD, 2012 data. Available at: http://stats.oecd.org/qwids/.

Canada's diminished developmental role in South Africa is understandable if one assumes that South Africa's middle income and emerging donor status mean it no longer faces developmental challenges. Indeed, it is hard for Canadian officials to reconcile the notion of apportioning more aid to South Africa when it gives over US$363 million in aid, to such countries as Burundi, Sudan, Zimbabwe and the Democratic Republic of Congo (Braude, Thandrayan and Sidiropolous, 2008: 3) and aims to increase its foreign aid provision from 0.18 percent to 0.2–0.5 percent of GDP (ibid.). But crucial assistance is still required in addressing societal issues such as HIV/AIDS, structural issues that cause income inequality, and poor primary and secondary education, among other issues. For Canada, reducing its ODA support despite these challenges, and given the track record of past program successes, is unfortunate. What is also remarkable is that the reduction in ODA has not been offset with other political programming or regional initiatives. Canada's contribution to regional initiatives such as the AfDB has been declining,[1] commitments to supporting the New Partnership for Africa's Development (NEPAD) were never fully realized (Akuffo, 2012) and Canada's role in the South African Development Community (SADC) is virtually non-existent. When it comes to South Africa, the impression is that Canada has reduced its aid activities to a skeleton program and essentially walked away. It appears that nothing is happening to build on the goodwill established through Canada's past contributions and role in South Africa, which would ensure that Canada remains a partner in South Africa's development. This is also evident when looking to the Canada-South Africa investment and trade ties.

## Trade Relations

There would seem to be a basis for a compatible economic relationship between the two countries. Both are well endowed with natural resources and capacity for extraction, have strong financial services sectors and important automotive components. Despite this, the Canada-South Africa trade relationship appears to be in decline.

Since the end of sanctions in 1994, the trade relationship has grown between Canada and the "Rainbow Nation" in dollar terms. South Africa and Canada have always maintained consistent trade linkages despite a dip during the period of international sanctions on the apartheid government applied in the late 1980–1994 period. At the end of sanctions in 1993, trade picked up to a level that was "almost triple the average of the sanctions years" (Freeman, 1997: 303). This was the beginning of a positive trend between Canada and South Africa, which was reinforced when negotiations for a Foreign Investment Protection Agreement (FIPA) began.

An analysis of Canadian trade statistics notes that bilateral trade increased by CDN$500 million from 1992 to 1997, reaching a total value of CDN$800 million (Statistics Canada, 2012). While this was a positive trend, it would take another seven years, until 2004, for bilateral trade between the two countries to hit the CDN$1 billion mark. The rapid growth of the trade relationship was not sustained post-1997, with only an additional CDN$200 million in bilateral trade between 1997 and 2004. The fact that South Africa refused to ratify the FIPA in 1997 provides some explanation for this, but what is even more noteworthy is that the value of the relationship has changed little since that time. There was a peak in 2007 when bilateral trade reached just over CDN$1.8 billion, but this fell with the global recession of 2008 and has not fully recovered. While trade between the two countries appears to be growing, reaching the CDN$1.6 billion mark in 2011, if one considers the value of the relationship in relative terms, another story becomes apparent — Canada has not grown as an export destination for South Africa since 1994, immediately following sanctions being lifted.

As Martin Nicol (2012) notes, "0.6% of SA exports went to Canada in 1994 — the first year after sanctions were lifted, 0.7% in 2010, with 0.7% the average and median for the sixteen-year period. This means that Canada's position as an export market for South Africa slipped from 22nd in 1999 to 30th in 2010." If one looks back to the bilateral trade relationship in the 1970s, before sanctions and economic boycotts became an issue, Canada was the destination for 2.6 percent of total South African exports (Freeman, 1997: 92). This suggests that Canada, as an export destination for South Africa, was more important in the 1970s than in 2010 (Keenleyside, 1983: 449-450).

On the imports side, a story of declining importance in Canada-South Africa relations is also evident. In 1994, approximately 1.4 percent of South African imports came from Canada, but only 0.8 percent in 2010 (Nicol, 2012). This means that Canada's position, in terms of imports to South Africa, is declining as a trade partner, down to twenty-ninth in 2010 (ibid.). To Canada, South Africa is its third-largest trading partner on the continent, falling behind Nigeria and Angola (Government of Canada, 2012).

According to past and present Canadian diplomats, the apparent reasons for this decline seemingly fall to problems that arise in doing business in

South Africa. Three concerns are consistently mentioned: first, unease exists over the tripartite alliance between government and unions, as this suggests a bias in the business environment; second, the costs associated with setting up a business in South Africa remain difficult for foreign enterprises due to its heavy regulatory environment; and third, increasing reports of government corruption scare away many Canadian investors. On the South African side, however, the reasons for the decline are not readily apparent.

These concerns have created a context where the importance of South Africa as a market for Canadian investment and trade (and vice versa) has, and is, declining in relative value terms since 1994. This would suggest that an important binding element typically used in Canadian foreign policy is not present; therefore, Canada really must do more and be more imaginative in looking for ways to give substance to its South African ties.

## THE RELEVANCE OF SOUTH AFRICA

For a long time, South Africa represented a successful case for how democracy, diplomacy and reconciliation can be a legitimate alternative to civil conflict, resulting in prosperity. Recent reports, however, claim that South Africa is in decline and that much of the hope inspired by the peaceful transition into a multiracial democracy have just not transpired (*The Economist*, 2012).

There are many internal challenges that South Africa faces, including a growing economic inequality that is demarcated along racial lines. Challenges persist relating to service delivery, housing, and primary and secondary education. Protests and strikes often reach the headlines in the international press, leading many to believe the country is in constant deadlock or economic paralysis. The tripartite alliance between the ANC, Communist Party and the Congress of South African Trade Unions has resulted in the emergence of a de facto one-party state that many believe is arrogant, corrupt and disconnected from the realities facing the majority of South Africans.

All of these challenges are real and present. They pose serious questions about the direction of South Africa and deserve interrogation. But despite these issues, South Africa continues to be a leader — democratically, economically and in regional governance institutions on the African continent. This means that South Africa is an important part of politics on the continent and a good partner for Canada to have.

## Democracy in South Africa

South Africa maintains strong democratic institutions, including a progressive constitution that enshrines political and socio-economic rights, and provides for checks and balances on the power of the government (Misra-Dexter and February, 2010). The electoral system, judiciary, civil society and press are also important actors in South Africa, providing a space for dissent and challenge to government even in light of the strong legislative majority the ANC maintains.

In particular, civil society and the media in South Africa remain strong and influential in the politics of the country, effecting change through widespread mobilization and use of the rule of law. This is best characterized by the opposition to the Protection of State Information Bill (the so-called "Secrecy Bill"), which has received widespread criticism for curtailing transparency and free speech. Such activism has resulted in important changes to legislation, which many consider insufficient and a constitutional court challenge is being prepared (Nkosi, 2011; Right 2 Know, 2012).

Stories of corruption and nepotism appear to be rising in South Africa, which is a worrying trend. South Africa ranks seventh within the region for corruption and sixty-fourth globally, while perceived continental competitors such as Nigeria rank thirtieth regionally and one hundred and forty-third internationally (Transparency International, 2011). The media and civil society are taking a leadership role in ensuring corruption and nepotism do not go unnoticed, using the courts to this effect. Within the ANC, commitments have been made to stem corruption with the proposal to establish an integrity commissioner that will maintain widespread powers to dismiss public servants engaged in corrupt behaviour.

All of this suggests that while corruption and nepotism may call into question the democratic advances made since 1994 in South Africa, the country is far from becoming a failed state.

## South Africa Is Economically Relevant

South Africa remains the largest economy in Africa and continues to post growth rates. In 2011, South Africa's GDP sat at US$408 billion and grew a modest 3.2 percent (World Bank, 2012a; *Mail and Guardian*, 2012). While this is a slowdown from previous years, it still represents continued growth, which is particularly impressive given the global economic climate. This slower rate of growth is compared against the six to seven percent annual rate experienced from 1993–2008 (Nedbank Group, 2011), and is increasingly compared to growth in Nigeria, which posted a 7.63 percent growth rate last year (Government of Nigeria, 2012; World Bank, 2012b). However, taking into account the systemic issues that Nigeria continues to have related to corruption, sectarian violence and service delivery, South Africa still dominates economically. Draper and Scholvin (2012) highlight how South Africa maintains critical infrastructure, enabling it to act as a hub for company headquarters, logistics and distribution, sourcing for regional markets and finance. South Africa is ranked forty-first globally as a place to do business, while Nigeria is ranked number 131 (World Bank, 2012a), and its GDP accounts for approximately 30 percent of the African continent's GDP. Its industrial output is 40 percent and mineral output 45 percent of the total output of the continent. In addition, it generates over 50 percent of Africa's electricity (Republic of South Africa, 2011). South Africa is also an important investor on the continent, providing over US$18.8 billion in foreign direct investment in 2010 (United Nations Conference on Trade and Development, 2011). This means that South Africa is, and will continue to be, important to the continent and, therefore, to Canada as well.

## South Africa Is Important

South Africa often plays an important role in continental governance frameworks and represents Africa on the international stage. It is the only African state to be part of the BRICS group, has just finished its second consecutive term on the United Nations Security Council, has played a central role in the African Peace and Security Architecture, and holds leadership positions in the SADC, the African Union (AU) and NEPAD.

With respect to security in the region, South Africa espouses a rhetoric of human security and the right to protect, but in practice eschews intervention

(Aboagye, 2012). This is in part due to economic reality — the costs of armed intervention and peacekeeping are significant — but also because of sensitivity to historical legacies (Flemes, 2009). Western nations often seem to forget that the continent still suffers from a preoccupation over colonialism. African states therefore appear hypersensitive to anything that encroaches upon their sovereignty. The AU's Common Defence and Security Policy and its Solemn Declaration on a Common African Defence and Security Policy embodies this sensitivity by privileging the respect for sovereignty and regime security (AU, 2004). While colonialism is past, the threat of neo-colonialism remains on the mind of many African leaders, particularly those that come from Marxist traditions. The reluctance of South Africa to intervene in some situations has elicited frustrated responses from nations such as Canada, particularly over the Democratic Republic of Congo (Cooper and Taylor, 2001) and Zimbabwe crises, but can also be seen in South Africa's response to the conflicts in Côte d'Ivoire and Libya (Aboagye, 2012).

## South Africa Is Relevant in Africa

Despite its challenges, South Africa continues to be strong democratically, economically and within continental governance frameworks. This suggests a level of influence unparalleled by any other African nation. Any consideration of engaging Africa or understanding its politics, therefore, should take heed of the influence of the "Rainbow Nation." If Canada is to retain any significant influence among African nations, it will have to enhance its ties with South Africa.

## RENEWING COOPERATION

The South African relationship reinforces the need for Canada to rethink its approach in Sub-Saharan Africa. In particular, Canada needs to develop an Africa engagement strategy that would emphasize a long-term approach and identify key partners on the continent beyond the countries that are currently the focus for Canadian aid (discussed in Part Three of this volume). As Akuffo (2012) notes, Canada has never maintained a coherent foreign policy towards Africa, which has led to an inconsistent presence. Even so, Canada maintains a positive reputation in South Africa and within the Sub-Saharan region, and needs to capitalize on this if it is going to be able to take advantage of a rising Africa.

It is possible that, with the Harper government's new policy of combining aid with Canadian economic interests, South Africa might stand to benefit due to a number of Canadian mining companies operating in the country. However, for the sustainability of Canada's influence in the region, it will be important to engage and partner with South Africa over areas of common interest. Here it is possible to identify regional economic development, international agricultural trade reform, regional security and development, and the advancement of democracy as areas of mutual interest (discussed in Part Two of this volume).

## Regional Economic Development

It appears to be a growing trend for countries in Sub-Saharan Africa to push any trade and investment negotiations to a regional level. This is meant to foster the regional integration that is considered key to building African economic development. South Africa appears to be following that trend, preferring regional arrangements for aid and trade over bilateral ones. This has direct implications for Canada's ability to strengthen its bilateral relationship with South Africa, as evidenced in South Africa's refusal to ratify the negotiated FIPA in 2006. Canada therefore needs to give consideration to initiatives that seek to advance regional activities and work with South African officials to identify those opportunities. Given that Canada has signed an agreement with South Africa for targeting its aid (Republic of South Africa, 2006), the mechanism already exists to facilitate this. As well, Canada is an important actor in the AfDB based in Pretoria, which offers real potential for building closer ties with South Africa under a regional guise. Taking advantage of ways to leverage Canada's existing inputs to advance South Africa's regional goals could help build stronger ties.

## International Agricultural Trade Liberalization

Canada and South Africa maintain a mutual interest in reforming agricultural trade. Both are members of the negotiating coalition, The Cairns Group, which explicitly seeks to achieve agricultural trade reform through the World Trade Organization (Cairns Group, 2012). In particular, the aim and intent is to address export subsidies and caps on agricultural trade quotas as they exist primarily in the European Union, United States and Japan. Canada is one of the founding members of The Cairns Goup, and the only country from the Group of Eight. South Africa is the only African member of The Cairns Group and joined during the Doha Development Agenda negotiations. Both countries are important actors in The Cairns Group and have been working closely together during the Doha negotiations. However, their impact and effectiveness at achieving reform in agriculture has been limited, despite efforts to develop frameworks for achieving subsidy elimination. Nonetheless, the partnership with Canada in this instance suggests a positive opportunity for the bilateral relationship, and ways to use this alliance to come together bilaterally should be explored.

## Regional Security and Development

Both South Africa and Canada have a mutual interest in ensuring that diamonds are not used to undermine the security and stability of governments in the region. Both countries need to reinvigorate the Kimberley Process discussion space as a context for dialogue over regional stability and the use of diamonds for supporting legitimate governments. As Ian Smillie notes in this volume, there is a positive history of cooperation and leadership between Canada and South Africa in this regard. However, such coordination has declined in recent years and needs to be revived. Canadian officials should find areas of mutual interest in this space.

## Advancement of Democracy

Canada and South Africa need to seriously consider how they can work together to resolve regional conflicts. The political instability in Madagascar and mounting violence from rebel insurgencies in Mali and the Central African Republic offer other opportunities for instilling a deeper sense of Canada-South Africa cooperation. As it currently stands, however, there is apparently little attempt in terms of a coordinated effort to resolve these issues. In Madagascar in particular, where a political crisis came about as a result of the military coup in 2010, both countries maintain significant economic and political interests in restoring stability to that country. Canadian and South African companies are both invested in the CDN$6.6 billion Ambatovy nickel and cobalt mining project, but are not cooperating or coordinating efforts to ensure a return to democracy occurs.

South Africa is working through SADC to restore stability and has been leading discussions with the Madagascar government to create a road map for a return to democracy. The Canadian government maintains an interest in the Madagascar situation through La Francophonie organization. Madagascar was suspended from La Francophonie following the military coup and Canada has been reporting back to members about Madagascar's progress towards restoring democracy.[2]

Canada has been supportive of the SADC process, which seeks to achieve a mediated settlement, but officials in Canada have not been directly engaged with South African officials or other SADC partners in discussions over strategy or providing technical assistance. It appears that Canada has been operating independently to pressure the Madagascar military-appointed government to resolve the political crisis based on the SADC plan. While both countries are engaged in the crisis and are seeking a common goal, they have taken different approaches to achieve this and have simply sought to "exchange information" rather than act in any coordinated way.[3]

## CONCLUSION

The present Canada-South Africa relationship is best characterized as ambivalent and at arm's length. If permitted to continue, such a situation has significant consequences for Canadian foreign policy interests in Africa. There is a strong foundation from which to rebuild this relationship; all that is required now is the political will to take advantage of areas of mutual interest and to build cooperative activities. Canada needs to develop an African engagement strategy in which relations with South Africa should be a strategic component. Canada has used aid and trade as important tools to advance development and foreign policy interests in the past, but in a context where these are either no longer appropriate or possible, identifying other ways to reinforce ties with South Africa is crucial. Canada's influence in the region depends on it.

## ENDNOTES

[1] For more information on Canada and the AfDB, see the chapter by Bruce Montador.

[2] Interview by author, Johannesburg, September 9, 2012.

[3] Ibid.

## WORKS CITED

Aboagye, Festus (2012). "South Africa and R2P: More State Sovereignty and Regime Security than Human Security?" In *The Responsibility to Protect: From Evasive to Reluctant Action?*, edited by Malte Brosig. Pages 29–48. Hanns Seidel Foundation, Institute for Security Studies, Konrad-Adenauer-Siftung and South Afrian Institute for International Affairs.

AU (2004). *Solemn Declaration on a Common African Defence and Security Policy.* Available at: www.au.int/pages/sites/default/files/Solemn_Declaration_on_CADSP_0.pdf.

Akuffo, Edward Ansah (2012) *Canadian Foreign Policy in Africa: Regional Approaches to Peace, Security and Development.* Ashgate Publishing Company.

Black, David (2012). "Between Indifference and Idiosyncrasy: The Conservatives and Canadian Aid to Africa." In *Struggling for Effectiveness: CIDA and Canadian Foreign Aid,* edited by Stephen Brown. Pages 246–268. McGill-Queen's University Press.

Braude, Wolfe, Pearl Thandrayan and Elisabeth Sidiropolous (2008). *Emerging Donors in International Development Assistance: the South Africa Case.* South African Institute for International Affairs.

Cairns Group (2012). "Background on The Cairns Group and the WTO Doha Round." Available at: www.cairnsgroup.org.

Cooper, Andrew and Ian Taylor (2001). "'Made in Africa' versus 'Out of Africa': Comparing South Africa's Non-Leadership with Canada's Leadership with the 1996 Crisis in Zaire." *Commonwealth and Comparative Politics* 39, no. 1: 23–41.

Draper, Peter and Sören Scholvin (2012). "The Economic Gateway to Africa? Geography, Strategy, and South Africa's Regional Economic Relations." South African Institute for International Affairs Occasional Paper No. 121. Available at: www.saiia.org.za/occasional-papers/the-economic-gateway-to-africa-geography-strategy-and-south-africa-s-regional-economic-relations.html.

Fairweather, Joan (2008). *The Road to Democracy in South Africa, Volume 3, International Solidarity, Part 2*. University of South Africa: Unisa Press and Hollywood: Tsehai Publishers.

Flemes, D. (2009) "Regional Power South Africa: Co-operative Hegemony Constrained by Historical Legacies." *Journal of Contemporary African Studies* 27 no. 2:135–157.

Freeman, Linda (1997). *The Ambiguous Champion: Canada and South Africa in the Trudeau and Mulroney Years*. University of Toronto Press.

Government of Canada (2010). "Capacity Building Technical Assistance Fund." Canadian International Development Agency. Available at: www.psu-southafrica.org/programmes-and-projects/capacity-building-technical-assistance-fund-cbtaf.html.

———— (2012). "Canada-South Africa Relations." High Commission of Canada to the Republic of South Africa. Available at: www.canadainternational.gc.ca/southafrica-afriquedusud/bilateral_relations_bilaterales/canada_sa-as.aspx?menu_id=7&view=d.

Government of Nigeria (2012). "Review of the Nigerian Economy in 2011 & Economic Outlook 2012–2015." National Bureau of Statistics. Available at: www.nigerianstat.gov.ng/pages/download/46.

Hornsby, David J. and Oscar Van Heerden (2013). "Canada-South Africa Relations: A Case of Middle Power (non)Cooperation? *Commonwealth and Comparative Politics* Special Issue, 51, no. 2: 153–172.

Keenleyside, Terence. A (1983). "Canada-South Africa Commercial Relations: 1977–1982: Business as Usual?" *Canadian Journal of African Studies* Special Issue 17, no. 3: 449–467.

*Mail and Guardian* (2012). "SA Economy's Growth Rate Rises to 3.2%." February 28. Available at: http://mg.co.za/article/2012-02-28-sa-economys-growth-rate-rises-to-32.

Misra-Dexter, Neeta and Judith February (2010). *Testing Democracy: Which Way is South Africa Going?* Institute for Democracy in South Africa.

Nedbank Group (2011). *Facts and Forecasts of Key Economic Variables.* October. Available at: www.nedbankgroup.co.za/pdfs/economic/economicForecasts/2011-10_yearlyForecast.pdf.

Nicol, Martin (2012). "Canada-South Africa Trade: 1994-2010." Canada-South Africa Relations Colloquium. University of the Witwatersrand, South Africa. May 14-15.

Nkosi, Milton (2011). "Will South Africa's 'Secrecy Bill' Become Law?" *BBC,* November 23. Available at: www.bbc.co.uk/news/world-africa-15860557.

OECD (2012). "Canadian ODA to South Africa." Query Wizard for International Development Statistics. Available at: http://stats.oecd.org/qwids/.

Republic of South Africa (2006). "General Agreement on Development Cooperation Between the Republic of South Africa and the Government of Canada." National Treasury. Available at: www.treasury.gov.za/comm_media/press/2006/2006112401.pdf.

———— (2011). *South Africa's Investor's Handbook 2011/2012.* Department of Trade and Industry. Available at: www.deloitte.com/assets/Dcom-SouthAfrica/Local%20Assets/Documents/sa_investors_handbook.pdf.

Right 2 Know (2012). Available at: www.r2k.org.za.

Statistics Canada (2012). "Trade Data Online." *Industry Canada.* Available at: www.ic.gc.ca/tdo.

*The Economist* (2012). "Cry, the Beloved Country: South Africa's Sad Decline." October 20–26.

Transparency International (2011). *Corruption Perceptions Index 2011.* Available at: http://cpi.transparency.org/cpi2011/results/.

United Nations Conference on Trade and Investment (2011). *World Investment Report 2011: Non-Equity Modes of International Production and Development.* United Nations.

World Bank (2012a). "South Africa." Available at: http://data.worldbank.org/country/south-africa.

——— (2012b). "Nigeria." Available at: http://data.worldbank.org/country/nigeria.

# Canadian Foreign Policy and Africa's Diaspora: Slippery Slope or Opportunity Unrealized?

David Carment, Milana Nikolko and Dacia Douhaibi

• • • • • • • • • • • • • • • • • • • •

## INTRODUCTION

Diaspora politics is the most significant Canadian foreign policy issue of the twenty-first century. It is more salient for a variety of reasons, including changing demography, declining fertility rates, shifts in priority immigrant countries and changes in refugee processing. Immigration is the only source of growth for Canada's population and two-fifths of all Canadians are first or second generation (Statistics Canada, 2009). Many new Canadians come from places where minorities are at risk, and human rights violations and open conflict are common. Diaspora communities occupy a unique and important position in Canadian politics, one that allows them to influence both their home and host government. They can exert pressure on their home government from abroad, free from political threats and fear of retribution, and they can lobby their host country to put pressure on their home government to enact policies favourable to their interests, ranging from calls for human rights progress and governance reform to constructive international trade policies.

This chapter argues that there is no clearly articulated and coherent diaspora policy in Canada, and asks how one might be developed. We believe that diaspora politics is a slippery slope because new Canadians — as Canada's economic, demographic and political future — are the most susceptible to this kind of "special treatment."

The terms "diaspora" and "diaspora communities" are loaded with various connotations and generalizations, and have been increasingly used to describe asylum seekers, refugees, immigrants, displaced communities, and ethnic and religious minorities at risk. The African Union (AU), for example, defines the African diaspora as "peoples of African origin living outside the continent, irrespective of their citizenship and nationality and who are willing to contribute to the development of the continent and the building of the African Union" (AMIP News, 2011). This chapter's definition of the African diaspora similarly means people who serve as the bridge between Africa and Canada. Diasporas are most commonly those born outside Canada, but may also include subsequent generations that maintain strong ties to the country of origin; the defining quality of a diaspora is a dynamic linkage with the country of origin (Matsuoka and Sorenson, 2001). These linkages may include: political lobbying; economic development, including remittances and investment; social tasks, including the promotion of the human; and cultural linkages, such as support for diaspora newspapers and media (World Bank, 2012; University for Peace [UPeace], 2006a). All of these activities can take place at the individual level (through family networks) or at the institutional level (through channels such as community or international organizations) (UPeace, 2006b).

The African-Canadian population is Canada's fastest growing ethnic minority and is particularly well established in Canada's largest cities. In 2001, the African-Canadian community was the third-largest minority group in Canada, after the Chinese and South Asian populations (Embaie, 2013). The 2001 census recorded 662,200 African-Canadians, representing just over two percent of Canada's total population and 17 percent of the visible minority population (ibid.). An increasingly ethnically diverse Canada makes diasporas a key battleground for political parties. While diaspora politics can be beneficial, it can also encourage new Canadians to bring their homeland disputes to Canada (Carment and Bercuson, 2008). In Canada, moreover, there appears to be no coherent principle underlying the motivations for politicians to support diaspora for political gain, nor ground rules for diaspora lobbying or for engaging diaspora in their host states. This may put Canada at a disadvantage when confronted with strong lobbying efforts from influential diaspora communities, and allows politicians leeway when courting these lobbies in exchange for foreign policy favours (ibid.).

This chapter examines the complex relationship between Africa's diaspora groups in Canada and their potential to influence foreign policy. The first and second parts of the chapter identify some of the pertinent linkages between diaspora and foreign policy at the home and host state level. The third section draws on Sudan and Somalia to show how diasporas interact with Canadian policy to shape foreign policy choices; the final section provides conclusions.[1]

## LEVERAGING INFLUENCE?

Like all diaspora, the African diaspora organize and lobby where their numbers are sufficiently large and concentrated, and where groups possess leaders with political skills and access to resources. The distribution of resources, crosscutting cleavages, leadership capabilities and group cohesion within Africa's various diaspora groups is extremely uneven, as the case studies demonstrate below. Many groups, mostly those of first generation immigrants from the poorest sub-Saharan states, are not as capable or experienced influencing and shaping policy processes as those from other regions (UPeace, 2006a). In theory, Canada has safeguards that inhibit foreign policy strategies that explicitly promote the agendas of specific diaspora groups. This is because elected leaders must satisfy multiple and diverse demands and overarching political constraints ensure that no single diaspora group can dominate and exploit the political process (Carment et al., 2012). The scattering and distribution of power in Canada's federalist system provides additional constraints because it gives over some authority for managing diaspora-related issues, such as language, culture and immigration to provinces and municipalities.

In reality, diasporas can and do influence policy through bloc voting, lobbying and by members of parliament (MPs) getting "captured" by constituent interests, which might be driven by the single-issue agendas of particular diaspora groups. The MP, looking to be elected, may align themselves with that diaspora agenda even though those local interests may not be important at the party level. Currently, we see situations where constituent interests find support at both the local riding level and at the party level. This makes support for specific diasporas very potent and often precarious.[2]

Some might argue that government attempts to win over and instrumentalize diaspora groups are legitimate as long as it does not hamper national interests. Others might suggest that because diaspora groups have a significant impact in the political realm in their home country, with the potential to both improve and impair political processes abroad, they need careful watching (Lum et al., 2012). In the Canadian context, ill-informed parliamentarians are often unaware of the intricate political agendas that diasporas benefit from back home and which they bring to Canada.[3] An extreme example of this can be seen in the case of The Toronto 18, a group of young Muslim men who conspired to storm Parliament Hill and detonate truck bombs in downtown Toronto in 2006 (Teotonio, 2012).

## THE ROLE OF POLICY

The policy frameworks adopted by home governments with respect to diaspora populations can have a substantial impact on a country's ability to capitalize on diaspora contributions to both development and peace.[4] To a large extent, positive and effective diaspora engagement depends on the existence of sound government policy designed to enable and encourage diaspora investment in areas of primary importance to the country. There are a number of policy initiatives that are explicitly aimed at developing relationships between home countries, host countries and diaspora communities. They range from the highly formalized to light and informal procedures. An example is the establishment of formalized regulatory systems, such as flexible citizenship laws, residency, visa access, political rights, portable pensions, social services and tax incentives for investment.

New Canadians also stimulate trade and investment because the informational advantages they hold improve investment by reducing the transaction costs of entry into home markets. For the banking and investment sector, diaspora connections are important for overcoming obstacles to resource transfer. Questions of diaspora labour mobility and retention issues are also very important for the Canadian economy. Given that more and more trade agreements include services issues, with respect to the World Trade Organization's protocols on movement of natural persons, there are important implications for trade.

On the development side, new Canadians with diaspora connections are now identified as key drivers of development through remittances, the transfer of human and social capital, and through direct support for democracy processes and peace building in fragile states. Health initiatives, brain circulation and professional networks are all well documented (The North-South Institute, 2010). But aid also acts as a "pull factor" for potential migrations; bilateral aid may actually increase skilled-worker migration to specific donors by enhancing information about labour market conditions in donor countries. In regards to pull factors, host countries such as Canada can ease this "brain drain" and contribute to development by creating policy frameworks conducive to flexibility in migration and investment in homelands.

Finally, questions of integration and positionality as determinants of Canadian security must be considered. Most research has shown the integration of new Canadians increases their capacity to participate positively. Diasporas have also become targets of manipulation and solicitation from insurgents in their countries of origin (Lum et al., 2012). In brief, while it may be true that diasporas utilize host country freedoms to lobby for political and partisan aims in home countries, such activity does not necessarily forward conflict to the host country.

## THE AFRICAN CONTEXT

Within the scope of strengthening the states of Sub-Sahara Africa, a critical role for diaspora is their ability to encourage trust and interdependence between conflicting groups and international organizations and interveners by providing important insights in the conflict and the actors involved (Hall and Swain, 2007). African diasporas in Canada can and do promote development in their countries of origin, but they do so selectively and the results can be uneven (Clark and Thomas, 2006; Okpewho and Nzegwu, 2009).

Canada's African diaspora are concerned both with making a life here and with maintaining links to countries of origin (Tettey and Puplampu, 2005). The nature of their relationship with Canada, the contributions that they make here and the linkages forged with countries of origin depend in large part on the ability of these diasporas to integrate into Canada, and to access programs and services here (ibid.). Added to this is the difficulty many diasporas face trying to be politically and economically involved with their homelands while trying to establish a home in Canada. These barriers are present in several African diaspora communities in Canada.[5] The following cases, South Sudan and Somalia, examine how these linkages play out. These are important cases because of the politics on the ground in each country, and the history of Canada's involvement in their conflicts. In each case, the question of representation arises: who should represent the diaspora communities, and how should the Canadian government utilize these representatives? Representation is a critical consideration for several reasons: to ensure that the interests of the diaspora community are properly understood; to prevent further factioning within the community as a result of uneven representation; and to ensure that any foreign policy decisions based on diaspora input or advice are in the best economic, political and/or social interests of the target country.

## Sudan/South Sudan

The majority of Sudanese immigrants, largely from the south, arrived in Canada from the mid-1980s on, as Sudan plunged into a prolonged period of internal conflict. Because the separation between Sudan and South Sudan is so recent, it can be hard to differentiate between the diaspora that come from each state; however, the focus in this section is the South Sudanese diaspora community. Since independence in 1956, protracted conflict rooted in deep cultural and religious differences, discordant views on the secular or Islamic character of the state and desire to control valuable oil resources in the border region between north and south Sudan resulted in two civil wars that in combination lasted for over 50 years, resulted in the death of over two million Sudanese people and displacement of over four million people (The Fund for Peace, 2010; US Department of State, 2010). The Comprehensive Peace Agreement (CPA), the final stage after more than three decades of peace negotiations, was formally signed on January 9, 2005. The referendum for the secession of the south, one of the cornerstones of the CPA, took place on January 9, 2011, and over 98 percent of voters chose to separate (BBC News, 2011). Secession of South Sudan occurred on July 9, 2011. The relationship between Sudan and South Sudan remains extremely unstable, and the challenges faced by South Sudan have led it to be labelled a pre-failed state, ripe for the outbreak of conflict (Chavez, 2011).

Canada is ranked sixth among source countries for refugees from Sudan. Sudan has approximately 967,500 emigrants, which consists of 2.2 percent of the population (World Bank, 2011). Of those, between 25,000 and 30,000 live in Canada, the majority being government-assisted refugees from South Sudan who came to Canada directly from refugee camps (Centre for Addiction and Mental Health, 2004). A significant number of South Sudanese in Canada were deliberately sent abroad by the Southern People's Liberation Army (SPLA) to become educated, send funds back to South Sudan to support the separation movement while working abroad and, upon return, help to build up the underdeveloped south (CBC Radio, 2010; Wheeler, 2008).

The population of Sudanese newcomers in Ontario is relatively young, moderately educated and underemployed (Wheeler, 2008). The Sudanese diaspora in Canada remain closely connected to Sudan, demonstrated by the regular and generous payment of financial remittances to both family members and friends in Sudan, membership in community or political organizations within Canada, communication with contacts in Sudan and frequent return trips home (The Mosaic Institute, 2009). These strong transnational linkages result in the transfer of both financial and social capital from the diaspora to Sudan, as well as between diasporas abroad. Financial remittances have been a significant source of direct financial contribution to Sudan, reaching US$3.178 billion in 2010 (World Bank, 2011). This can be compared with net foreign direct investment inflows, which were US$2.6 billion in 2008 (ibid.). Official development assistance was US$2.4 billion in 2008 and exports totalled US$13.3 billion (ibid.). Within Canada there are political organizations, such as the SPLA — which has numerous chapters across Canada representing a sizable number of South Sudanese — and a less formal network of Sudanese community associations and cultural associations in most large cities across Canada that represent the South Sudanese community. The diaspora community has also further divided into ethno-specific associations.

The history of conflict between the centralized government in Khartoum and the recent secession of South Sudan from the north has created a complex diaspora community, lacking a common national interest. The "diversity within diversity" of the South Sudanese population in Canada has been noted as a unique challenge (Centre for Addiction and Mental Health, 2004). The diversity of the South Sudanese community, the different interests at play and the fact that most South Sudanese are first generation immigrants have limited the capacity of the diaspora to advocate for government support of South Sudanese matters. An example of successful policy intervention from Canada occurred in 2003, when pressure from domestic civil society groups, the Sudanese community and the United States pushed Talisman to sell its interests in what is now South Sudan, because the Government of Sudan was almost totally reliant on oil revenues for its war effort against the south and Darfur. While the South Sudanese diaspora tends to have limited impact through advocacy and lobbying, it has had a great impact on some of the key actors involved on the ground at home, supporting a range of rebel leaders financially and politically.

Canada is involved on the diplomatic front in Sudan and South Sudan, through its active participation in peace processes, bilateral relations, multilateral initiatives and peace building. Since 2006, the Government of Canada has contributed more than CDN$885 million toward humanitarian assistance, development and peace building in the former Sudan. In support of the new nation and the UN Mission in the Republic of South Sudan (UNMISS), the Canadian Forces (CF) formed Task Force Sudan, comprised of 14 CF personnel who work with UNMISS (Department of National Defence, 2012). Three core areas have been prioritized by the Government of Canada (2011): aid, both humanitarian assistance and early recovery; security, in particular support for UN peacekeeping missions; and diplomacy through advocacy work and peacebuilding activities. In this case, working closely with key members of the diaspora community in Canada may help ensure the success of Canadian initiatives in Sudan and South Sudan. The challenges here are ensuring that Canadian priorities align with Sudanese and South Sudanese diaspora interests, and the location of representative leaders in the diaspora that can accurately speak for the larger ethnically diverse communities.

## Somalia

The Somali diaspora makes substantial contributions to the Somali economy and livelihoods through remittances, humanitarian assistance, and participation in recovery and reconstruction efforts. Somali diasporas play a role in both conflict and peace building, supporting the clan in times of conflict, yet intervening in support of local reconciliation and state building, which has been seen to be a critical component of success (Sheikh and Healy, 2009). The transfer of financial remittances to family members in Somalia are a well-established practice and substantial amounts of money move into the country. Remittance flows were estimated at up to US$1 billion in 2004, and represented 23 percent of household income; approximately 40 percent of households received some level of support (ibid.). In addition, members of the diaspora have returned to Somalia to assume leadership positions in the state, political parties, cabinet, the parliament and the civil service in Somalia, Somaliland and Puntland (ibid.).

Canada has one of the largest Somali diaspora populations in the world, most of whom live in Toronto. The Somali diaspora form the most prominent African diaspora community in Canada. The 2006 census indicates that 37,790 people claim Somali heritage (Statistics Canada, 2006), although government figures put the number much higher at 170,000 (Government of Canada, 2012). This number is significant as it means that in light concentrations, the Somali diaspora may have political leverage.

The Somali diaspora has remained very intimately connected with the homeland. As is common for African diasporas, Somalis in Canada have experienced barriers to employment despite having many qualified professions. This has been attributed to discrimination, language barriers and limited recognition of skills and training from Somalia (CBC News Edmonton 2011; CBC News Toronto, 2012). This has led to much higher levels of unemployment within the Somali community than the general population, a fact noted in Somali media (Santur, 2010). As a result, many members of the Somali diaspora with Canadian citizenship return to live, work and invest in Somalia. It is estimated that there are 15,000 Canadian citizens in Somaliland alone (ibid.), significantly strengthening unofficial ties between Canada and Somalia. Underemployment of youth is also tied to the two big issues that plague the diaspora community in Canada, both affecting national security and the conflict dynamic in Somali: recruitment into Al-Shabab and gang violence. The Somali diaspora community came to Canada to flee violent civil conflict, but an ironic twist has seen members of the Somali youth seduced back into the conflict in the homeland as a result of their marginalization in Canada. Discrimination and a sense of exclusion are felt widely across the Somali community, particularly due to the fact that the majority of Somalis in Canada are Muslim (McGown, 1999). Young Somali-Canadians need more opportunities to gain employment within Canada or they may remain at high risk of being recruited into extremist organizations and gangs (Mackrael, 2012). Despite these challenges in the Somali community, many of which could be helped through programs in Canada to facilitate employment of Somali youth and discourage anti-Islamic rhetoric, there is willingness in the community in Canada to promote peace building in Somalia, and there are requests for government support (Rae, 2011). There is also evidence of increasing engagement with Canadian political channels to support Somali interests.

Somali online media, for example, has promoted candidates that would help support Somali interests in a recent Ontario municipal election (Hiiraan Online, 2006; Rae, 2011). In one municipality, a Somali woman ran for office. This, although not linked to politics at the federal level, does demonstrate that members of the Somali community are not only interested, but are getting involved, in Canadian politics. This is in spite of, or perhaps in reaction to, the many barriers that have been noted to integration of Somali-Canadians (Van Lingen, 2013; McGowan, 1999). As members of the large Somali community become increasingly proficient navigating the Canadian political system, they will gain the tools to lobby for support at higher government levels. The future may see Somali-Canadians running for provincial or federal office as well.

Liberal MP Bob Rae has suggested that Canadian agencies need to listen to the diaspora, who know what is happening in Somalia and how to help. The first step in this process is for the Government of Canada to begin meeting with members of the Somali community. Further evidence of the peace directive in the diaspora community is the presence of community organizations such as the Somali Canadian Diaspora Alliance. The vision of this organization is "to strive for a sovereign and peaceful Somalia that is politically, socially and economically independent and just. A Somalia that is united and free from institutionalized tribalism" (Somali Canadian Diaspora Alliance, 2007). This points to the fact that, similar to the Sudanese diaspora communities, there are opportunities to engage the community with the potential for creating peaceful relations both within Canada and Somalia. The difficulty here, again, is who in the Somali community would best represent the interests of the large diaspora community and how the government would move forward with recommendations from that community.

## CONCLUSIONS

As the two cases suggest, Africa's diasporas carry their homeland interests with them and maintain active connections with their countries of origin (Carment and Samy, 2012). These relatively young diaspora communities have already made inroads working with various arms of the Canadian government to address concerns in their home countries. As a result, there is a need to develop a functional, positive relationship between more of Africa's diasporas and policy makers in Canada that brings benefits back to the countries from which these diaspora are drawn. We also observe that to some extent, Africa's diaspora possess specific knowledge that appears to be lacking within Canada's policy-making community and Parliament. Though these have demonstrated a willingness to contribute to security dialogue and provide expert advice on trade and investment and development, the results have been uneven.

We argue that development assistance, with a focus on strengthened social networks and remittances, stands out as an area that need to be better understood as a policy tool. Most significantly, diaspora are a force for mobilizing resources through individual and household investments and increasingly through collective donations to fund development projects in their home communities.[6] These factors are often thought to contribute to a homeland's resilience, which refers to a coping ability that allows a country to withstand or recover from economic shocks, and are reflected in macroeconomic stability, microeconomic market efficiency, good governance and social development. These impacts and processes within diaspora homelands can provide valuable insight for Canadian policy makers on priority areas and culturally sensitive issues which Canadian programs themselves may be ill trained to address.

Over time, diaspora communities may increasingly influence policy decisions as the communities grow in size and political mobility. Formalized linkages could reinforce their role as vital human conduits for guiding human, social and economic capital into their home countries; capital which is capable of contributing to democracy promotion, state rebuilding and development.

Canada, as the host of many African diaspora communities that come from fragile homelands, can support these groups towards that stabilizing role. In addition, because of the relationship between diasporas and the country of origin, any attempt at creating diaspora policy would also necessitate a clear understanding of the "push" and "pull" factors at work between diasporas and homeland governments.

For example, remittances, in addition to providing for the basic necessities of poor households and communities, can lead to improvements in welfare and development through something such as more investments in health and education. Contrary to other resource flows, such as foreign aid, remittance flows tend to be also countercyclical and more stable. However, migration in large numbers represents a loss of skills — the so-called brain drain — for the source countries, and remittances may not have long-term impacts on growth and development if they are consumed rather than invested. Part of the challenge, therefore, is to ensure that there are net benefits of remittances and migration for source countries, and that policies in host countries can contribute to these net benefits.

Identifying appropriate diaspora "experts" is also a major challenge. The key figure the government may choose, or alternatively, who would present themselves, may lack proper representativeness. Continuity between the often small minority of politically active diaspora organizations and the larger majority who they claim to represent would have to be ensured.

In conclusion, as the main source of growth for Canada's population, the importance of diaspora in Canada will only continue to grow, influencing policy and economic choices. Since its inception, Canada has always been shaped by diaspora communities, but today's diaspora are truly transnational populations in a position to influence both home and host governments, shape their security and influence trade, development and investment policy preferences. To this end, more work must be done to assess diaspora linkages specific to the Canadian context and to clarify how the potential benefits of diaspora can be sufficiently documented, strategized and made policy relevant independent of political interests.

# ENDNOTES

1    It is interesting to note that finding information on African diaspora groups in Canada is somewhat of a challenge. More research must be done on understanding the demographics and behaviours of Canada's diaspora communities.

2    Consider, for example, the effort by the Department of Foreign Affairs and International Trade to organize a foreign policy around a "global citizens" agenda. Recognizing that out-migration from Canada is increasing, there has been a perceived need to "capture and instrumentalize" those Canadians living abroad (primarily in the United States, but also elsewhere), and to harness their energies for some sort of common collective good.

3    By playing the "diaspora card," Canada's leaders are opening up the country to the possibility of exploitation by other countries looking to disrupt its internal affairs by using diaspora to lobby or influence our leaders; politicians competing for the support of specific diaspora leads to the classic problem of outbidding. In an effort to curry favour, political parties try to "outbid" and outflank the other. Escalatory outbidding can force a government to commit to policies that it might not otherwise choose — policies that many Canadians might find extreme or unnecessary — just to win the votes of particular constituencies. In the case of the current government, being right of centre means that it can hold a more extreme position on some diaspora issues without fear of being "outflanked" by more centrist or left leaning parties.

4    For a comparative study of several different policy approaches, see Kathleen Newland and Erin Patrick (2004), "Beyond Remittances: The Role of Diaspora in Poverty Reduction in their Countries of Origin," *Migration Policy Institute,* July, available at: www.eldis.org/static/DOC17672.htm.

5    There are two ways in which African diaspora provide support. First, diaspora members may provide expertise to their homeland in a post-conflict environment as peace builders, business investors or by working with local non-governmental organizations (UPeace 2006a; 2006b). Second, those who do not return may serve as a source of guidance, information, new ideas, best practices and appropriate technology.

Diaspora remain active at a distance — through dialogue with contacts at home, visits and involvement in organizations that are involved on the ground in home countries.

[6] Consider Sub-Saharan Africa. The World Bank has been asked to provide expected outcomes related to several "bankable" projects including: the proposed African Diaspora Investment Fund; an Africa continent-wide Diaspora Professional Skills database; an expanded African Diaspora Development Marketplace; the African Union Commission's (AUC's) Volunteer Program; and the African Institute for Remittances (AIR). On remittances, the Africa Development Professional Group, with a European Commission grant and in partnership with the African Development Bank and International Organization for Migration, are facilitating the establishment of the AIR in the AUC.

## WORKS CITED

AMIP News (2011). "Africa Union Defines Diaspora." Available at: www.amipnewsonline.org/?p=660.

BBC News (2011). "South Sudan Referendum: 99% Vote for Independence." BBC News Africa. Available at: www.bbc.co.uk/news/world-africa-12317927.

Carment, D. and D. Bercuson (eds.) (2008). *The World in Canada: Diaspora, Democracy, and Domestic Politics.* Montreal: McGill-Queen's University Press.

Carment, D. and Y. Samy (2012). "The Dangerous Game of Diaspora Politics." *The Globe and Mail,* February 10. Available at: www.theglobeandmail.com/commentary/the-dangerous-game-of-diaspora-politics/article544912/.

Carment, D. et al. (2012). "Canadian Foreign Policy and Diaspora." Paper presented at the International Studies Association, San Diego, April.

CBC News Edmonton (2011). "Somali-Canadians Urged to Help Police Solve Homicides." CBC, July 5. Available at: www.cbc.ca/news/canada/edmonton/story/2011/07/05/edmonton-somali-homicide-campaign.html.

CBC News Toronto (2012). "Somali-Canadian Community Fears Further Loss of Life." CBC, July 12. Available at: www.cbc.ca/news/canada/toronto/story/2012/07/12/toronto-somali-canadian-community-fears-more-violence.html.

CBC Radio (2010). "Part 3: Cuban Jubans: Interview with Dr. Okony Simon Mori." CBC Radio, April 14. Available at: www.cbc.ca/thecurrent/episode/2010/04/14/april-14-2010/.

Centre for Addiction and Mental Health (2004). *The Study of Sudanese Settlement in Ontario — Final Report*. Available at: http://atwork.settlement.org/downloads/atwork/Study_of_Sudanese_Settlement_in_Ontario.pdf.

Chavez, Edgar (2011). "Recognizing the New Sudan: Innovation, Investment and Capacity Building." Peacefare.net, February 17. Available at: www.peacefare.net/?page_id=1798.

Clarke, Kamari Maxine and Deborah A. Thomas (eds.) (2006). *Globalization and Race: Transformations in the Cultural Production of Blackness*. Durham, NC: Duke University Press.

Department of National Defence (2012). "Canada's Role in the Republic of South Sudan." National Defence and the Canadian Forces, January. Available at: www.forces.gc.ca/site/tml/article-eng.asp?id=2&y=2012&m=01.

Embaie, Michael (2013). "Speech of Michael Embaie at Black History Month Celebration." Speech, Intercultural Dialogue Institute, Calgary, February 28. Available at: http://calgary.interculturaldialog.com/uncategorized/speech-of-michael-embaie-at-black-history-month-celebration/.

Government of Canada (2011). "Canada's Engagement in Sudan: Priorities and Objectives." Government of Canada — Sudan, December. Available at: www.canadainternational.gc.ca/sudan-soudan/engagement.aspx?lang=eng&view=d.

——— (2012). "Somalia." Canada-Somali Relations Fact Sheet. September. Available at: www.canadainternational.gc.ca/kenya/bilateral_relations_bilaterales/canada-somalia.aspx?menu_id=59&view=d.

Hall, Jonathan and Ashok Swain (2007). "Catapulting Conflicts or Propelling Peace? Diasporas and Civil Wars." In *Globalization and Challenges to Peace Building,* edited by Ashok Swain, Ramses Amer and Joakim Öjendal. London: Anthem Press.

Hiiraan Online (2006). "Ontario Municipal Election: Somali Canadian Prospective." Hiiraan Online, November 10. Available at: www.hiiraan.com/news2/2006/nov/ontario_municipal_election_somali_canadian_prospective.aspx.

Mackrael, Kim (2012). "Parents, Government Urged to Collaborate for Sake of Somali Diaspora." *The Globe and Mail,* July 18. Available at: www.theglobeandmail.com/news/national/parents-government-urged-to-collaborate-for-sake-of-somali-diaspora/article4426819/.

Matsuoka, Atsuko Karin and John Sorenson (eds.) (2001). *Ghosts and Shadows: Construction of Identity and Community in an African Diaspora.* Toronto: University of Toronto Press.

McGown, Rima Berns (1999). *Muslims in the Diaspora: The Somali Communities of London and Toronto.* Toronto: University of Toronto Press.

Lum, Brandon et al. (2012). "Diasporas, Remittances and State Fragility: Assessing the Linkages." *Ethnopolitics: Formerly Global Review of Ethnopolitics* DOI:10.1080/17449057.2012.744217. Available at: www.tandfonline.com/doi/abs/10.1080/17449057.2012.744217.

Okpewho, Isidore and Nkiru Nzegwu (eds.) (2009). *The New African Diaspora.* Bloomington: Indiana University Press.

Rae, Bob (2011). "Somali Diaspora Can Help Canada Lead." Bob Rae, MP, July 21. Available at: http://bobrae.liberal.ca/uncategorized/somali-diaspora-can-help-canada-lead/.

Santur, Hassan Ghedi (2010). "The New Expats — Many Somalis Came to Canada Looking for a Better Life. They Found it Back in Africa." WardheerNews.com, November 12. Available at: http://wardheernews.com/News_10/Nov/12_the_new_expats.html.

Sheikh, Hassan and Sally Healy (2009). *Somalia's Missing Million: The Somali Diaspora and its Role in Development: March 2009.* Report for the UN Development Programme. Available at: www.so.undp.org/index.php/Somalia-Stories/Forging-Partnerships-with-the-Somali-Diaspora.html.

Somali Canadian Diaspora Alliance (2007). "Our Vision." Available at: www.somalidiasporaalliance.com/index.php.

Statistics Canada (2006). "Ethnic Origins, 2006 Counts, for Canada, Provinces and Territories — 20% Sample Data." Available at: www12.statcan.ca/census-recensement/2006/dp-pd/hlt/97-562/pages/page.cfm?Lang=E&Geo=PR&Code=01&Table=2&Data=Count&StartRec=1&Sort=3&Display=All&CSDFilter=5000.

———— (2009). *Birthplaces of Immigrant Arrivals, 1963 to 1965.* Available at: www65.statcan.gc.ca/acyb02/1967/acyb02_19670220004-eng.htm.

Teotonio, Isabel (2010). "Toronto 18." Thestar.com. Available at: www3.thestar.com/static/toronto18/index.html.

Tettey, Wisdom J. and Korbla P. Puplampu (eds.) (2005). *The African Diaspora in Canada: Negotiating Identity and Belonging.* Calgary: University of Calgary Press.

The Fund for Peace (2010). Available at: www.fundforpeace.org/web/index.php?option=com_content&task=view&id=454&Itemid=903.

The Mosaic Institute (2009). "Profile of a Community: A 'Smart Map' of the Sudanese Diaspora in Canada." Available at: www.mosaicinstitute.ca/uploaded/tiny_mce/File/Sudanese_Report.pdf.

The North-South Institute (2010). "The Diaspora Giving Back: Strengthening Health Care Systems in Sub-Saharan Africa." Policy Brief. Available at: www.nsi-ins.ca/content/download/African%20Diaspora_finalV2.pdf.

UPeace (2006a). *Expert Forum: Capacity Building for Peace and Development: Roles of Diaspora Final Report: Toronto, Canada, October 19-20, 2006.* Diaspora Conference 2006. Available at: www.unitar.org/ny/sites/unitar.org.ny/files/UPEACE%20Report.pdf.

———— (2006b). *Capacity Building for Peace and Development: Roles of Diaspora: High Level Expert Forum: Toronto, Canada, October 19-20 2006. Booklet 1.* Available at: www.upeace.org/documents/news/2351_Booklet_1_UPEACE.pdf.

US Department of State (2010). "Background Note: Sudan. Bureau of African Affairs."

Van Lingen, Bethany (2013). "New Research Details Barriers for Somali-Canadian Youth." CTV News Online. Available at: http://toronto.ctvnews.ca/new-research-details-barriers-for-somali-canadian-youth-1.1180265.

Wheeler, Skye (2008). "Cuba to Juba: South Sudanese Doctors Come Home." Reuters Online, July 2. Available at: www.reuters.com/article/2008/07/03/us-sudan-cuba-idUSL1848504120080703?pageNumber=2.

World Bank (2011). *Migration and Remittances Factbook 2011.* Washington, DC: World Bank Publications.

———— (2012). *World Bank Africa Diaspora Program.* Available at: www.worldbank.org/afr/diaspora/.

# Canadian Nation Building in Africa: Building Whose Nation?

Chris Brown

● ● ● ● ● ● ● ● ● ● ● ● ● ● ● ● ● ● ●

## INTRODUCTION

This chapter examines the Canadian contribution to nation building in Africa in the post-independence period, focussing on Sub-Saharan Africa and official Canadian government actions. It is organized into four sections. The first section argues that Canada has relatively few linkages to Africa that would establish a basis for a clear Canadian national interest on the continent. It considers Africa within Canadian foreign policy and makes the case that Canadian decision makers have an unusually wide degree of autonomy with respect to their Africa policy. The second section examines the concept of nation building; it argues that over time this concept has undergone a significant shift in meaning. The third presents a brief overview of Canadian foreign policy towards Africa over the last 50 years, including a consideration of Canadian contributions to African nation building, as that term has been variously understood. It emphasizes the inconsistent and episodic nature of Canada's engagement with the continent. At times, Canada has been an important player in African affairs, and Africa has loomed large in the Canadian consciousness; at other times, Canada has seemingly withdrawn from the continent and Africa has disappeared from Canadian foreign policy debates. This record shows the Canadian contribution to nation building in Africa to be mixed, at best. Finally, the concluding section argues that the only way to understand the vagaries of Canada's Africa policy is to understand that it is fundamentally not about Africa, but instead about Canada; it is a policy designed to build the Canadian nation.

## AFRICA IN CANADIAN FOREIGN POLICY

In 1960, Douglas Anglin published an article calling for the development of a Canadian foreign policy towards Africa, arguing that Canada did not have one at that time. In discussing the potential foundations for such a policy, he reviewed the existing connections between Canada and Africa, and concluded that they were very minor (Anglin, 1960). Though the scale and scope of Canada-Africa relations have grown enormously since that time, Anglin's basic point remains true today — that the starting point for any analysis of Canadian foreign policy towards Africa must be the recognition that Africa is largely peripheral to Canada's core national interests, whether those are defined in national security or in economic terms. Compared to other regions of the globe, Canada has relatively few ties to Africa, and those ties that do exist are comparatively minor.

Unlike its major European allies, Canada was not formerly a colonial power in Africa, and has had little historical connection to the continent. Until recently, Canada did not have significant immigrant communities of African origin. This has begun to change in the last decade or so, though it is still generally true that African diaspora groups are not major players within the Canadian political system.[1] Most significantly, Canada has never developed strong economic ties with Africa. When Anglin wrote his article, Africa accounted for just under 1.5 percent of Canadian exports and less than 0.5 percent of Canadian imports (ibid.: 294). These ratios remained remarkably stable over the next 50 years; though, in the last decade, significant oil imports from Algeria, Angola and Nigeria have boosted Africa's share of Canadian imports from 0.76 percent in 2000 to 3.02 percent in 2011 (Industry Canada, 2013). The story is similar with respect to investment and capital flows. Anglin (1960) found just 20 Canadian companies operating in Africa, with total private foreign investment of CDN$40 million, amounting to less than three percent of the Canadian total. By 2011, annual Canadian foreign direct investment in Africa had risen to CDN$3 billion, but this accounted for only 0.4 percent of Canadian direct investment that year; at no point in the last decade has the figure surpassed one percent of the total (Statistics Canada, 2013).

The consequence of these comparatively weak ties between Canada and Africa is that Canadian policy makers are relatively free to shape Africa policy as they wish. Canada has no overriding security or economic interests in Africa that compel government action; there is no powerful "Africa lobby" to which the government must pay attention if it wishes to gain re-election. Put simply, Canada's Africa policy is a matter of *choice*, not *necessity*. As others have observed, this has often meant that Canada's Africa policy has a strong values orientation, as Canadian governments have used their Africa policy to project their values abroad. Edward Akuffo (2012) emphasizes the moral character of Canada's Africa policy and labels it "non-imperial internationalism," while David Black (2010) suggests that Africa has constituted a "serial morality play" in Canadian foreign policy.

## NATION BUILDING

Before turning to a history of Canadian foreign policy in Africa, and its contributions to African nation building, it is necessary to discuss the concept of "nation building" itself. In common usage, and sometimes even in academic literature, nation building is often confused with state building. In the standard political science definitions of the terms, the "nation" refers to a *group of people*, while the "state" refers to a *set of institutions*. Benedict Anderson (1983) defines the nation as an "imagined community"; that is, a large group of people with a shared subjective sense of belonging. In Max Weber's (1919) classic formulation, the state is a set of institutions that claims a "monopoly on the legitimate use of force" within a given territory and over a given population. Nation building, therefore, becomes the process of building shared national identity amongst the citizens of the state, while state building is the process of building the capacity and legitimacy of state institutions.

In the first few decades after independence, nation building (as defined above) was a major focus of political action by African states. The argument was that colonialism had left African states with disparate populations who lacked a sense of common national identity. Much of the push for "modernization" was associated with an attempt to build these new national identities, hopefully leaving behind more parochial ethnic identities. Nation building efforts were led by African states themselves, though Canada and other countries were certainly supportive of the endeavour.

Following the American-led interventions in Afghanistan and Iraq in the early 2000s, the common meaning of nation building underwent a significant change. The neo-conservative proponents of these wars used the phrase "nation building" to refer to the process of rebuilding war-torn countries after the removal of the former regime. Since much of the work of rebuilding these countries involved (re)building state institutions, the "new" nation building became much closer to the older concept of state building. Significantly, this new nation building was led by external actors, who saw it as the necessary condition for a peaceful withdrawal from the countries they had occupied. In Africa, there was no equivalent to the invasions of Afghanistan and Iraq, but there was a significant upsurge in intrastate conflict following the end of the Cold War. As some of these conflicts moved towards resolution, the new sense of nation building (efforts to rebuild shattered states and societies) soon became a major activity in Africa. As discussed below, Canada was one of the external actors that participated in these new nation-building activities in Africa.

## CANADA'S AFRICA POLICY

What, then, has been the history of Canada's foreign policy in Africa during the independence era, and what have been Canada's contributions to African nation building? Obviously, in a chapter of this length it is impossible to tell the full story of the Canada-Africa relationship over the last 50 years; what follows is a selective account. Highlighted is the inconsistent and episodic nature of Canada's Africa policy, with periods of active engagement separated by periods of indifference and neglect.

The first major African issue that confronted Canadian policy makers in the independence era was South Africa's renewed membership in the Commonwealth, following the whites-only referendum in 1960 that resulted in South Africa becoming a republic. Canada, like the United Kingdom and the other "white" dominions, was politely critical of racial discrimination in South Africa, but reluctant to take any concrete action against a traditional ally; the "new" Commonwealth members, led by India, were adamant that the Commonwealth could not survive with racist South Africa as a full member. At the 1961 Commonwealth Prime Ministers' conference, Canadian Prime Minister John Diefenbaker proposed that the Commonwealth adopt a resolution reaffirming its commitment to the principle of racial equality. This neatly finessed the problem, as South Africa subsequently withdrew its application for renewed membership.

Starting in the later 1960s, development assistance became a major pillar of Canada's Africa policy. Canada took a leadership role in the new enterprise of international development assistance, with Prime Minister Lester Pearson chairing the UN expert commission, which in 1969 established the widely agreed upon target that donor countries should give 0.7 percent of their gross national income as official development assistance (ODA) (Commission on International Development, 1969). The Canadian International Development Agency (CIDA) was founded as a separate agency under the terms of the Foreign Affairs and International Trade Act of 1968. As David Morrison (1998) discusses in his history of CIDA, development assistance has enjoyed widespread support among the Canadian public over the years. Even though academic experts and others are frequently critical of CIDA, the public at large tends to believe that it is doing a good job (Morrison, 1998: 269). Indeed, for many Canadians, CIDA embodies values of humane internationalism that they hold dear.

While Africa is only a minor economic partner of Canada, it has always been a major focus of CIDA activity. Disbursements have varied over the years, but throughout CIDA's existence African countries have typically been the recipient of more than one-third of total Canadian ODA (Morrison, 1998: 466). From the beginning, CIDA has been careful to balance its African aid program between anglophone and francophone countries. Although the list is ever changing, CIDA's countries of focus in Africa traditionally included a judicious mix of French- and English-speaking countries.

Because of Africa's prominence in Canada's development assistance program, in many respects Canada's Africa policy has been aid policy.[2] Aid has been the dominant lens through which Canadians have understood Africa and the major vehicle through which the Government of Canada has engaged with Africa. As has been repeatedly pointed out by academic critics of CIDA, however, Canada has frequently been a fickle and inconsistent development assistance partner (Brown and Jackson, 2009; Morrison, 1998). After an initial period of enthusiasm and growth subsequent to its creation, CIDA suffered a period of retrenchment and reorientation in the late 1970s and early 1980s as the Trudeau government struggled with recession and stagflation (Morrison, 1998). This pattern of ebb and flow in ODA commitments was repeated in subsequent years.

In the latter part of the 1970s and through to the 1980s, an increasing focus of Canada's Africa policy was the anti-apartheid struggle in South Africa and the liberation struggle in southern Africa more generally. As Linda Freeman (1997) argues, Canada was at best an "ambiguous champion" of the liberation struggle. A wide array of church groups, non-governmental organizations and other civil society actors in Canada pushed the government to take a more decisive stand against racial discrimination in southern Africa. For many years Canada hesitated, reluctant to get ahead of its Western allies in imposing sanctions on the apartheid regime. The government of Brian Mulroney, however, decided to make southern Africa a centrepiece of its foreign policy. Prime Minister Mulroney made a bold statement at the United Nations in 1985, pledging to "invoke total sanctions" against South Africa should it fail to reform (Brown, 1990). Although critics, such as Freeman, are skeptical about the true depth of Canada's commitment at the time, and although there were many missteps along the way, there is no doubt that Canada did play an important role in supporting the successful UN-led transition to Independence in Namibia in 1990 and in supporting the end of apartheid in South Africa (ibid.).

With the end of apartheid, however, came a marked decline in Canadian interest in Africa. After making a major contribution to the Namibian independence process, Canada contributed very few soldiers or other personnel to subsequent UN peacekeeping missions in Africa. Meanwhile, CIDA suffered a series of budget cutbacks as the Jean Chrétien government sought to bring the federal budget deficit under control. CIDA suffered more than other government departments, absorbing a 33 percent cut to its budget (with African programming within CIDA cut back proportionally) at a time when overall federal government expenditure declined five percent in real terms (Brown and Jackson, 2009: 16).

In the late 1990s and into the early 2000s, Africa suddenly returned to the centre of Canada's foreign policy. This was the period of the "human security agenda," championed by Foreign Affairs Minister Lloyd Axworthy. When Canada assumed the rotating presidency of the UN Security Council in April 2000, it laid out a five-point program arising from the human security agenda, with four of the five points related directly or indirectly to Africa (Brown, 2001: 196). In these years, Canada was actively involved in the Kimberley diamond certification process,[3] the process leading to the 1997 Ottawa treaty banning land mines and the development of the "Responsibility to Protect" doctrine; all these initiatives had primarily African referents. As well, in line with the "new" nation building, Canada actively engaged with the African Peace and Security Architecture (APSA).[4] It contributed to capacity building of the APSA and provided direct support for the resolution of a number of conflicts, most importantly in Darfur. On the other hand, in keeping with its recent record, Canada contributed very few boots on the ground to these missions. Renewed Canadian engagement with Africa peaked with Prime Minister Chrétien's championing of African concerns at the 2002 Kananaskis Group of Eight (G8) Summit. For the first time, Chrétien made partnership with Africa a major focus of the G8. His successor, Paul Martin, went further, pledging that Canada would double its aid to Africa over a five-year period and declaring that henceforth 14 of the 25 CIDA countries of focus would be from Africa.

Almost as soon Africa appeared at the centre of Canadian foreign policy, it seemed to disappear again. The Stephen Harper government, first elected in 2006, apparently has little interest in Africa. It followed through on the commitment to double aid to Africa, albeit in part through the use of some accounting "sleights of hand."[5] On the other hand, in 2009 it changed the CIDA countries of focus, reducing African representation to seven out of the reduced list of 20; breaking with long-standing practice, it also upset the English-French balance by leaving only one francophone country on the list. More broadly, it declared its commitment to a regional focus on the Americas and to an emphasis on trade and investment over development assistance, both of which seemed to leave Africa out. All this has led many observers to ask if the current government is once again taking Canada "out of Africa" (Black, 2009).

Did Canada's engagement with Africa over the last 50 years contribute to nation building on that continent? Development assistance and liberation support were not explicitly justified in nation-building terms, though it could certainly be argued that they broadly contributed to that project, as the term was originally understood. More recently, Canada's role in conflict resolution and post-conflict reconstruction has frequently been justified in nation-building terms, as it is now defined. Either way, Canada's record with African nation building has been mixed, at best. Canada can certainly point to some important achievements in its overall Africa policy, despite the inconsistencies noted earlier. Looking more narrowly at post-conflict reconstruction, Canada's contribution has certainly been helpful, but it is too small to have made a decisive difference. However one defines nation building, therefore, it cannot be argued that Canada has made a decisive contribution to nation building on the African continent.

## CONCLUSION: EXPLAINING CANADA'S AFRICA POLICY

If Canada has been an inconsistent interlocutor with Africa, how are we to explain this record? The argument of this chapter is that Canada's Africa policy is fundamentally about Canada, not Africa. In order to explain the vagaries of Canada's Africa policy it is necessary to understand the domestic political context in which that policy has been formulated and implemented. As argued in the first section, Canadian governments have an unusual degree of freedom with respect to their Africa policy; it is a policy of choice, not necessity. The declared African goals of Canada's policy were real and they mattered, of course, but the underlying logic driving Canada's Africa policy was a desire to project a certain image of Canada on the international and, more importantly, the domestic stage. At times, this meant that Africa was close to the centre of Canadian foreign policy; however, at other times, for instance when budgetary pressures were intense or the government had other priorities, Africa could just as easily disappear from Canadian foreign policy.

It is possible here to sketch in only the broadest terms these domestic determinants of Canada's Africa policy, though they have been debated extensively in the Canadian foreign policy literature. One determinant is that since the days of Lester Pearson, Canadian governments have wished to project an image of humane internationalism. Canada's development assistance program, as well as its peacekeeping role, is especially important in this regard. Another important driver of Canadian policy is the commitment to multilateralism. In the African context, *this* has meant support for UN and Commonwealth initiatives and a commitment to work through these institutions whenever possible. Multilateralism helps differentiate us from the United States and it reinforces our commitment to international law. A third driver is Canada's never-ending national unity crisis. Until 2009, CIDA maintained a rough parity in its anglophone and francophone countries of focus in Africa. The Harper government's decision to upset this balance says as much about its approach to the national unity file as it does about its approach to Africa; it is no coincidence that the new Parti Québecois government recently announced that it intends to "repatriate" the aid file in response (The Canadian Press, 2013). Historically, Canadian governments have assiduously balanced support for the Commonwealth in Africa with support for its french language counterpart, La Francophonie. Finally, a fourth driver of Canada's Africa policy is multiculturalism. As Canada has become more culturally diverse at home through immigration, it has been increasingly important to emphasize a commitment to racial equality abroad. This was evident as early as Diefenbaker's response to the crisis surrounding South Africa and the Commonwealth, and became even more salient under Mulroney and the struggle against apartheid.

In conclusion, this chapter argues that at its core, Canada's Africa policy has been about projecting an image of Canada as a humane and tolerant country, bilingual and multicultural in character, respectful of international law and working through international institutions, which is committed to policies designed to help those in need and to fight against all forms of racial discrimination. In other words, Canada's Africa policy has been about telling ourselves who we are, or at least who we would like to be. It has been about building the Canadian nation.

## ENDNOTES

[1] See the chapter by David Carment, Milana Nikolko and Dacia Douhabi.

[2] See the chapter by Stephen Brown.

[3] See the chapter by Ian Smillie.

⁴    See the chapter by Edward Ansah Akuffo.

⁵    See the chapter by Stephen Brown.


## WORKS CITED

Akuffo, Edward (2012). *Canadian Foreign Policy in Africa.* Burlington VT: Ashgate.

Anderson, Benedict (1983). *Imagined Communities.* London: Verso.

Anglin, Douglas G. (1960). "Towards a Canadian Policy on Africa." *International Journal* 15: 290–310.

Black, David (2009). "Out of Africa? The Harper Government's New 'Tilt' in the Developing World." *Canadian Foreign Policy* 15, no. 2: 41–56.

———— (2010). "'Africa' as Serial Morality Play in Canadian Foreign Policy." Paper presented to the annual meeting of the Canadian Association of African Studies, Carleton University, Ottawa, May.

Brown, Chris (1990). "Canada and Southern Africa 1989: Autonomy, Image and Capacity in Foreign Policy." In *Canada Among Nations 1989: The Challenge of Change,* edited by Maureen Appel Molot and Fen Osler Hampson. Pages 207–224. Ottawa: Carleton University Press.

———— (2001). "Africa in Canadian Foreign Policy 2000: The Human Security Agenda." In *Canada Among Nations 2001: The Axworthy Legacy,* edited by Fen Osler Hampson, Norman Hillmer and Maureen Appel Molot. Pages 192–212. Oxford: Oxford University Press.

Brown, Chris and Edward T. Jackson (2009). "Could the Senate be Right? Should CIDA be Abolished?" In *How Ottawa Spends, 2009-2010: Economic Upheaval and Political Dysfunction,* edited by Allan T. Maslove. Pages 217–245. Montreal and Kingston: McGill-Queen's University Press.

Commission on International Development (1969). *Partners in Development.*

Freeman, Linda (1997). *The Ambiguous Champion: Canada and South Africa in the Trudeau and Mulroney Years.* Toronto: University of Toronto Press.

Industry Canada (2013). "Trade Data Online (TDO)."

Morrison, David R. (1998). *Aid and Ebb Tide: A History of CIDA and Canadian Development Assistance.* Waterloo: Wilfrid Laurier University Press.

Statistics Canada (2013). "CANSIM 376-0051: International Investment Position, Canadian Direct Investment Abroad and Foreign Direct Investment in Canada, by Country."

The Canadian Press (2013). "Quebec Seeks Own Global Aid Agency: Canada's Policy Doesn't Match Quebec Values, International Relations Minister says of CIDA." *Ottawa Citizen,* February 7.

Weber, Max (1919). *Politics as a Vocation.*

# Part Two:
# Security and Conflict Management

• • • • • • • • • • • • • • • • • • • • • • • •

# Remedying State Fragility in Africa

## Robert I. Rotberg

● ● ● ● ● ● ● ● ● ● ● ● ● ● ● ● ● ●

Sub-Saharan Africa no longer is the fabled, deeply troubled, dark subcontinent. Most of its constituent countries are growing economically, delivering significant social enhancements to their inhabitants and progressing politically. A number of the region's nation-states are increasing their per capita GDPs more rapidly than their Asian counterparts. Poverty is diminishing. Trade between Sub-Saharan Africa and the rest of the world has tripled since 2000, and attracted more private foreign investment than official aid handouts since 2005. Its share of global foreign direct investment has quadrupled since 2000. Almost everywhere in the subcontinent there is the exciting bustle of improvement and of takeoff. Sub-Saharan Africa's much lamented infrastructure deficits are being erased, thanks to China. Furthermore, Africans are much healthier than they were, with startling improvements in child mortality being recorded across half of the subcontinent; dictators are fewer, democrats more common; the intrastate wars of the subcontinent are claiming fewer lives; and almost everywhere in Sub-Saharan Africa there is hope for the future and an upwelling of pride. Sub-Saharan Africa is no longer the "basket case" of yore, about whose future the rest of the world once despaired. Africa is ready at last to play an increasingly important role in the affairs of the world. Major positive changes, in sum, have already transformed what once was a chilling outlook for most of the subcontinent into a future that is potentially much more warm and uplifting.

At a mining investors' conference in Toronto in March 2013, Robert Freidland, one of Canada's best known and most successful entrepreneurs, pronounced Africa the place to be. "There's incredibly large potential to make money," he said. "When you go to Africa to invest, when you work in Africa, you become part of an astonishing success story," he continued. "By 2025," he predicted, "…630 million people…will live in 37 megacities." Building those cities will demand the metals and other resources of Africa. "Africa is definitely open for business," he concluded (Friedland, 2013).

Many, including the International Monetary Fund (IMF), various consultancies and experienced analysts, strongly believe that Sub-Saharan Africa has turned the corner. "Something deep is at work. These countries are on a different path from the one they were on in the past." This "turnaround is neither cyclical nor temporary. It is not just a blip on the screen…" (Radelet, 2010).

President Ellen Johnson Sirleaf of Liberia echoes this favourable optimism. What is going well in Liberia, she writes, is similar to a transformation occurring across a number of other sub-Saharan African countries. "Dictators are being replaced by democracy. Authoritarianism is giving way to accountability. Economic stagnation is turning to resurgence. And… despair is being replaced by hope — hope that people can live in peace… that parents can provide for their families, that children can go to school and receive decent health care, and that people can speak their minds without fear" (Johnson Sirleaf, 2010).

A rapidly swelling, ambitious and globally conscious middle class is one of the key drivers of this new momentum almost everywhere south of the Sahara, just as it was a few decades ago in Asia. Twenty years ago, Africa's middle class was much smaller, and powerless. Now there is a coterie of entrepreneurs and executives that is much less dependent than before on governments for favours, beneficial regulations and permits, and contracts. The rise of middle-class independence and an independent mindset are signs of an Africa, as Johnson Sirleaf proclaims, very much on the rise.

This is the new Africa that has begun to banish the miseries (and the miserable public relations) of the past. Whereas many observers in times past despaired of Sub-Saharan Africa, and murmured that bad news seemed to overwhelm anything else coming out of Africa, now there are true success stories, demonstrable improvements in governance and democracy, and a brighter outlook all around. Twenty-five years ago, only Botswana and Mauritius were full democracies. Today, there are elected democracies in a large proportion of the subcontinent's states. Additionally, in many Sub-Saharan African countries, formal rules are better respected and political institutions are taking hold.

Propelled to some important extent by significant drivers of economic uplift such as the dramatic spread of mobile telephone capabilities and China's pulsating appetite for African resources, Sub-Saharan Africa, for the first time in more than 60 years, has a golden interlude in which it, and sub-Saharan people, can take advantage of abundant new opportunities. The African renaissance could be at hand, no doubt driven by a new generation of gifted leaders, by a new emphasis on strengthened governance, by a new willingness and desire to play a central role in the global commons, and by a determination to overcome the ethnic and acquisitive challenges that have, for too long, held its states from becoming nations.

But as we rightly emphasize the new positive, the road ahead for Sub-Saharan Africa is not obstacle free. The challenges are many, and serious. There are long-standing, and several surprising, even alarming, new barriers that could derail this long-overdue great leap forward.

Sub-Saharan countries are about to expand their populations exponentially. Many small and weak states will double or triple their inhabitant numbers in the next 30 years. Several of the subcontinent's more populous nations will take their places among the largest countries on the planet. Cities will mushroom. Youth numbers will surge and dominate country after country.

As one Sub-Saharan African state after another becomes much larger than could have hitherto been imagined or envisaged, existing challenges will neither be erased nor avoided. Sub-Saharan Africans will still have to contend with the scourge of disease and reduced life expectancy and productivity, with massive educational deficits at secondary and tertiary levels, with an absence of potable water, with energy shortfalls, with being landlocked, and with weak road and rail infrastructures. Together with its burgeoning population, these are Sub-Saharan Africa's key natural, physical and geographical challenges.

There are also man-made challenges; the remaining civil conflicts and simmering wars of some parts of the subcontinent detract from development as well as create worsening outcomes for the civilian populations that are directly affected. In nearly all countries, corruption prevails and hinders developmental progress. Weak rule-of-law regimes, internal insecurities, inhibited political participation, limited transparency and accountability, and a widespread disrespect for fundamental human rights all contribute to poor governance and its counterpart, slower economic growth. A legacy of irresponsible leadership (military coups and despotic adventurism) has brought about this lack of good governance and a deepening of the policy challenges that the subcontinent must now overcome if its future is going to be strong.

Finally, there are those nation-states where another attempt to rig an election or distort the democratic process could reignite internal fires — for example, in Guinea, Ethiopia, Madagascar, Swaziland and Zimbabwe, to mention only five among a number of likely possibilities.

Whether or not each of these diagnoses is widely shared, the transformation of Africa from a region where hostilities between ethnic, geographical, linguistic or religious groups are always raw and contentious into a region where everyone feels they are an integral part of and a valued contributor to the nation-state project is still ongoing. Distrust (political more than ethnic) across communities is rampant and widespread. Grievances are legion. Resource avarice abounds. So too do zero-sum approaches to wealth and political advantage. The inability of many of the nation-states of Africa to keep their citizens safe and secure or to provide them with a reasonably adequate quantity and quality of essential political goods means that minorities often feel oppressed and ethnicity, or some other separate identity, often trumps national solidarity. People feel threatened, especially when they believe that they and people similar to them are being preyed upon rather than protected by a central government — or by a ruling cabal that constitutes a regime in power. Likewise, if wealth opportunities are shared unequally or are channelled to a preferred group, anger intensifies and fuels antagonism.

Anywhere an African polity does not fulfill the functions of a modern nation-state and discriminates against some of its own people; anywhere African leaders look after themselves, their lineages and their kin rather than their entire citizenry; anywhere leaders in Africa appear to steal from their people; anywhere in Africa that is consumed by flamboyant corruption and criminality; anywhere in Africa dominated by greed without a social conscience; and anywhere in Africa lacking a strong separation of power and rule of law, plus a military subordinate to civilians, is at risk of a countervailing popular reaction and cataclysmic civil conflict. This is precisely what has happened so many times in Sub-Saharan Africa (as well as in 2011 and 2012 in North Africa and the Middle East). These are the realities, among others, that hold Africa back. Without close leadership attention to the new approach to peacemaking that Africa's emergent middle class now demands, even China's warm economic embrace of Africa will be unable to create the proper foundations for a new progressive African order.

Much of Sub-Saharan Africa remains weak (or fragile, to use the donor-friendly appellation). The geographical expression we call Somalia continues to be collapsed, even though Somaliland (its northern third) is an adequate, if weak, state capable of delivering a reasonable amount of political goods to its citizens. Indeed, it has done so despite the absence of international recognition since 1993. But southern Somalia and Puntland are appropriately labelled collapsed and failed, respectively, because of the absence, until now, of much freedom from violence (thanks to warlordism and piracy), and of the active antagonism of the al-Qaeda-affiliated al-Shabaab movement. The latter has been ousted from the port city of Kismayo in Jubaland and it no longer controls much of southern Somalia, but at the time of writing, it remains a formidable force of potential destabilization.

The category of failed states is currently occupied, as it has been for two decades, by the Democratic Republic of Congo, both the Sudan and South Sudan, the Central African Republic and Guinea-Bissau, and now by once-democratic Mali. Failed states and collapsed states deliver very little governance (adequate political goods) to their citizens. In addition, they are violent — each year they have war-related deaths in excess of a minimum figure provided by the Uppsala data set and as recorded and explained in earlier editions of the *Index of African Governance* (Rotberg and Gisselquist, 2007; 2008; 2009).

Death (and rape) numbers continue to be very high in much of the eastern Congo, South Sudan, the southern (Kordofan and Blue Nile) and Darfur portions of the Sudan, the Central African Republic (a fallout from a coup in late March 2013, from battles with the Lord's Resistance Army and from the wars of the Sudan), Guinea-Bissau (from drug-related attacks), and Mali's north, where three Tuareg-inspired insurgencies conspired against the Malian state and have now largely been pushed into the Sahara by French, Chadian and ECOWAS (Economic Community of West African States) soldiers.

Much of the rest of Sub-Saharan Africa consists of weak (or fragile) states. The rankings and scores in recent annual compilations of the *Index of African Governance* indicate that there are a dozen or so strong, well-managed, well-governed and well-led states, starting with Mauritius, Cape Verde and Botswana, but also including the Seychelles, South Africa, Namibia, Ghana, São Tomé and Príncipe, Tanzania, Zambia, Malawi and Benin. Sub-Saharan Africa's other 37 states can be classified as weak, a few as somewhat weak (Gabon, Rwanda, Mozambique), and the remainder as gradations of weakness down to very weak.

Weak African states are those that exhibit middling to poor scores according to the *Index of African Governance*. (The Human Development Index, Freedom House, Worldwide Governance Indicators and other measures all jibe with the Index.) This means that these states deliver insufficient, but not dismal, helpings of security, rule of law, participation, transparency, respect for human rights, economic opportunity and human developmental potential to their citizens. (All of the above, as explained at length in my writings, constitutes governance, writ large.) In some places, educational opportunity is better than in others, or health outcomes are stronger. Corruption is less rampant in some countries than in a neighboring weak state. The Republic of Congo, for example, may be a tad less corrupt than the Congo across the river. In one or two places, such as Nigeria, which is almost a failed state, there are frequent episodes of violence. Some countries are safer (less crime) than others. Uganda was once safer than Kenya, but may be less so now. But, as a collective, weak African states are inherently poorly governed and demonstrably fragile. Their populations are dramatically at risk and donors (Canadians and other like-minded nations in particular) must think twice before spending monies in countries where the likelihood of overcoming weakness without major governmental reforms or new, responsible leadership is either poor or uncertain.

Human agency brought Africa to its current state of disarray. Human agency must, equally, provide the wisdom and energy to meet Africa's critical challenges and to chart a successful path forward. Those are the striking conclusions of an analysis of the determining role of leadership in all developing societies, as well as of a broad understanding of Africa's history since 1960. Leaders clearly make a difference; the smaller and the more fragile the state, the more leadership actions are substantial and critical. Hence, the failed states of Africa never failed by themselves or on their own. They were driven to failure and to internal warring by purposeful leadership actions. Likewise, those few African states that have never known internal conflict, that have long been fully participatory with high incomes and high social returns per capita, and those polities that today seek to emulate Botswana and Mauritius, are all well led, with strong political cultures and well-established political institutions.

Intrastate conflict occurs in Africa and elsewhere not primarily because of colonial legacies or poorly drawn borders, not because of ancient hatreds between peoples, not exclusively because of competition for scarce resources, and not completely because of innate avarice. Instead, it is the failure of the modern nation-state in Africa and elsewhere to perform adequately — to deliver the essential political goods that are fundamental to the existence of a nation-state and that satisfy the expectations of its citizens — that causes ruptures of trust, the breaking of the implicit social contract between the state and its citizens and outbreaks of reactive war. Conflict is also protective. Minorities (and sometimes majorities) strike back against authority when they fear for their lives and their rights, or anticipate predatory assaults by the state. Conflict is rarely anomic, offensive or without a recognizable trigger — real or perceived state-delivered discrimination, deprivation and oppression.

Improved governance will strengthen the weaker countries of Africa, enable them to prosper, and avoid state failure and the clash of arms that depresses individual standards of living and reduces the social safety net. If the leaders of Africa could begin to condemn despotism amid their ranks, if they could shun those among their fellow heads of state who compromise the rights of citizens, if they could thus bolster the chances that democracy would take root in more, rather than fewer, countries then, and only then, will the civil wars of Africa diminish in number, frequency and lethality. Otherwise, Africa will continue to struggle to catch up with Asia and Latin America, where the good governance battle has largely been won, and internal wars are now rare.

Africa, especially its emerging middle class, wants to free itself from conflict so that it can truly banish intrastate conflict and consequently join the global village of economic growth. There is no other easy path to prosperity.

Weak (or fragile) states will remain mired in their weakness until Sub-Saharan Africa benefits from strengthened governance and strengthened leadership.

The road ahead for major donors is, therefore, clear. So are the recommendations for action:

- Funds spent specifically on nurturing leadership are well advised. That is, donors should first build capacity for leadership among future political leaders — persons drawn from the ranks of existing younger members of parliament and deputy ministers. They can do so by sponsoring intensive learning about leadership workshops for carefully chosen persons of prospective influence and prominence. Employing a curriculum first created by the African Leadership Council in 2004, these workshops could be introduced in selected African countries on a trial basis and then extended to many more if the "experiment" is judged successful. Canada could, optimally, organize such leadership training in conjunction with like-minded Scandinavian donors, and by drawing on the expertise of those who established and developed the African Leadership Council.

- A cohort of emboldened, enlightened, younger, aspirant political leaders across a number of African countries could reinforce each other's learning and behaviour. The workshop experiences should acculturate them to the arts of leadership. As a group, they will be socialized together and should, thus, gradually develop an esprit de corps to uphold positive leadership values. The object is to develop more leaders in the mould of Seretse Khama, Nelson Mandela and John A. Kufuor, and fewer mendacious tyrants in the footsteps of Robert Mugabe, Daniel arap Moi, Idi Amin and Isaias Afewerki.

- Good governance is fostered by responsible leadership, not just political institutions. In the pre-institutional environment in which most sub-Saharan states find themselves, it is essential to strengthen leadership capacity for good, precisely in order to strengthen the possibility of good governance, and to create a political culture of democracy. Only then are positive political institutions capable of being established and strongly implanted in the body politic of young, struggling, weak and fragile states. Only then do they become fully-fledged nations needing little outside assistance. Only then do they begin to provide the essentials of prosperity — safety, security and rule of law — for their inhabitants. The perfect circle closes and the social contract becomes fulfilled for the inhabitants of African states only when these positive political and social factors are fully in place.

A final, overall, recommendation is that Canada and other like-minded donors should focus almost exclusively on the leadership-governance problem in Sub-Saharan Africa. There is no better way to strengthen Africa's capacity for development and better outcomes.

## WORKS CITED

Freidland, Robert (2013). Speech given at the annual Prospectors and Developers Association of Canada Conference in March. Quoted in "Head to Africa to Join 'an Astonishing Success Story'" by Pat Jordan in *The Globe and Mail,* March 6.

Johnson Sirleaf, Ellen (2010). "Introduction." In *Emerging Africa: How 17 Countries are Leading the Way*, by Steven Radelet. Page 3. Washington, DC: Center for Global Development.

Radelet, Steven (2010). *Emerging Africa: How 17 Countries are Leading the Way.* Washington DC: Center for Global Development.

Rotberg, Robert I. and Rachel M. Gisselquist (2007). *Strengthening African Governance: The Index of African Governance, Results and Outcomes.* Cambridge, MA. World Peace Foundation.

———— (2008). *Strengthening African Governance: The Index of African Governance, Results and Outcomes.* Cambridge, MA. World Peace Foundation.

———— (2009). *Strengthening African Governance: The Index of African Governance, Results and Outcomes.* Cambridge, MA. World Peace Foundation.

# WHAT HAS CANADA (NOT) DONE?

## Drawbacks of Strategically Targeting Limited Resources

As of early 2013, the Canadian International Development Agency (CIDA) and the Department of Foreign Affairs and International Trade (DFAIT) each maintained a list of priority countries on which to focus, and by examining these two lists, Canada has chosen to focus on only a few African nations.[2] For DFAIT, they are Sudan, South Sudan and the Democratic Republic of the Congo (DRC). CIDA engages in Ethiopia, Ghana, Mali, Mozambique, Senegal, Sudan, South Sudan and Tanzania. The logic of strategically targeting Canada's limited resources to only a few pre-selected countries makes sense; however, upon deeper examination, this approach is problematic for a number of reasons. For example, Canada is unable to respond as easily to emerging conflicts in other countries, since effective peace building often requires that good working relationships with local partners are in place before any new work can be initiated. It can often be difficult for new actors to gain entry into a conflict. Having a good reputation with local actors can sometimes help overcome this problem, but this can take many years of working together to build.

Focussing Canada's efforts on only a few pre-determined countries might also make it more difficult to take a regional approach to peace-building efforts in Africa. Drug trafficking is a major problem in the small West African country of Guinea-Bissau. Numerous actors, both there and internationally, including the United Nations Integrated Peace-building Office in Guinea-Bissau, have stressed that a regional focus involving all the relevant stakeholders working together in a coordinated manner is required in order to effectively tackle this issue and help create stability in Guinea-Bissau. Limiting Canada's official engagement in the West African region makes it more difficult to operate in a regional mode.[3] Tracking and capturing Joseph Kony, leader of the Lord's Resistance Army, a guerilla group in Uganda, has become a regional matter, since he is reputed to move in and out of the DRC, Uganda and parts of Sudan undetected. Closely coordinated efforts occurring simultaneously in many countries will likely be required to bring Kony to justice. Addressing the conflict in the Mano River Union region is another issue that requires a wide approach since it transcends state boundaries.[4] Employing a regional focus is necessary to effectively address many other peace-building problems and Canada should, perhaps, reconsider its decision to focus on only a few select African countries.[5] Canada would, however, have to find a way to effectively resolve the dilemma between using targeted assistance provided to only a few pre-selected countries and employing a wider regional approach.

## Lack of Financial Support for Peace-building Activities

Canada has predominately focussed on funding humanitarian assistance in all of its various forms — there is actually very little money given for true peace-building activities, such as conflict resolution workshops, mediation and dialogues. According to figures from DFAIT, Canada has provided more than CDN$24 million since 2006 to support mediation efforts in places such as Sudan, Afghanistan, Pakistan, Colombia, Central America and the DRC. This includes more than CDN$1.3 million towards building the in-house capacity of the UN Mediation Support Unit, CDN$1.1 million to develop the mediation support capacity of the Organization of American States and more than CDN$200,000 to help establish mediation support mechanisms in the African Union (AU) and the Economic Community of West African States (ECOWAS). In contrast, Canada spent over CDN$347.5 million dollars on the 2011 military intervention in Libya. In terms of humanitarian assistance, Canada was the seventh-largest donor of official humanitarian aid in 2010, providing US$550 million in aid (Global Humanitarian Assistance, n.d.). Nearly half of Canada's humanitarian assistance was provided to Africa (ibid.) making it the most important continent for Canadian foreign aid (Brown, 2013). This means that in 2010 alone, Canada spent more than 20 times the amount it provided for all of its peace-building efforts between 2006 and 2012. Canada should, therefore, examine why it doesn't provide greater support for peace building and undertake it more often. Certainly, it would not make sense to increase peace-building efforts without concrete results from earlier activities; however, there is evidence that past peace-building efforts by Canadians have raised Canada's profile on the international stage and produced some very impressive results.

## Notable Canadian Peace-building Achievements

Canadians have led a number of notable peace-building efforts over the last 60 years. During the Suez Crisis in 1956, Canadian Forces were part of a pioneering peacekeeping formation, proposed by Lester B. Pearson, then Canada's secretary of state for external affairs, deployed to help stabilize the situation. Pearson was awarded a Noble Peace Prize in 1957 for his efforts. Canada was also instrumental in developing the Responsibility to Protect (R2P) norm established in 2005 that aims to prevent mass atrocities such as genocide and ethnic cleansing. Former Foreign Affairs Minister Lloyd Axworthy's efforts led to the adoption of the Ottawa Convention — an international treaty banning the use of land mines — in 1997. In the same year, Axworthy was nominated for the Noble Peace Prize and in 2003 he was made an Officer of the Order of Canada. The Fowler Report (named after Canadian diplomat Robert Fowler, who led the UN commission that produced the report), helped to raise awareness about conflict diamonds and eventually sparked the creation of the Kimberley Process in 2003, which aimed to prevent conflict diamonds from entering the market. Lastly, former Prime Minister Brian Mulroney was awarded the Companion of the Order of Canada in 1998 for his efforts to end apartheid in South Africa, and his other notable achievements.

## Canada No Longer a Trusted Mediator?

A December 2012 op-ed argued that some of Canada's foreign policy decisions from last year, such as closing its embassy in Iran and voting against the Palestinian bid for observer state status at the UN, have removed any possibility of Canada playing a future mediation role in the Middle East (Carment, 2012). Building on the point made earlier in this chapter — that having local partners in place is often a necessary prerequisite — it is also important to note that a mediator cannot be imposed upon the conflicting parties. Rather, one must be invited by the parties to intervene, and this usually only occurs if both parties trust the mediator. Trust often needs to be earned; the same op-ed argued that Canada has recently made an intentional shift towards becoming a "warrior nation," which has negatively affected the country's image as a trusted mediator (ibid.). While there has been substantial debate on whether or not this is true, it cannot be the sole reason that Canada is not a more active mediator on the world stage. According to a study by Peter Jones, discussed later in this chapter, Canada has not been a major actor in very many mediation efforts over the last 20 years. Nevertheless, Canada should, perhaps, consider whether it is currently perceived on the world stage as a trusted mediator and what kind of image it would like to project in the future.

Another factor to consider is that, unlike some European countries that have adopted mediation as their "national brand," Canada has simply not made mediation a high-priority foreign policy goal.[6] Finland, for example, recently adopted a National Action Plan for Mediation,[7] which sets out the rationale for making mediation a major part of its foreign policy. Canada currently does not have an overarching policy on mediation to guide its efforts, or any plans to develop such a policy.[8] Moreover, Akuffo (2013: 2) argues that, "since 2006 the Conservative government of Stephen Harper has substantially reduced Canada's support to African-led peace and security initiatives as the government shifted Canadian foreign policy focus to Latin America, Afghanistan, and emerging economies." Furthermore, because Canada's policies are driven by the prime minister (ibid.: 7), leadership from his office will be required before Canada undertakes more peace-building efforts in Africa.

Clearly, without "champions" and advocates within the government, peace building will continue to be underutilized as a tool for advancing Canada's interests in Africa. Zartman and Touval (1996: 452) argue that because mediators are motivated by self-interest, they will intervene only when they believe a conflict threatens their interests or presents an opportunity to advance their interests. As the last section of this chapter describes, Canada can meet many of its interests by focussing on peace-building and post-conflict reconstruction efforts in Africa.

## Canada's Recent Peace-building Efforts

This is not to say that Canada has not supported any peace-building efforts. Although not focussed directly on Africa, Canada has supported efforts to draft the new UN guidance on mediation document (UN, 2012). This important document defines the parameters for the mediation efforts of the United Nations and its member nations and signals the United Nations's intent to make mediation a high priority. Similarly, Canada has provided some modest funding to the UN's Mediation Support Unit. All of this has occurred against a backdrop of Canada's increasing withdrawal from working with the United Nations. Canada's recent efforts to help create peace in Africa via the United Nations have been, at best, a minimal effort.

Canada has also undertaken some recent efforts to support the implementation of peace agreements in Sudan and Darfur. Canada chairs the Sudan-South Sudan Contact Group of like-minded countries that supports peace efforts in Sudan and South Sudan (Organisation for Economic Co-operation and Development [OECD], 2012). In Darfur, Canada serves on the Implementation Follow-up Commission and the Joint Ceasefire Commission (ibid.). A major issue of concern, however, is a lack of support for Canadian non-governmental organizations (NGOs) and peace-building practitioners. Canada's support is often channelled to multilateral institutions, which means that there are very few Canadian peace-building NGOs currently operating in Africa with Canadian funding. Many talented young professionals who want to represent Canada abroad as peace builders have been forced to join NGOs from other countries. In a move illustrative of this pattern, the government recently cut the core funding of Peacebuild[9] (formerly known as the Canadian Peacebuilding Coordinating Committee), a network of Canadian NGOs and institutions, academics and individuals engaged in a wide range of activities that address the causes and consequences of violent conflict. Peacebuild had previously enjoyed a good working relationship with earlier governments and it served as a valuable platform for generating policy and planning new joint peace-building projects among its members.

## Signs of Support for Canadian Peace Building

On the other hand, there are some signs within the last year of a possible move towards greater support for Canadian peace builders. DFAIT, for example, is currently building a new database of Canadian experts that it can utilize, from time to time, for special assignments overseas as requests for support come into Ottawa. This move stems, in part, from a recent study commissioned by DFAIT. Peter Jones, associate professor at the University of Ottawa, was tasked with identifying all Canadians who have mediated in an official capacity (that is, on behalf of the Canadian government) in the last 20 years. His study identified 47 individuals who fit these criteria, 35 of whom he was able to interview. Jones identified 18 cases where Canadian officials (serving or former) were involved. Of these, Canada led or co-led four processes at the official level, and one at the "Track 1.5" level. Canada made a significant contribution to another seven processes and a more modest contribution, usually in the form of financial support, to another three processes.[10] Jones' landmark study represents the first time that DFAIT has taken a retrospective look at its own international mediation experience and capacity.

These two important steps may signify a shift towards building and supporting Canadian peace-building talent, but much more work remains to be done in order to truly engage the Canadian peace-building community and support its efforts in Africa and elsewhere. In sum, there is nothing unique per se about the Canadian approach to peace-building and post-conflict reconstruction in Africa, despite the fact that there is a rich and deep pool of expertise to draw upon. What becomes evident from this examination is that Canada's approach is far from unique and there are multiple areas where improvements could be made. There exists, therefore, an important and timely opportunity for Canada to rebrand itself as an innovator in this area. In doing so, Canada may also inspire other countries with a similar approach to peace building to follow suit.

## CHARTING THE WAY FORWARD

Since there are few Canadian peace-building efforts in Africa to point to in recent years, we can instead look at missed opportunities. This allows us to rethink our peace-building and post-conflict reconstruction agenda in Africa, and learn from the successes, as well as the errors and omissions, in order to help chart a way forward.

### Opportunities for Canada to Play a Peace-building Role

Canada could be playing a more decisive peace-building role in a number of conflicts in Africa: in the DRC, where the March 23 Movement rebels have advanced; in Guinea-Bissau, where coups and instability are ongoing; in the Central African Republic, which has recently experienced a coup; in Nigeria, which is struggling to control violence initiated by militants; and in Guinea, which is currently dealing with a major political crisis related to delayed elections. Moreover, Canada could take steps to help prevent post-election violence that might still arise in Kenya and, more generally, undertake activities aimed at preventing election-related violence from occurring in other countries with upcoming elections.[11] The need to tackle African conflicts has been recognized by the head of the International Monetary Fund, Christine Lagarde, who recently said that conflict is the main threat to African growth (Bavier, 2013).

If current events are any indication, there is no shortage of opportunities for Canada to play a supportive role in promoting peace in Africa. In the future, however, Canadian foreign policy on peace building in Africa needs to begin with a clear statement of its goals. In this regard, Canada should commit to supporting the growth of multicultural, fully democratic and inclusive states in Africa that have well-established rule of law and basic human rights guarantees for all of their citizens. This should be considered an overarching peace-building goal to strive for.

## Canadian Peace Building Should Recognize the Linkages between Peace, Security and Development

Being absolutely transparent about its interests and goals would help Canada build its credibility and earn trust, which is a necessary prerequisite for positive and constructive engagement with its partners in Africa. Canada also needs to recognize the interdependence between peace, security and development, and how this can create a favourable climate for Canadian businesses to operate in. More precisely, in supporting the growth of peace by making international mediation, conflict resolution and other peace-building activities a cornerstone of its foreign policy in Africa, Canada would increase its soft power (defined as the ability to influence others without using coercion or force), while at the same time creating new trade and investment opportunities. There is, thus, an important role in the future for Canadian businesses to play in advancing Canada's peace-building agenda in Africa. DFAIT would be wise to devise a new strategy that outlines how it will engage the business community in order to advance mutual interests in Africa. Certainly, the recent announcement concerning the creation of a new Department of Foreign Affairs, Trade and Development presents a timely opportunity for Canada to translate these linkages into new foreign policies.

## Canadian Peace Building Should Focus on both the Short and Long Term

No matter which phase of the conflict cycle Canada is intervening in (preventative, after violence has already broken out, or during the post-conflict phase), it needs to keep a long-term focus. It is now a well-established fact that foreign aid, development assistance and peace-building effectiveness are adversely affected by short-term approaches. Notwithstanding the need for short-term, rapid responses to emerging crises, addressing deeper, structural issues that impede peace requires a long-term approach. Staff turnover at DFAIT and CIDA, changes of government and short funding cycles are all factors that hinder Canada's ability to take long-term approaches to peace building in Africa.

## Canada Should Focus on Preventing Violent Conflicts

Canada can take an even more proactive and progressive approach to building peace by focussing on the prevention of violent conflicts in Africa. This new focus on prevention could be achieved through supporting and working with regional mechanisms like the AU and ECOWAS. These actors already have early warning and response mechanisms in place and they can often be mobilized very quickly. Canada is already supporting the AU's current stabilization efforts in Mali, but it needs to provide this kind of support more often in other emerging conflicts. Part of achieving this goal might mean broadening the list of counties Canada will engage with to include all African countries. For example, the entire Sahel region is, at the moment, very volatile and could benefit from Canadian conflict-prevention efforts. If prevention fails to avert the eruption of violent conflict, however, then Canada needs to plan to engage more specifically on peace building. While a great deal of money is spent on humanitarian assistance and related activities, the government needs to direct funds explicitly towards peace-building activities such as dialogues and peace processes.

Canada must also ensure that it maintains a conflict-sensitive approach in its post-conflict reconstruction efforts in Africa that builds the capacity of local actors to prevent the outbreak of future violent conflicts.

## There Are Many Possible Peace-building Roles for Canada

It is important to note that Canada does not need to, nor should it always expect to, take the lead role in peace-building efforts in Africa. Leadership can be demonstrated in other ways and there are many support tasks that could be done, ranging from coordination to norm setting to specialized information collection and analysis, to monitoring and supporting the implementation of peace agreements. In terms of norm setting, Canada has, for example, worked with the G7+ to develop norms for engagement in fragile states and it should continue this work to develop and implement the New Deal for Engagement in Fragile States.[12] The New Deal can serve as an important guide for Canada's actions in Africa.[13]

## CONCLUSION

In sum, Canada's approach should place a primary focus on preventing violent conflict from occurring in the first place, mediating its resolution if prevention fails and then, lastly, undertaking post-conflict reconstruction activities that will help prevent the outbreak of future conflict by building local capacities to prevent and resolve future conflicts in a non-violent manner in keeping with the overall goal of supporting the growth of multicultural, fully democratic and inclusive states in Africa. There are, without a doubt, many reasons why Canada should not carry on with "business as usual" in Africa. There is a need for Canada to re-examine its peace-building policies, as outlined in the suggestions made in this chapter.

## ENDNOTES

[1]  Akuffo (2013) argues that a similar pattern has also occurred in terms of Canada's security engagement with Africa.

[2]  In its March 2013 federal budget, the government announced that it planned to merge CIDA with DFAIT to form one super-ministry, the Department of Foreign Affairs, Trade and Development.

[3]  For a detailed analysis on the need for taking a regional approach to counter West African drug trafficking, see A. Bybee (2012), "The

Twenty-first Century Expansion of the Transnational Drug Trade in Africa," *Journal of International Affairs* 66, no. 1.

4    For an excellent overview of this conflict, see: www.c-r.org/conflicts/mano-river-union-0.

5    For a detailed discussion of the necessity of building peace across state borders, see A. Ramsbotham and I. W. Zartman (eds.) (2011), *Building Peace Across Borders*, Accord: An International Review of Peace Initiatives, Issue 22, London: Conciliation Resources.

6    For example, it is only within the last two years that a full-time mediation focal point position has been created at DFAIT.

7    See Ministry for Foreign Affairs of Finland (2011), *Action Plan for Mediation,* available at: www.pbsbdialogue.org//documentupload/49151944.pdf.

8    In 2005 and 2006, there were some initial explorations on how to build a Canadian international mediation capacity, including a DFAIT "Fast Talk" session on conflict prevention during which this topic was discussed (Storie, 2006). These initial deliberations, however, never led to any wider consultations or the creation of a new policy.

9    David Lord, personal communications, April 5, 2013.

10   Peter Jones, personal communications, December 5, 2012.

11   The Toronto-based Sentinel Project for Genocide Prevention indicated that there was a high chance for violence to occur in Kenya due to the elections. This would have been a perfect opportunity for Canada to undertake conflict prevention actions. See: http://thesentinelproject.org/kenya-annual-report-update-high-risk-rating-remains-in-effect/.

12   The G7+ is a group of fragile and conflict-affected countries that have united to form one collective voice on the global stage. The countries are: Afghanistan, Burundi, Central African Republic, Chad, Comoros, Côte d'Ivoire, the DRC, Guinea-Bissau, Guinea, Haiti, Liberia, Papau New Guinea, Sierra Leone, the Solomon Islands, Somalia, South Sudan, Timor-Leste and Togo.

13   See International Dialogue on Peacebuilding and Statebuilding (2012), "A New Deal for Engagement in Fragile States," available at: www.pbsbdialogue.org//documentupload/49151944.pdf.

## WORKS CITED

Akuffo, E. (2013). "Canada's Engagement with African Regional Peace and Security Architecture: Constructivist Analysis and Implications for Policy." In *Canada-Africa Relations: Looking Back, Looking Ahead — Canada Among Nations 2013,* edited by Rohinton Medhora and Yiagadeesen Samy. Waterloo: CIGI.

Bavier, J. (2013). "IMF's Lagarde says armed conflict 'Enemy No. 1' of African growth." *The Globe and Mail*, January 7. Available at: www.theglobeandmail.com/report-on-business/international-business/african-and-mideast-business/imfs-lagarde-says-armed-conflict-enemy-no-1-of-african-growth/article7009427.

Brown, S. (2013). "Canadian Aid to Africa." In *Canada-Africa Relations: Looking Back, Looking Ahead — Canada Among Nations 2013,* edited by Rohinton Medhora and Yiagadeesen Samy. Waterloo: CIGI.

Carment, D. (2012). "Canada's led itself into a corner." *The Globe and Mail*, December 6. Available at: www.theglobeandmail.com/commentary/canadas-led-itself-into-a-corner/article6003394/.

Global Humanitarian Assistance. Country Profiles: Canada. Available at: www.globalhumanitarianassistance.org/countryprofile/canada.

OECD (2012). *Improving International Support to Peace Processes: The Missing Piece.* OECD Publishing: Conflict and Fragility.

Storie, F. (2006). "A Canadian International Mediation Capacity." In *CIIAN News.* Pages 4–7. Ottawa: Canadian International Institute of Applied Negotiation. Available at: www.ciian.org/assets/newsletters/CIIAN-Newsletter-Summer2006.pdf.

United Nations (2012). *Guidance for Effective Mediation.* New York: United Nations. Available at: www.un.org/wcm/webdav/site/undpa/shared/undpa/pdf/UN%20Guidance%20for%20Effective%20Mediation.pdf.

Zartman, I. W. and S. Touval (1996). "International Mediation in the Post-Cold War Era." In *Managing Global Chaos: Sources of and Responses to International Conflict*, edited by Chester Crocker, Fen Osler Hampson and Pamela Aall. Pages 463–473. Washington: United States Institute of Peace Press.

# Canada's Engagement with African Regional Peace and Security Architecture: Constructivist Analysis and Implications for Policy

### Edward Ansah Akuffo

• • • • • • • • • • • • • • • • • • • •

## INTRODUCTION

This chapter provides an analysis of Canada's support for the African Peace and Security Architecture (APSA) that was established by the African Union (AU) to promote peace and security in the African region. Its central argument is that Canada's security role in Africa is informed by its moral identity on the African continent. It further argues that even though Canada's moral image is an important international capital, it must back its morality with substantial and sustainable material and financial support for peace and security if it is to maintain its influence and competitiveness on the African continent in the twenty-first century. The chapter draws on constructivists-inspired theoretical framework, "non-imperial internationalism," to provide an understanding of

Canada's security role in Africa. The central element of this framework is Canada's moral identity, which connotes "the normative image of Canada that motivates or shapes the behaviour, interests, and activities of Canada in the global arena generally and on the African continent specifically. Canada's moral identity entails how Canada perceives itself as caring, a good international citizen, and as a humanitarian and moral actor. The other side of the coin is the construction of Africa as the 'other' which is conflict-ridden and poor and, hence, requiring the benevolent support of Canada especially through development assistance and peacekeeping" (Akuffo, 2012: 2). The result of the construction of Africa as poor and conflict-ridden is the lack of Canada's Africa strategy that clearly articulates the pursuit of long-term mutual security and economic interests with African states and organizations.

Canada's moral identity is rooted in its historical relationship with Africa as a non-colonizer, and sustained by the objectives of development assistance and peacekeeping — the two pillars of Canadian activism in Africa. To this end, although there can be episodic shifts, Canada's moral identity is a structural phenomenon that does not necessarily change with a change of government or government policy towards Africa. Thus, the maintenance of moral identity appears to be a norm in Canada's approach to Africa that is largely driven by the prime minister and Canada's relations in multilateral institutions, such as the United Nations. The discussion in this chapter sheds light on why the African continent lies at the margins of Canadian foreign policy, and why there is a need for a stronger and long-term partnership between Canada and the AU to promote peace and security in Africa. It concludes with suggestions on how to strengthen Canada-AU cooperation generally and, more specifically, on security.

## CONTEXTUALIZING CANADA'S SECURITY ENGAGEMENT IN AFRICA

Canada's security engagement in Africa at the turn of the twenty-first century can be understood within the context of rising (human) security concerns, especially in the 1990s, and the subsequent transformations of African regional institutions to respond to these challenges. Africa's post-Cold War insecurity, the result of violent conflicts, was often met by half-hearted interventions and inaction, especially by the United Nations and Western powers.[1] This contributed to the Economic Community of West African State (ECOWAS) intervention in Liberia in 1990 without a Security Council authorization. As well, the 1994 Rwanda genocide[2] may have prompted other African interventions such as the Southern African Development Community (SADC) interventions in Lesotho and the Democratic Republic of the Congo in 1998. These interventions demonstrated "an awakening of the conscience" and the willingness of African leaders to take an active role to promote peace, security and stability on the African continent.

This "new thinking" among African leaders brought institutional innovation in Africa's approach to peace, security and development. The New Partnership for Africa's Development (NEPAD) was launched in 2001, followed by the transformation of the Organisation of African Unity (OAU) into to the AU in 2002, to address the twin challenges of security and development in Africa. As the African leaders embraced the slogan of "African solutions to Africa's problems," the AU established the APSA for the prevention, management and resolution of conflicts. The APSA includes the AU Peace and Security Council, Panel of the Wise, Continental Early Warning System (CEWS) and an African Standby Force (ASF) that will be fully operational by 2015.

The institutional transformations in Africa had significant impacts on Canada's security role in the region. Under the Liberal government of Jean Chrétien, Canada's foreign policy took a major, positive shift in support of the peace and security capacity building of the AU and sub-regional organizations, especially the ECOWAS. The NEPAD framework now provided an avenue for the funding of Africa's security initiatives. Canada became the mouthpiece for NEPAD in the international community and led the Group of Eight (G8) to establish an Africa Action Plan to help implement the priorities that are set out in the NEPAD document (NEPAD, 2001). The Chrétien government established a CDN$500 million Canada Fund for Africa (CFA), within the context of the Africa Action Plan, to implement those priorities, which include trade reforms, democracy, investment and the promotion of peace and security (ibid.). The CFA allocated CDN$4 million and CDN$15 million to the AU peace and security capacity building, and West Africa peace and security initiatives, respectively. The Liberal government's engagements reflected an overall policy of placing Africa at the center of Canada's international cooperation (CIDA, 2003; 2004; 2006). Nevertheless, there was a resource-commitment gap in the Liberal government policy in view of the overwhelming security challenges on the African continent. The lack of significant Canadian resource contribution to Africa's peace and security capacity building has persisted since Prime Minister Stephen Harper's Conservative government came to power in 2006. As will be discussed later, both Liberal and Conservative governments have spent far more resources (including financial, material and personnel) on the "war against terror" in Afghanistan than in Africa since the turn of the twenty-first century. Generally speaking, the lack of adequate Canadian material support for Africa's peace and security was compounded by the Harper government's shift in Canadian foreign policy focus to Latin America, Afghanistan and emerging economies.

## NON-IMPERIAL INTERNATIONALISM AND CANADA'S MORAL IDENTITY IN AFRICA

Like all states, Canada's foreign policy is anchored on the pursuit of national interests. In this light, Canada has developed and maintained stronger ties with its traditional allies — such as the United States, France and the United Kingdom, as well as other Western nations — through treaties and other international arrangements, such as the G8. Arguably, beyond the Euro-Atlantic region, Canadian governments (over time) demonstrate less commitment in terms of foreign policy. In the case of the African continent, Canada's engagement, even though influenced by economic and security interests, has followed a "moral trajectory." Although economic and security interests are prominent in Canada's internationalism in Africa, Canada's overall foreign policy orientation is embedded in the maintenance of moral identity — the pursuit of humane-oriented foreign policy objectives, including human rights, human security and poverty alleviation (Akuffo, 2012).

As noted earlier, Canada's moral identity is the core element of the non-imperial internationalist approach to Canadian foreign policy in Africa. Non-imperial internationalism draws on constructivists' approach to international relations that focus on the role of ideas in shaping the identity and interests of actors in the international system (Onuf, 1989; Ruggie, 1998; Wendt, 1995; 1999). What follows is a brief outline of some of the mutually reinforcing ideas of the non-imperial internationalist approach which projects Canada's moral identity: first, Canada has never been a colonial power in Africa;

second, Canada perceives itself as developed, which in turn portrays Africa as the "other" — poor and conflict-ridden; third, Canada has historically been an active supporter of and a voice for African initiatives, such as NEPAD; fourth, Canada does not impose its views, especially on Africa's regional organizations; finally, and more importantly, Canada enjoys a reciprocal image in Africa[3] as non-belligerent, friendly and sensitive to Africa's interests (Akuffo, 2012). It is important to recall that Canada's moral identity is not only historically produced through diplomatic interactions, but it is anchored on development assistance and peacekeeping through which Canada promotes humane-oriented goals, such as human rights and poverty reduction. Canada's moral image sets it apart from its closest allies, which are perceived by African officials as belligerent or (neo-) colonial powers. This is in spite of the fact that Canada, like its allies, plays an active role in the exportation of the neo-liberal ideology of the free market through global institutions such as the International Monetary Fund, the World Bank and the World Trade Organization. These organizations are generally criticized for undermining economic development and contributing to the increasing gap between both peoples and states in Africa on the one hand, and advanced industrialized societies on the other hand. Ironically, the neo-liberal agenda of NEPAD was one of the main reasons why Canada supported it; yet, this did not undermine Africa's perception of Canada as a moral actor. Following this analogy, Canada could be described as a moral superpower in Africa, when one takes a historical view and compares Canadian foreign policy behaviour with its key allies on the African continent.

## A NEW AFRICA AND CANADA'S SUPPORT FOR AFRICAN PEACE AND SECURITY INITIATIVES

Unlike the OAU, the establishment of the AU and APSA and the launching of NEPAD, which has now been integrated into the AU system, project a new image of Africa (NEPAD, 2010). The AU's positive image as a security-, development- and human rights-oriented organization attracted the Chrétien government (which played a leadership role in the creation of the G8 Africa Action Plan) and the CFA that, among other things, supported AU and ECOWAS peace and security initiatives. Unlike its predecessor, the OAU, the

AU's new image was consistent with the "good international citizen" image that Canada portrays in the global arena.

The policy transformations that took place in Africa coincided with Canada's new-found role as a global leader to promote human security. Through the active involvement of then Minister of Foreign Affairs, Lloyd Axworthy, Chrétien's Canadian foreign policy was framed as the protection of people during violent conflicts — freedom from fear. The Chrétien government played leadership roles to establish global institutions: the International Criminal Court, which has the jurisdiction to try individuals for war crimes, genocide and crimes against humanity; the 1997 Ottawa Treaty to ban anti-personnel land mines; the Kimberly Process Certification Scheme on conflict diamonds; and the Responsibility to Protect (R2P), that redefines sovereign as a responsibility of states and the international community to protect human rights. Canada worked with African states at the diplomatic level to establish these innovative institutions to protect and promote human security.

The single most important policy innovation that appears to have informed Canada's closer partnership with the AU to protect human security in Africa was the incorporation of the "just cause" principles of the R2P — the need for the international community to intervene in situations of large-scale loss of life, including genocide and ethnic cleansing — into the legal institutions of the AU (AU, 2000). The AU is the first intergovernmental organization to entrench the R2P threshold for intervention into its Constitutive Act. According to Article 4 (h) of the Constitutive Act of the AU, the AU has the right to intervene in "member states in respect of grave circumstances, namely: war crimes, genocide, and crimes against humanity" (ibid.). In this regard, the AU did not only give its backing to intervention through the R2P doctrine, but its action also supported the entrenchment of international humanitarian law in international affairs through the establishment of the International Criminal Court. In sum, the transformation of African institutions and Canada's own foreign policy focus on human security provided the motivation for the Government of Canada's support to APSA. This suggests that the AU's new identity and interest were consistent with Canadian foreign policy goals.

Drawing on Canada's experience in peacekeeping, Chrétien's Liberal government focussed on building the capacity of the ASF. The CDN$15 million of the CFA (allocated for peace and security initiatives in West

Africa) supported several projects, including the establishment of the "African Peacekeeping Centers of Excellence (APCE) made up of the Kofi Annan International Peacekeeping Training Center (KAIPTC) in Accra, Ghana that offers peace support training at the operational level; the African Center for Strategic Research Studies (ACSRS) which is part of the National War College in Abuja, Nigeria that offers training at the strategic level; and the Ecole de Maintien de la Paix in Bamako, Mali which concentrates on training at the tactical level" (Akuffo, 2012: 131).

Canada's support for AU regional peace and security capacity building falls far short of its spending in Afghanistan alone. For instance, the incremental cost in Afghanistan from 2001 to 2011 was estimated at CDN$11.3 billion (Government of Canada, 2011). A 2008 report, *Fiscal Impact of the Canadian Mission in Afghanistan,* put the overall spending at CDN$18.1 billion by 2011, and acknowledged that the lack of transparency and consistency made figures difficult to estimate (Office of the Parliamentary Budget Officer, 2008; CBC News, 2008). According to the Government of Canada (2010), "Canada has provided a total of $26 million since 2005 on programs that build African capacity to conduct peace operations." More specifically, Canada has spent CDN$11 million on ASF training since 2005, including support for peacekeeping training centers in Kenya and South Africa (ibid.). This spending includes the Harper government's announcement in 2008 to provide CDN$10.3 million of the Global Peace and Security Fund (GPSF) over three years to support police and civilian training, as well as to improve the institutional capacity and coordination of the APCE (Akuffo, 2012: 133). The training of the ASF involves Canadian organizations. As the Embassy of Canada (2012) in Addis Ababa noted, "the Pearson Centre and CANADEM [Canada's Civilian Reserve]…have enabled the actual sharing of the Canadian expertise in a flexible and responsive manner along quality standards." Nevertheless, it can be argued that an increase in Canada's security spending in Africa to the tune of what was spent in Afghanistan will go a long way to provide training to the ASF and support other institutions of the APSA that would, in turn, contribute to building a long-term partnership between Canada and the AU.

Aside from ASF training, Canada has provided support to the AU during times of conflict. In the 1990s, Canada provided support for OAU intervention in Burundi and Rwanda. The most elaborate Canadian assistance to an

African-led intervention came in the Chrétien government's provision of equipment and logistical support to the AU Mission in Sudan (AMIS), which intervened in the Darfur crisis in 2003 until the joint AU and UN hybrid force (UNAMID) took over in January 2008. Among other things, the Canadian military provided 105 armoured personnel carriers, vests and protective helmets to AMIS. In addition, Canada supported AMIS operations in the area of logistics. Canadian experts assisted in operating the AU's information analysis cell, which was part of the Darfur Integrated Taskforce, charged with the overall mandate to bring peace and security to Darfur.

After Prime Minister Harper came into power, his Conservative government maintained Canada's support (equipment and logistics) to the African forces in the UNAMID. This ensured some consistency in Canada's overall approach to the Darfur crisis. As co-chair with the United States of the Friends of UNAMID Group, Canada has provided CDN\$255 million since 2006 in voluntary contributions for peace and security in the Sudan (Government of Canada, 2012). The Canadian military launched Operation Saturn (January 2008), a military task force, to assist UNAMID capacity building in areas such as intelligence, logistics, administration and civil-military cooperation; this demonstrated consistency as it came on the heels of Operation Augural (July 2005), which assisted the AMIS (National Defence and the Canadian Forces, 2012). Canada fell short, however, of deploying "boots on the ground" as part of the military personnel that carried out the day-to-day operations in the field. Moreover, the number of Canadian military personnel who were deployed to assist AMIS and UNAMID remained very small; for instance, Operation Saturn was made up of a six-man team. The overall Canadian Forces contribution in Darfur reflects the decline in Canadian peacekeeping contribution to the United Nations since the late 1990s. It is noteworthy that Canada has contributed less than 200 peacekeepers to UN peacekeeping operations in each year since the mid-2000s (UN, 2012). If this trend continues, it may undermine Canada's influence in Africa: the "home" of UN peacekeeping operations.

Both the Chrétien and Martin governments' support to AMIS was linked to the long-term capacity building of the ASF. This constituted an important shift in Canadian foreign policy that has hitherto concentrated on multilateral and bilateral relations with African states in the areas of development assistance and UN peacekeeping. Yet, Canada's overall support to the ASF demonstrates the negative construction of Africa in Canadian foreign policy, which shows a dialectical or mutually linked relationship between development assistance and peacekeeping that reinforces Canada's foreign policy and moral identity in Africa. Through the support for APSA, the two policy arenas of development assistance and peacekeeping became interlinked both in theory and practice, and helped to espouse the same ideas and interests of the Canadian government. In the theoretical realm, Canada's support to the ASF capacity building appears to have been conceived by the Government of Canada (both Liberal and Conservative) as development assistance. Corollary, development assistance and peacekeeping are perceived as Canada's "benevolent activity" towards an African continent that has little geostrategic interests to Canada. In effect, development assistance and peacekeeping carry the notion of "help," the promotion of Canadian values (such as human rights and the rule of law) and are seen by Canada and NGOs as the solutions to the predicaments of African states and people. At the practical level, therefore, the Canadian government (especially Chrétien's Liberal government) used CIDA as the main implementation institution of the CFA and the support for APSA, even though the Department of Foreign Affairs and International Trade (DFAIT), Department of National Defence, CANADEM and the Pearson Centre were involved in the implementation process at different levels.

The Government of Canada established the Stabilization and Reconstruction Task Force (START), supported by the GPSF, as a unit within DFAIT in 2005, to provide leadership and coordinate government responses to international crises and to "deliver effective programming in support of conflict management and peace-building, peacekeeping and peace operations" (DFAIT, 2012a). Since 2005, START's Global Peace Operations Programme has supported the AU's peace and security institutional capacity building, including support for the African forces in the UNAMID (DFAIT, 2012b). It is important to note, however, that within the context of the CFA's support for NEPAD priorities, CIDA appears to have played an overarching role, including in the areas of Canada's support for APSA, as evidenced in the January 2011 report, *Canada Fund for Africa: Summative Evaluation Executive Report,* authored by CIDA's Evaluation Directorate (CIDA, 2011). Even though the report mentions START, it is not clear as to the specific role the unit played to implement the peace and security aspects of the CFA.

The use of CIDA itself, and what appears to be a limited role played by START, to provide institutional support for the implementation of the peace and security priorities of NEPAD demonstrates some (bureaucratic) conservatism in Canada's approach to Africa generally, and a certain lack of urgency or priority that is accorded to Canada's security engagement in Africa, specifically. This foreign policy approach suggests Canada's involvement in Africa is a moral duty to help a continent in need of political and economic "rescue." This echoes former UK Prime Minister Tony Blair's assertion that the political and economic situation in Africa "is a scar on the world's conscience" (McGreal, 2002). Indeed, the moral obligation discourse has been employed by both the Liberal and Conservative governments in recent years to explain their engagements in Africa. According to former Prime Minister Chrétien, Canada's leadership role to promote NEPAD in the G8 was "a moral obligation for us [Canada] who have a lot to share with those who have not much" (Tibetan News, 2002). Similarly, Prime Minister Harper expressed his support for the NATO (North Atlantic Treaty Organization) intervention in Libya in 2011: "assisting them is a moral obligation upon those of us who profess to believe in this great ideal" (Milewski, 2011).

This discussion suggests that Canada's security engagement in Africa is not borne out of a carefully crafted, long-term Africa strategy that seeks to build partnerships with African regional organizations and states to promote Canada's overall national interest.[4] For the most part, Canada is pulled into Africa by virtue of association in international organizations, such as the United Nations — the key actor for engaging in peacekeeping operations in post-independence Africa. Canada's security engagements in Africa generally follow its commitment to UN multilateralism and the organization's role in promoting international peace and security. To some extent, this helps to sustain Canada's middle-power role and multilateralist tradition in the international arena (Keating, 2012).

More importantly, Canada's security role in Africa is event-driven and reactionary due to the lack of an Africa strategy, which suggests that from Lester B. Pearson to Stephen Harper, Canada's prime minister has been the most influential factor that drives Canada's engagement in Africa. This has been the case despite civil society groups — including NGOs, government departments and key Canadian personalities (such as Robert Fowler, Stephen Lewis and Romeo Dallaire) — playing important roles to keep African issues on Canada's foreign policy agenda. As much as Canada upholds its international obligations in the United Nations, Canada's active engagement, or otherwise, in African issues is heavily influenced by the motivation and interest of the prime minister (Akuffo, 2012). This pattern has generated ad hoc, inconsistent and unsubstantial Canadian security engagement in Africa since the launching of the "made in Africa policy," NEPAD, and the transformation of the OAU into AU. The tokenism of Canadian resources to the APSA attests to this general trend of Canada's security engagement in Africa. Perhaps the recent announcement in the 2013 Budget to merge CIDA into DFAIT will make way to reshape Canada's approach to Africa and help lift Africa from the margins of Canada's security policy (Flaherty, 2013: 240-241).

## CONCLUSION

Canada's maintenance of moral identity shapes its peace and security engagement in Africa. Perceptions not only have meaning, they also shape actual behaviour in the real world and consequently the interests that states pursue. By perceiving Africa as poor and conflict-ridden, Canada has focussed its foreign policy on development assistance and peacekeeping, with CIDA playing a central role in Canada's engagement in Africa. The objectives that underscore these arenas of foreign policy portray Canada as a "helper-state" and Africa as an "impoverished continent," allowing Canada to occupy a moral high ground — moral actor — in its relationship with Africa. Nevertheless, Canada needs to rethink its approach to Africa if it is to have a major impact on improving peace and security, and to be able to develop market opportunities for Canadian business in a competitively emerging African economy; although bedevilled with scarce resources, the AU appears poised to take a leading role in the promotion of these areas in Africa. Its interventions in states such as Sudan, Somalia and the Comoros Islands, and its strong opposition to the NATO intervention in Libya, attest to its demand for seriousness and respect in the international community as far as Africa's security in concerned.

The rejection of Canada by African states in the UN Security Council vote in 2010 suggests that the influence of Canada's moral identity has a limit as far as the real needs of African states are concerned. Canada's moral identity will always be necessary but insufficient to support its foreign policy goals in a new and competitive Africa. The security and development challenges on the African continent that help to shape Canada's role and define its moral identity are well known; yet, the ongoing political and economic transformations in African states,[5] and the configuration of power in the AU has given Africa a stronger voice in world affairs. The AU needs material and financial support as it makes frantic efforts towards improving security, economic integration and consolidating the gains from democracy.

Africa has options, including material support and strategic partnerships, as major economic powers are reorienting their policies toward the continent to position themselves for an emerging African economy in the twenty-first century. The European Union, United States and emerging economies such as China, Brazil and India, see the strategic importance of Africa and have placed the continent firmly on their foreign policy agendas as they make significant investments on the continent. China has a poor human rights record in Africa, and Canada's key allies (the United States, France and the United Kingdom) have historical baggage as colonial or belligerent powers. Despite these issues making Canada appear as the best choice, the danger is that its morality may not be enough to support its long-term foreign policy goals if it does not back this international capital with significant and long-term support to the AU and African states in their efforts to promote peace, security and development. The growth of Canadian mining interests in Africa and the signing or ongoing negotiations of Foreign Investment Promotion and Protection Agreements with several African states should motivate Canada to put more resources in its security engagement with the AU.[6]

Arguably, what the AU needs is a real partnership with Canada to sustain Canada's comparative advantage as a moral actor on the continent. From an ideational standpoint, the perception of Canada by African officials as friendly and non-belligerent puts it high and above other external actors on the continent, as far as historical circumstances and moral conduct in foreign policy is concerned. Yet, Canada's interest in maintaining a moral image in and of itself through its tokenist material support to the AU will not provide long-term solutions to the security and development challenges in Africa.

Canada must rethink its perception of Africa. The political and economic changes that are taking place in Africa provide a timely opportunity for Canada to recognize the strategic value of its moral image in Africa, and link it to substantial and long-term material support for the APSA and the development of long-term strategic partnership with Africa's regional organizations. The Department of National Defence and the Armed Forces should play a more active role in Canada's security engagement with the AU. Although the Harper government's training support for counterterrorism in states such as Niger is an important innovation in Canada's security engagement in Africa (Chase, York and Freeze, 2013), it should not distract Canada from building on its niche in supporting the APCE that provides training to the ASF. Moreover, Canada should extend its support to AMIS in the areas of intelligence, administration and civil-military relations to a long-term support for the AU's CEWS — which, when fully operational, will help to prevent the outbreak of violent conflicts in African states — and in this way, Canada will overcome what appears to be an inherent moral dilemma in its policy towards Africa. This is especially important as political leaders, especially prime ministers, profess to uphold a "moral obligation" towards Africa and do not want to be seen as having material interests in the continent, and therefore contribute little in terms of substantial material in investments and trade that would help to address the real needs of African states and peoples on the one hand, and support Canada's national interests on the other hand. Canada needs a balanced and responsible African strategy that blends security and economic interests with the maintenance of moral image that would serve the mutual interest of Canada and states in Africa.

## ENDNOTES

[1]   See Charles C. Pentland (2005), "The European Union and Civil Conflict in Africa," *International Journal* 60, no. 4: 919–936.

[2]   The international community "watched" as over 800,000 Tutsis and moderate Hutus were butchered to death with machetes within a span of 100 days.

[3]   Here, Africa is used to mean the views expressed by officials of the AU, ECOWAS, think tanks and non-governmental organizations (NGOs). For details see Akuffo, 2012.

[4]   Although the meaning of national interest is contested by various theoretical approaches, it is used here to mean both material and

ideational interests in security, trade, investment and the maintenance of Canada's moral image on the African continent.

5   The list includes Botswana, Ghana, Senegal, Tanzania, Sierra Leone, Kenya, Uganda and Morocco.

6   See Edward Ansah Akuffo (2013), "Beyond Apartheid: Moral Identity, FIPA's, and NEPAD in Canada South Africa Relations," *Commonwealth and Comparative Politics* 1, no. 2: 173–188. See also DFAIT (2013), "Negotiations and Agreements," March 25, available at: www.international.gc.ca/trade-agreements-accords-commerciaux/agr-acc/index.aspx?lang=eng&view=d.

## WORKS CITED

Akuffo, Edward Ansah (2012). *Canadian Foreign Policy in Africa: Regional Approaches to Peace, Security, and Development.* Burlington, VT: Ashgate Publishing Company.

AU (2000). *The Constitutive Act of the African Union.* Lome, Togo. July 11.

CBC News (2008). "Canada's Afghan Mission Could Cost up to $18.1B." *CBC News Canada,* October 9. Available at: www.cbc.ca/news/canada/story/2008/10/09/afghanistan-cost-report.html.

CIDA (2003). *Canada Fund for Africa: New Vision New Partnership.* Ottawa: CIDA.

——— (2004). *Canada and the G8 Action Plan: Maintaining the Momentum.* Ottawa: CIDA.

——— (2006). *Canada Fund for Africa: Delivering Results.* Ottawa: CIDA.

——— (2011). *Canada Fund for Africa: Summative Evaluation Executive Report.* Ottawa: CIDA.

Chase, Steven, Geoffrey York and Colin Freeze (2013). "Ottawa Contributing to Fight in Mali by Training Niger Forces." *The Globe and Mail,* January 13.

DFAIT (2012a). "About the Stabilization and Reconstruction Task Force." July 16. Available at: www.international.gc.ca/START-GTSR/about-a_ propos.aspx?view=d.

――― (2012b). "The Global Peace Operations Program." July 16. Available at: www.international.gc.ca/start-gtsr/gpop-pomsp.aspx?view=d.

Embassy of Canada (2012). "AU POLCIVEX — Exercise NJIWA: Official Opening — 31 Oct 2012 — AU HQ: Remarks from the Embassy of Canada." Speech given at the AU Headquarters, October 31. Addis Ababa. Available at: www.peaceau.org/uploads/au-polcivex-njiwa-31-oct-2012-canada-speech.pdf.

Flaherty, James M. (2013). "Jobs, Growth, and Long-Term Prosperity-Economic Action Plan 2013." Available at: www.budget.gc.ca/2013/doc/plan/budget2013-eng.pdf.

Government of Canada (2010). " Canada's Support for Peace and Security." June 22. Available at: www.acdi-cida.gc.ca/acdi-cida/ACDI-CIDA.nsf/eng/FRA-619132148-ND7.

――― (2011). "Cost of the Afghanistan Mission 2001-2011." June 27. Available at: www.afghanistan.gc.ca/canada-afghanistan/news-nouvelles/2010/2010_07_09.aspx?view=d.

――― (2012). "Canada supporting Peacekeeping in Darfur: Past, Present, Future." December 4. Available at: www.canadainternational.gc.ca/sudan_south_sudan-soudan_soudan_du_sud/assets/pdfs/supporting.pdf.

Keating, Tom (2012). *Canada and World Order: The Multilateralist Tradition in Canadian Foreign Policy. 3rd edition.* Don Mills: Oxford University Press.

McGreal, Chris (2002). "Blair Confronts 'Scar on World's Conscience.'" *The Guardian,* February 7. Available at: www.guardian.co.uk/world/2002/feb/07/politics.development.

Milewski, Terry (2011). "Moral Imperatives: Why Libya?" *CBC News,* March 24. Available at: www.cbc.ca/news/politics/canadavotes2011/realitycheck/2011/03/moral-imperatives-why-libya.html.

National Defence and the Canadian Forces (2012). "Operation Saturn." October 2. Available at: www.cjoc.forces.gc.ca/exp/saturn/index-eng.asp

NEPAD (2001). "The New Partnership for Africa's Development (NEPAD)." October. Available at: www.nepad.org/system/files/framework_0.pdf.

———— (2010). "Decision of the Integration of The New Partnership for Africa's Development (NEPAD) into the Structures and Processes of the African Union including the Establishment of the NEPAD Planning and Coordinating Agency (NPCA)." Available at: www.nepad.org/system/files/Decsion%20of%20the%2014th%20Assembly%20on%20Integration%20of%20NEPAD.pdf.

Office of the Parliamentary Budget Officer (2008). *Fiscal Impact of the Canadian Mission in Afghanistan.* October 9. Available at: www.pbo-dpb.gc.ca/files/files/Publications/Afghanistan_Fiscal_Impact_FINAL_E_WEB.pdf.

Onuf, Nicholas (1989). *World of Our Making.* University of South Carolina Press.

Ruggie, John (1998). *Constructing the World Polity: Essays on International Institutionalization.* New York: Routledge.

Tibetan News (2002). "Canadian Prime Minister Urges Rich Countries to do More for Africa." Available at: www.tibetinfor.com/en/news/2002/06/c063283.htm.

UN (2012). "Troop and Police Contributors Archive (1990–2011)." Available at: www.un.org/en/peacekeeping/resources/statistics/contributors_archive.shtml.

Wendt, Alexander (1995). "Anarchy is What States Make of it: The Social Construction of Power Politics." In *International Theory: Critical Investigations,* edited by James Der Derian. New York: New York University Press.

———— (1999). *Social Theory in International Politics.* Cambridge University Press.

# Part Three:
# Trade, Investment and Governance

# Canadian Trade and Investment in Africa

Victoria Schorr and Paul Hitschfeld

• • • • • • • • • • • • • • • • • • • •

## INTRODUCTION

Sub-Saharan Africa is a continent of increasingly rapid growth and positive change. For historical reasons, Canada has not been as commercially involved on the continent as other nations, making penetrating these markets often very difficult for Canadian companies outside of the mining sector. As Sub-Saharan African markets expand and Canada increasingly seeks to diversify its overseas markets, this is an ideal time for Canada to strengthen its commercial ties with Africa. Due to their lack of experience on the continent and the continuing challenges of entering African markets, the Canadian government will need to increase its support to Canadian companies in order to kick-start the process. Further commercial engagement will benefit not only Africa, but Canada as well.

## AFRICA: THE NEXT GLOBAL GROWTH POLE?

Though it is seldom discussed in Canadian circles, globally, Africa is being described as the global growth pole of the future (United Nations Economic

Commission for Africa [UNECA], 2012). Indeed, on May 21, 2012, *The Atlantic* published an article with the bold title, "The Next Asia Is Africa: Inside the Continent's Rapid Economic Growth" (French, 2012). Even during the economic crisis, African countries continued to have positive growth rates and are projected to experience a growth rate of 5.1 percent in 2012; this is the second-highest growth rate in the world, just behind Asia (International Monetary Fund [IMF], 2012). Indeed, African economies have recovered quickly from the global financial crisis, with real income per capita rising by 4.7 percent in 2011 and a trade surplus of US$5 billion (UNECA, 2012).

Much of these improved terms of trade are due to the high price of commodities, especially in minerals and petroleum. Africa is wealthy in natural resources and more deposits are being found every month.[1] This has helped the continent's governments to increase their foreign exchange reserves, an important safeguard in today's highly volatile market, however, the continent's growth has not solely been due to the commodities sectors. A report by the African Development Bank (AfDB) projects that by 2030, African consumer spending will explode from US$680 billion in 2008 to US$2.2 trillion (2011). A recent report by McKinsey & Company (2012a) details this growing consumer class and reports that "by 2020, more than half of African households are projected to have discretionary incomes." The UNECA report (2012) also states, "as in previous years, domestic demand supported growth in many countries, and is becoming as important as the export market in some countries…And with rising incomes and urbanization, the domestic consumer market is growing, becoming an important source of growth."

This growing consumer class is just one result of a positive demographic dividend — a large young population that is the engine of any growth economy. With almost 200 million people aged between 15 and 24, Africa has the youngest population in the world, and the number of young people in Africa is estimated to double by 2045 (African Economic Outlook, 2012). The World Bank (2012a) reports that 10 million youth enter the Sub-Saharan African labour force every year. As shown in Figures 1 and 2, this youth population will increasingly have secondary school education rates, an important requirement for the manufacturing and industry sectors. Equally, a McKinsey report (2012b) notes a significant shift in spending habits among youth (those under 35), as well as a growing optimism for the future, resulting in higher consumer spending trends, which indicate these changes will reflect future spending norms. This cohort is often aptly referred to as the "Cheetah Generation"; anxious and excited about the future but also impatient and eager for jobs and growth.

**Figure 1: Africa Is Experiencing a Rapid Growth of Educated Young People (20–24 year-old cohorts by education, 2000–2030)**

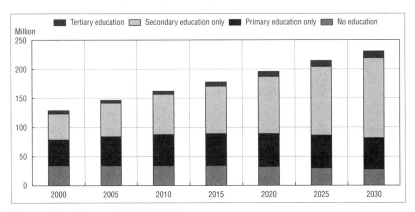

Source: African Economic Outlook, 2012.

**Figure 2: Education Levels in Africa (percent of total population)**

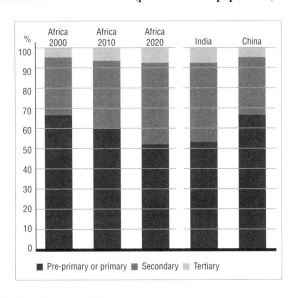

Source: Mo Ibrahim Foundation, 2012.

While this demographic dividend is often promoted as a positive, in fact this youth bulge could be an enormous asset or liability depending on job availability. As the World Bank's *World Development Report* (2012b) and the African Economic Outlook (2012), organized by the Organisation for Economic Co-operation and Development (OECD), highlight, significant gains in employment will be required to ensure that African growth rates continue apace.

On the one hand, large numbers of unemployed youth would not bode well for future growth and stability. Jobs must be created for these workers; something that only the private sector can do on the scale needed. On the other hand, if able to create jobs, these youths will enable African economies to enter the next stage of development, producing low-price consumer goods. This level of production, however, will require industrial infrastructure (i.e., power, water, transportation), a better business climate (i.e., laws, governance, tax codes) and the capacity to enter foreign markets (i.e., marketing skills, trade deals, business savvy, credit). This process of industrialization, manufacturing and marketing to overseas customers will come about mostly as a result of the efforts of African entrepreneurs, but partnerships with Canadian firms could facilitate the flow of goods between Canada and African countries.

Africa's growth and change is attracting companies, businesses and investment from all over the world. Ernst & Young's annual report shows growing attention and interest from the private sector globally toward Africa (2012). This perception is only slowly attracting Canadian businesses. As mentioned, while not all African economies are growing from natural resource extraction — Ethiopia being an obvious example — nevertheless, most African economies are based around commodities and the selling of those commodities abroad. In this, Canada and Africa have an enormous shared interest: to use and grow from the rich natural resources we have. These natural resources include not only the mining sector, but also forestry, fishing and agriculture. Canada also shares a similarly low population density with many African countries. While Africa has significant infrastructure challenges, Canada has experience in providing electricity, roads and other services to disparate areas with small populations. Canada provides these services often through public-private partnerships, a model that is difficult but can be successful when tightly controlled. Although Canada does not immediately come to mind for many as having a competitive advantage in Africa, our shared demographics and resources on their own offer much in terms of competitive business models.

## IMPORTANCE OF THE PRIVATE SECTOR IN DEVELOPMENT

It is well accepted that the private sector has an important role in the development of countries, and Africa is no exception. According to the AfDB, "We believe that private sector development is fundamental for creating inclusive growth through employment creation...Africa's private sector accounted for more than 80 percent of total production, two-thirds of total investment, and three-fourths of total credit to the economy over the 1996-2008 period. It was also responsible for 90 percent of formal and informal employment" (2011). This has also been stated clearly by the report of the Standing Committee on Foreign Affairs and International Development at the Canadian House of Commons in November 2012 (Government of Canada, 2012b).

At this time, most of the private sector in Africa is informal and carried out by small- and medium-sized enterprises (SMEs). As mentioned, these are the primary job producers in any economy and, outside of farming, are what most Africans are employed in. The informality of these enterprises and markets are a significant issue for African countries because it means that African governments have a hard time garnering accurate statistics, in implementing taxation and in ensuring that laws and regulations are abided by. In this, the private sector has been shown to help formalize and organize these markets, usually incurring significant profits in the process. The examples of Nakumat in Kenya and Shoprite in South Africa are well-known case studies (Mahajan, 2008).

Finally, partnerships between non-governmental institutions (NGOs) and the private sector have been proven to achieve enormous positive impacts. The best known pioneer of such partnerships is the Global Public-Private Partnership for Handwashing with Soap, which included Unilever, Proctor & Gamble, Colgate-Palmolive and other companies (Collender, 2010).[2] This initiative has even been transferred back to the developed world in order to encourage better sanitary practices.

## CANADA-AFRICA TRADE RELATIONS

What is the current situation between Canada and Africa in terms of trade? According to Industry Canada data, Figures 3a and 3b show the amount of imports and exports between Canada and the continent.[3] There is a noticeable decrease of both imports and exports in 2008 due to the global financial crisis. Since then, however, exports to Sub-Saharan Africa have recovered and imports from the continent are now double the 2008 peak.

**Figure 3a: Exports from Canada to Africa**

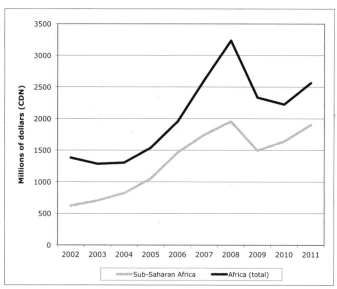

Source: Industry Canada, 2011 and authors.

## Figure 3b: Imports to Canada from Africa

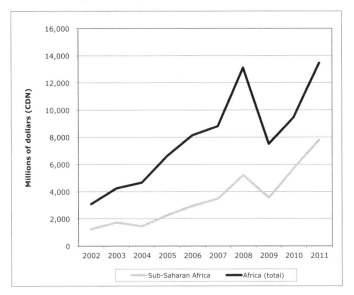

Source: Industry Canada, 2011, and authors.

What are we trading? Nearly 75 percent of Canada's imports from Sub-Saharan Africa are in oil and petroleum products. Gold, gems, cocoa beans and uranium are the next main imports, but none constitute more than five percent of our trade with the continent. In terms of exports, approximately 20 percent of our trade is in wheat,[4] with no other products having more than 10 percent, and most only constituting four or five percent of products exported to the continent. As such, given that our trade is almost entirely in oil and wheat, this trade relationship, while increasing, is still highly volatile.

While these trade patterns indicate an increase in the volume of Canada-Africa trade relations, especially in terms of oil imports, this trade is still minimal and leaves Canada with a very low trade profile in Africa. According to the International Trade Centre, Africa's share of imports to Canada is still only about three percent, while Canada's exports to Africa constitute less than one percent — with no African country having more than 0.2 percent of Canada's export trade. That said, in 2011, bilateral trade between Canada and Nigeria totalled over CDN$2.7 billion, an increase of 44 percent since 2010 and 300 percent compared to 2009 (Government of Canada, 2012a). Bilateral trade between Canada and Ghana in 2011 also increased to CDN$321 million, a 61 percent increase over 2010 (ibid.). Nevertheless, when compared to other countries, Africa is not heavily concerned about trade with Canada. China, the United States and the European Union are Africa's main trading partners, with significant markets and financial power. As of late, Brazil and India are also garnering much attention, and South Africa's economic relations with the rest of the continent are formidable. So why are trade relations between Canada and the continent so low? Is Canada doing enough to ensure competitiveness, especially when such powerhouses as the United States, European Union and China are seeking access to Africa's markets? Can Canada compete?

The Government of Canada has recently made inroads with regards to foreign investment promotion and protection agreement (FIPAs) with the continent, perhaps now realizing the significant economic potential on the continent. The Minister for International Trade, Ed Fast (2012), announced that he will lead a trade mission to Ghana and Nigeria in early 2013, accompanied by Canadian companies in the extractive and infrastructure sectors (Government of Canada, 2012a). Similarly, FIPAs were signed with both Senegal and Tanzania in late 2012 and Benin in early 2013, in addition to the FIPA signed with Madagascar in 2008. According to the Government of Canada, negotiations towards other FIPAs are underway with Burkina Faso, Cameroon, Côte d'Ivoire, Ghana, Morocco, Tunisia and Zambia (2012a).

These upcoming FIPAs will need to be buttressed by a renewal of the Market Access Initiative for Least Developed Countries (MAI), expiring in 2014. The MAI was passed in 2002, with the objective to "encourage foreign development in the least developed countries through duty-free and quota-free access to the Canadian market for exports from these countries thereby promoting economic growth" (Government of Canada, 2003). The OECD commended this agreement and other initiatives at diminishing barriers to trade in its peer review of Canada (2012). While the MAI is for all least developed countries (LDCs) and not only Africa, 34 African countries qualify under the agreement. Sadly, however, few African countries have taken advantage of this agreement. According to *The Rising Africa Magazine*, while countries like Bangladesh and Cambodia have used this agreement quite successfully to export their textiles to Canada, the MAI has not been sufficiently promoted in Africa by the government and has resulted in countries and companies not knowing that it can apply to them (CCAfrica,

2012a). By comparison to the United States' African Growth and Opportunity Act (AGOA) agreement, Canada's is more generous in terms of value-added country origin requirements,[5] but Canada's MAI was not promoted by the Canadian government in the way that the United States made AGOA a high-profile initiative.[6] As well, since most African economies export commodities and raw goods, these are already duty-free without the MAI. Though 15 African countries have registered with Canada to export their textiles and clothing under the MAI, few have ever exported such products to Canada in any significant number (CCAfrica, 2012a).

Finally, the issue of types of goods to be traded is an important one. Since nearly all African LDCs export mostly raw commodities, many of which Canada also exports, it is not surprising that most African countries have not taken advantage of the MAI. Indeed, most countries that could benefit from trade with Canada are not LDCs. If Canada wishes to encourage development and growth in Africa, allowing access to more processed (and thereby higher value) goods should be a priority. Equally, some of the tariff barriers on food stuffs should be re-evaluated. For example, Botswana has high quality organic beef that it is currently not allowed to export to Canada (Seretse, 2012). It is obviously important to ensure the quality and health of food stuffs, but Canada should be open to such products from Africa if they are shown to comply with Canadian food safety standards.

## CANADIAN INVESTMENT ON THE CONTINENT

While trade data is useful in determining Canada's economic relations with the continent, this data reflects the trade in products only. According to the Canadian International Development Platform (CIDP), in 2009 the largest single sector for global Canadian foreign direct investment (FDI) was in finance and insurance (CIDP, 2009). This was followed by mining, and the oil and gas sector. This is consistent with Canadian domestic markets, where financial institutions (banks and insurance companies) and mining are the largest sectors (ibid.). Most of the world's finance and monetary exchanges outside of governments, however, occur through company-to-company (including subsidiaries) payments,[7] making it hard to determine actual FDI flows.

In order to encourage Canadian investment on the continent, the Canadian government previously offered financial support to developing countries through its aid program in order to help finance support in increasing local production capacity and eventually their export capacity. In 1990, support was offered to Canadian firms through the Canadian International Development Agency's Industrial Cooperation Program (INC). This was financed at CDN$60 million per year, with about CDN$20 million going to support Canadian private sector activities in Africa. In the 2000s, the program was reduced in size due to pressures on aid funding in general, as well as a lack of clear program success. In 2010, the INC program was moved to the Department of Foreign Affairs and International Trade, with a total global budget of CDN$20 million per year. The program was suspended in 2012, again for budget and program impact reasons. This initiative, however, was often only utilized by companies who were ahead of their time and willing to expand into Africa before its recent economic takeoff. Given the growth of African markets, a redesigned program could be relaunched — albeit with a lower subsidy element — if the Government of Canada were to promote an expansion in business relations with the continent.

As well, in 2001, Canada considered, but later shelved, the idea of creating a Development Finance Institution (DFI) (as exists in all other Group of Seven donor countries). Though the timing may not have been right a decade ago, a DFI with a focus on medium- and larger-size investments in Africa may be appropriate now. The benefits of a DFI is that public finances can be given for private endeavours on an investment basis; accruing interest and not placing an ongoing cost to the treasury because returns can be reinvested upon future endeavours.

Meanwhile, Export Development Canada (EDC) — a Crown corporation — is Canada's export credit agency and offers financial advice, risk management solutions and financing for Canadian companies wishing to expand their businesses internationally. In 2011, EDC supported 457 Canadian companies in 46 African countries and had a total of CDN$2.39 billion in transactions, of which CDN$1.71 billion took place in Sub-Saharan Africa (CCAfrica, 2012a). In addition, under the Canada Account, on rare occasions when a significant investment is in the national interest, EDC may be used to authorize support for transactions for which it would usually not be able. Similarly, the Canadian Commercial Corporation, also a Crown corporation, is active on the continent but could be beefed up with respect to African markets.

Outside of government, there are several mechanisms to expand business and investment that are currently in place. CCAfrica is a national organization with the expressed mandate to encourage Canadian-African business relations. This mandate includes all sectors ranging from education and health, to finance and natural resources. CCAfrica provides advising services, conducts trade missions, hosts conferences and has discussions with many government departments in order to better facilitate trade, investment and business relations between Canada and the continent.

Finally, there are several NGOs, such as Trade Facilitation Office of Canada, that offer support to businesses of various sizes that wish to expand their business linkages with LDC partners. Even still, there is little investment from Canadian companies on the continent outside of the mining sector — which is usually able to finance itself without the assistance of governments or organizations.


## CANADA, AFRICA AND MINING

Canadian companies are actively involved on the continent within the mining sector, showing no signs of slowing. Given the constant new discoveries of natural resources in Africa and Canada's active mining sector — locally as well as abroad — this trend of Canadian mining companies active on the continent will likely continue in the coming decades. Canadian capital markets are one of the largest sources of capital for the mining and oil and gas industries globally (CIDP, 2009). For this reason, in order to fully understand our economic relations, the mining and extractives sector must be addressed.[8]

According to the Toronto Stock Exchange (Shahnawaz, 2012), as of 2011, Canada had 185 mining companies active on the continent with a total of 684 mining properties. The North-South Institute estimates that about CDN$1 billion of equity capital was raised in Canada in 2011 for mining projects in Africa (ibid.). It also reports that Canada is listed as first in the world for the listed mining companies worldwide, first in listed oil and gas companies worldwide, first in global mining and global gold S&P/TSX Indices (Standard & Poor's/Toronto Stock Exchange), first in listed clean technology companies worldwide and second in the world for the number of listed companies (ibid.). According to Natural Resources Canada, in 2011 more than CDN$30 billion of Canadian mining assets were in Africa.[9] Since this amount does not include liquid assets and writeoffs, the total amount of investments is likely even higher.

Canada's role in the mining sector, both in Canada and abroad, has raised concerns over corporate social responsibility (CSR).[10] While the mining sector is often scrutinized for CSR practices, as our companies outside of the extractives sectors become more involved on the continent, other sectors will need to be aware of and address CSR issues. For example, mines are often evaluated for their environmental impacts, but construction companies can also have environmental externalities, labour relations issues and other CSR concerns. Similarly, the types of investments of Canadian banks and funds need greater scrutiny in order to make sure they are investing in non-corrupt assets. Moreover, while an SME in Canada may consist of 400 people or more, in Sub-Saharan Africa a company with only 100 employees can constitute a medium or even large enterprise. This means that even a small Canadian company can be a relatively big player in most African markets and may represent Canada, positively or negatively, in the country where it operates. In this way, CSR is far more than only a mining issue, it is a global issue that will likely continue to be the focus of attention by many stakeholders, both Canadian and international, in the years to come.

## THE FUTURE OF CANADA'S BUSINESS WITH THE CONTINENT

What is the likely future for Canadian private sector involvement on the continent? While any prediction is always tenuous at best, the trends in Canada's trade relations, Africa's growth rates, and the growing role that Africa will assume internationally, means that some forecasts are more likely than others.

Given the steadily rising amounts of imports from Africa to Canada, despite the brief drop during the global financial crisis, it is likely that this trade will continue. Exports are also likely to rise, and Canada is likely to remain a major player in the extractives sector, if only because many Canadian companies are involved in this industry in Canada and will naturally expand into other regions of the world where these skills and experiences are practical.

As Africa becomes the next global growth pole, Canada's interactions with the continent will dramatically increase once Canadian businesses — notoriously cautious — see their competitors making significant profits on the continent.[11] This was the process observed with regards to Canadian investments in the Asian Tigers and is likely an indication of Canada's future in Africa. Such behaviour would unfortunately result in Canadian companies playing catch-up: trying to gain access to already saturated markets, resulting in less profit and not helping Africa in its early market maturation.

In order to avoid being late to the table, there are several measures that would be appropriate from the Government of Canada and private sector to promote business on the continent. The government should take a more active role in encouraging trade. This can be done through increasing the number of embassies, bolstering trade commissioner services on the continent and increasing the number of high-level missions to the continent. The government should also ease visa restrictions to allow for more bilateral trade missions and to better facilitate market research. Encouraging more direct flights and shipping lines — instead of going through Europe — will help to promote greater trade and exchange. In addition, the government could expand its focus towards mutual taxation agreements in support to the signing of more FIPAs. Further, as the case of Botswana beef shows, a review by the Government of Canada of our current tariff arrangements, perhaps in tandem with our increasing FIPA negotiations, would be appropriate.

In terms of the private sector, Canada must diversify outside the mining sector, especially as other sectors inherently use larger workforces and can thereby take advantage of the demographic dividend. This chapter has offered several ways in which Canada can diversify its business relations in Sub-Saharan Africa. Canada is a leader in the energy sector, and electricity and energy needs will only continue to rise on the continent. Canada has expertise in forestry, fishing and eco-tourism. It is important that the private sector learn of these opportunities rather than investing solely in the extractives sector. Investing in Africa is more than mines.

As Canada has shown, public-private partnerships, especially in the case of public goods such as water and electricity provision, are excellent ways of ensuring citizens receive services efficiently at an affordable price.

Though these partnerships are by no means perfect and must be watched carefully, Canada can be a leader in demonstrating how they can be used most effectively. For example, it has been a well-documented problem that African countries were encouraged to privatize their public electricity companies but could find few buyers. The reluctance of private investors to enter utilities markets is because most African countries' populations are too poor to pay for electricity at the price it would actually cost for the company to generate it. Equally, given the low population densities in many African countries, the cost of supplying electricity to disparate, poor, rural, small markets would simply not be profitable for companies. At the same time, it is very well-documented that government utility companies are inefficient, especially over the long term. While such public-private partnerships are still only in the trial stages for most African countries, this is one area in which Canadian policy makers and companies have great experience and advantage.

With regard to aid and the private sector, though it has taken some time to accept, most development observers now recognize that as important as institutional strengthening is, job creation in the private sector is also a key component for economic growth and political stability. Job creation for the millions of African teenagers and young adults entering the job market every year means the majority will need employment in private enterprises. As a result of the near-collapse of the Word Trade Organization's Doha Round, countries are increasingly making bilateral or regional trade agreements. Canada, recognizing that differences in economic strength and technological capacity means that such trade deals are at times negotiated between very unequal countries, has turned to the aid program to help finance support to developing countries in order to increase their production and eventually their export capacity. For example, the Government of Canada has begun to provide financial support to mining companies operating in Africa, with the objective of helping to launch local development activities for local suppliers and producers. This is a new trend in aid programming, and not one that meets with wide support from the Canadian development community.

A further step that is being tried, but not yet fully developed, is to enhance trade capacity building with local business climate improvement measures and more direct support to developing country exporters. This would contribute significantly to the revenue of developing countries, especially in the creation of local entrepreneurs. Whether the aid program would be the best way to do this, or whether it should be put into the hands of more business-knowledgeable institutions, still needs to be considered.[12] National interest should involve increasing trade between Canada and Sub-Saharan African countries. Indeed, Canada must take the lead on this as we are not a primary concern for African countries and will not be targeted by them.

If Canadian companies outside of the mining sector do become more involved, there are several lessons that can be learned from others already on the continent. Charles Field-Marsham (2012)of Kestrel Capital Management advocates for four pillars to success on the continent: "be polite, patient, persistent, and passionate." Canadian companies, while certainly polite, may not have all these qualities, especially when it comes to their first time ventures on the continent. Barriers to businesses — such as banking services, local suppliers, power supply, local housing, cost of living, access to doctors and long processing times at ports — can sometimes mean that Canadian companies will have to be especially resilient. Infrastructure deficits, while an opportunity for Canadian companies to become involved, can also be a significant deterrent to business and makes running any operation difficult. For this reason, trade offices must exist and explanations of differences between markets need to be elucidated. This is especially the case when it comes to the manufacturing and services sectors, as they require very different skills, infrastructure and business climates than the mining sector.

As such, companies should form partnerships or create wholly-owned subsidiaries,[13] as these are often the most sustainable businesses and are easier than starting from scratch. Canadian companies should find African entrepreneurs and SME owners in which they see potential; these local businesses know the climate, know the markets, know the competitors and know what sells. Canadian businesses can offer expertise and financing but they must be active members in these businesses and cannot simply invest from afar on a short-term basis (White, 2012). Just as brands and client relationships take time to build, investors need to understand that sometimes they will be organizing and formalizing markets, and that this will take time (Mahajan, 2008).

Another very important factor is that Canadian companies should be prepared to do stress tests or trials. As stated by Eliot Pence (2012), from the Whitaker Group, "pilot projects can help refine the business case and entry strategy while limiting expenditure and exposure." Equally, not all of

Africa is the same; the continent is huge and has many different markets. Business partners need to listen to what their local entrepreneurs, owners and partners say in order to not only market products successfully, but also to ensure they are following the laws of the country (or countries) they are in. Lastly, businesses need to be prepared to innovate with regards to payment structures and product sizes. The credit and banking markets throughout most of Africa are very weak, meaning that many customers may buy only small amounts of a product on a daily basis.

Kestrel Capital Management shows that the rate of return on FDI in Africa has averaged 29 percent since 1990 and yet, while it has 400 clients across 20 countries, none are from Canada.[14] Most experts, including the authors, attribute Canada's lack of involvement on the continent to Canadians' inaccurate and outmoded perceptions of the continent.[15] Chris Roberts of the University of Calgary says, "Canadians must get beyond the outdated and dismissive images of Africa, ones that overly focus on Africa's problems that cause opportunities to be missed" (CCAfrica, 2012b). While it is by no means easy to run a company in Sub-Saharan Africa, companies from all over the world have been able to adapt to the rapidly changing circumstances on the continent.

## CONCLUSION

Canadians need to understand that in the future, and sooner than we think, we will need Africa more than Africa will need us. Canadian companies do have advantages and expertise that are needed on the continent. Africa is a continent of growth and change. Though Canadian companies are active on the continent, much ground has been lost in the last decade as Canada has been reluctant to engage this new Sub-Saharan Africa. If Canada's business relations with the emerging Asian economies is an indication, the private sector on its own will likely be slow and several years behind much of the world. This would be to the detriment of both Canada and Africa, though more for the former than the latter. On the other hand, if the government takes a more proactive role to retool partnership mechanisms and increase services that will enable the Canadian private sector to be a full partner in Africa's economic takeoff, such a costly delay may be averted. Canadians need to recognize that in discussions about emerging markets, African markets must be included. Canada-Africa business relations are still in their infancy and the actions that are taken in the next couple of years will determine our relations for the next decade and perhaps several decades into the future.

## Acknowledgements

The authors wish to give special thanks to Lucien Bradet, president and CEO of the CCAfrica, for his support and advice on the production of this chapter. The authors would also like to extend their thanks to all those who helped by contributing their knowledge and experience to ensure this chapter's quality. Any errors are the fault of the authors and in no way reflect the input of our esteemed colleagues.

## ENDNOTES

[1]  See the Canadian Council on Africa's (CCAfrica's) news clippings service.

[2]  For a Canadian example, see Grand Challenges Canada, available at: www.grandchallenges.ca/.

[3]  It is important to note that there are few direct shipping routes between Canada and Africa, meaning most goods are shipped via Europe. For this reason, the data given may be lower or higher than is actually the case.

[4]  This statistic includes food aid from Canada, indicating the volume of trade in wheat may not constitute strictly commercial activity.

[5]  Canada only requires that 20 percent of the value added comes from the LDC country itself, allowing that another 20 percent may be from Canada, a developing country or another LDC. The remaining 60 percent of value added may come from any country.

[6]  For a detailed look at AGOA, see Witney Schneidman and Zenia Lewis (2012), *The African Growth and Opportunity Act: Looking Back, Looking Forward*, Brookings Africa Growth Initiative.

[7]  For examples, see the Tax Justice Network's investigations, available at: www.taxjustice.net/cms/front_content.php?idcatart=2&lang=1.

[8]  The following two chapters in this section discuss this in further detail, so only an overview will be given here.

[9]  Direct communication with Natural Resources Canada, December, 2012.

10    CSR has been defined in several ways and will be discussed further in the next two chapters in this section. Its importance, however, deserves some attention here.

11    According to a draft government foreign policy document written in September 2012, the Government of Canada is also concerned that the Canadian private sector is too timid when it comes to foreign investment and that this should change.

12    There is debate on both sides as to whether aid should be distributed through the private sector or through NGOs. See Jeroen Kwakkenbos (2012), "Private Profit for Public Good? Can Investing in Private Companies Deliver for the Poor?" In *Aid and the Private Sector: Catalysing Poverty Reduction and Development?*, edited by The Reality of Aid Report International Coordinating Committee.

13    For an example, see Dessau's acquisition of the Chilean firm MG Ingenieros S.A.

14    See Schneidman and Lewis, 2012.

15    For an example of how perceptions of Africa impact FDI globally, see Victoria Schorr (2011), "Economics of Afro-Pessimism: The Economics of Perception in African Foreign Direct Investment," *Nokoko* 2.

## WORKS CITED

AfDB (2011). *The Middle of the Pyramid: Dynamics of the Middle Class in Africa.* AfDB Market Brief. Available at: www.afdb.org/fileadmin/uploads/afdb/Documents/Publications/The%20Middle%20of%20the%20Pyramid_The%20Middle%20of%20the%20Pyramid.pdf.

African Economic Outlook (2012). "In Depth: Promoting Youth Employment in Africa." Available at: www.africaneconomicoutlook.org/en/in-depth/youth_employment/.

CCAfrica (2012a). *The Rising Africa Magazine,* October.

———— (2012b). *The Rising Africa Magazine,* December. Available at: http://issuu.com/ccafrica/docs/the_rising_africa_issue_3/1.

CIDP (2009). "Canadian Foreign Direct Investment Overseas." North-South Institute. Available at: http://cidpnsi.ca/blog/portfolio/canadian-foreign-direct-investment-overseas-quick-review/.

Collender, Guy (2010). "Development Matters: Global Handwashing Day: Why it Matters and its Growing Success," Development Matters, London International Development Centre podcast audio, July 22. Available at: http://soasradio.org/content/development-matters-global-handwashing-day-why-it-matters-and-its-growing-success.

Ernst & Young (2012). *Building Bridges: Ernst & Young's Attractiveness Survey 2012: Africa.* Ernst & Young: Emerging Markets Center.

Fast, Ed (2012). "Address by Minister Fast to Canadian Council on Africa, 10th Anniversary Symposium." Speech given at the Canada-Africa Symposium: Looking Forward — The Next Decade, October 16. Ottawa.

Field-Marsham, Charles (2012). Speech given at the Canada-Africa Symposium: Looking Forward — The Next Decade, October 16. Ottawa.

French, Howard W. (2012). "The Next Asia Is Africa: Inside the Continent's Rapid Economic Growth." *The Atlantic,* May 21.

Government of Canada (2003). "Introductory Guide to the Market Access Initiative for the Least Developed Country and the Least Developed Country Tariff." Ottawa: Canada Border Services Agency. Available at: www.cbsa-asfc.gc.ca/publications/pub/rc4322-eng.html#d.

——— (2012a). "International Trade Minister to Lead Trade Mission to Africa in Early 2013," news release, October 16. Available at: http://news.gc.ca/web/article-eng.do?nid=701469.

——— (2012b). *Driving Inclusive Economic Growth: The Role of the Private Sector in International Development.* Report of the Standing Committee on Foreign Affairs and International Development, House of Commons.

IMF (2012). *World Economic Outlook: Growth Resuming, Dangers Remain.* World Economic and Financial Surveys.

Industry Canada (2011). "Trade Data Online (TDO)." Available at: www.ic.gc.ca/eic/site/tdo-dcd.nsf/eng/Home?OpenDocument#tag.

Mahajan, Vijay (2008). *Africa Rising: How 900 Million African Consumers Offer More Than You Think.* New Jersey: Pearson Education, Inc.

McKinsey & Company (2012a). *The Rise of the African Consumer.* McKinsey Global Institute.

Mo Ibrahim Foundation (2012). *African Youth: Fulfilling the Potential.* Dakar: Mo Ibrahim Foundation.

OECD (2012). *Canada 2012 DAC Peer Review.* Development Assistance Committee. Available at: www.oecd.org/dac/peerreviewsofdacmembers/ canadapeerreview2012.pdf.

Pence, Eliot (2012). "Navigating Africa: 17 Lessons from the Ground." How We Made It In Africa, November 18. Available at: www. howwemadeitinafrica.com/navigating-africa-17-lessons-from-the-ground/22215/.

Seretse, Tebelelo (2012). "Botswana, Its Strengths and Weaknesses." Speech given at the Canadian International Council's Africa Study Group, November 7. Ottawa.

Shahnawaz, Shishir (2012). "Canada's Policies and Strategies for Africa's Growth and Private Sector Development." Paper presented at Africa-Canada Forum — CCIC Colloquium 2012: Economic Growth, the Private Sector and Sustainable Development: Where is Africa Heading?, Ottawa, Canada, October 30-31.

UNECA (2012). *Economic Report on Africa 2012: Unleashing Africa's Potential as a Pole of Global Growth.* UN Economic Commission for Africa.

White, Ben (2012). "Top 5 Mistakes Made by Investors in Africa." Venture Capital for Africa, April 12. Available at: http://vc4africa.biz/ blog/2012/04/12/top-5-mistakes-made-by-investors-in-africa/.

World Bank (2012a). "Jobs are a cornerstone of development, says World Development Report 2013," press release, October 1. Available at: www. worldbank.org/en/news/2012/10/01/jobs-cornerstone-development-says-world-development-report

———— (2012b). World Development Report 2013: Jobs.

# Mining Codes in Africa: Opportunities, Challenges and Canada's Position

Hany Besada and Philip Martin

• • • • • • • • • • • • • • • • • • •

## INTRODUCTION

The mining and extractive sector constitutes a significant and increasingly important share of exports and tax revenues for much of Africa, and holds enormous potential to finance the rapid infrastructure development and private sector-led socio-development projects that are needed for sustainable broad-based economic growth and poverty reduction. From 2000 to 2011, natural resource extraction constituted a major component of real GDP growth in over 15 resource-rich African states, including over half of all growth in Equatorial Guinea, Ghana and the Democratic Republic of Congo (DRC) (International Monetary Fund [IMF], 2012: 65). With high commodity prices and the rise of emerging economies, in particular the BRICS (Brazil, India, China and South Africa), driving more ambitious investment strategies among multinational mining companies, increased international attention — in Canada and elsewhere — is now being directed to harnessing Africa's resources for socio-economic development.

In this chapter, we seek to illustrate the contemporary but still evolving policy environment in Africa's mining sector. In particular, we highlight the liberalization of Africa's regulatory regimes since the late 1980s, as well as the recent wave of voluntary "good governance" initiatives in the extractive industry. We also consider Canada's role and perspective, both as a dominant investor in the African mining sector and as a country aspiring to be a global leader in responsible business practices and the promotion of sustainable development. While Canada is well-positioned to be an influential development partner and leading international investor in Africa's extractive sector, it also finds itself exposed to the vulnerabilities associated with operating in regions of political instability and civil strife, endemic corruption and low governance capacity. This is in addition to the inability on the part of the Canadian government to hold Canadian mining companies accountable for their corporate behaviour outside the country, due to the lack of enforcement regimes.

Finally, we assess future trends and policy challenges for Canada and other international actors operating in Africa's mining sector. Rising investment from emerging economies and continued pressure on host-country governments to intervene more forcefully in the extractives industry will be the key issues determining the role that the extractive sector plays in resource-rich African states in the immediate future. Navigating these challenges successfully will demand innovative, implementable and inclusive governance strategies, as well as best practices over the continent's natural resources that promote transparency and shared benefits for host countries, foreign investors and local communities.

## THE LIBERALIZATION OF AFRICA'S MINING REGIMES

Africa's mining regimes have undergone fundamental changes since the post-independence era. While many post-colonial African governments adopted a nationalistic approach to their countries' natural resources by way of state-engineered development and national economic planning, the sector underwent significant reform beginning in the late 1980s. Guided by international financial institutions (IFIs), many African governments moved to attract greater foreign investment through decreased regulation, liberalized social and labour policies, and more private sector-friendly ownership and taxation schemes (Campbell, 2004; 2009). Liberalized mining codes were presumed to benefit resource-rich countries by providing host governments with increased export earnings and royalties, generating employment for domestic communities, and facilitating technological transfer, improved physical infrastructure and the creation of downstream industries (Hilson and Maconachie, 2009: 54). From the 1980s to the early 2000s, Africa experienced three successive waves or "generations" of liberalization in its minerals and extractives sector (Campbell, 2004; 2009). One of the first generational cases occurred in Ghana in the mid-1980s, where the IMF applied substantial pressure on the government to amend its Investment Promotion Act and allow for greater foreign investment in the country's mining sector. In line with the dramatic free-market restructuring of mining regimes in these first generation reforms, foreign investors were granted a number of incentives for doing business in Ghana, including the right to repatriate their profits, exemption from paying duties on imported equipment and complete ownership of business ventures in the country (Akabzaa, 2009). A second generation of mining codes unfolded in the early to mid-1990s, continuing the trend of liberalization and privatization, but with nominal recognition of the need for certain social and environmental regulations (Campbell, 2004). In the case of Guinea, for example, the 1994 Plan National d'Action pour l'Environnement and the 1995 Mining Code set forth "the protection of the environment" as a responsibility for operating companies. However, these rules remained non-binding on multinational companies, and governments held little enforcement capacity for their implementation (ibid.: 34). Finally, a "third" generation occurred from the end of the 1990s, with countries such as Mali, Madagascar and Tanzania opening up their mining industry to foreign investment. While these regimes legislated a greater role for the state to facilitate and regulate extractive operations than in previous generations of reform, local administrators possessed inadequate capacity to effectively monitor and enforce these codes (Sarrasin, 2004; Butler, 2004). In effect, most environmental, social and accountability measures became heavily reliant on "self-regulation" by private sector operators.

The recent growth of natural resource exports — which accounted for approximately one-quarter of the 4.9 percent annual real GDP growth across Africa from 2000 to 2008 (Roxburgh et al., 2010) — has resurrected debates over the developmental benefits of natural resource exploitation.

While Western governments and international organizations have credited this surge for reviving stagnating African economies, others argue that the long-term economic and social benefits of mining in Africa have hardly been impressive (Labonne, 2002; Aykut and Sayek, 2007). Liberalized regulatory frameworks are perceived to maximize benefits for privately owned foreign companies and a small subsection of local elites, rather than provide broadly shared benefits to affected communities (Campbell, 2009). Natural resource dependency also insulates national leaders from public pressure, since they do not rely on taxation of their populations for revenue, with an established correlation between resource abundance and political corruption (Tsui, 2011; Ross, 2012). States like the DRC, Angola and Equatorial Guinea appear trapped by a "resource curse," where economic rents gained from the export of minerals and petroleum permit governments to neglect taxing personal or corporate incomes, divert public revenues to patron-cliental networks and deplete natural resources without reinvesting in assets to diversify the national economy (Hilson and Maconachie, 2009: 59-60).

At the community level, the promised benefits and linkages of resource exploitation have also been scrutinized. As a recent study by the African Development Bank (AfDB) notes, few of the inputs into capital-intensive mining activities in Africa over the last decade have been sourced locally. Rather, equipment, machinery and consumables are most often imported (Gajigo, Mutambatsere and Ndiaye, 2012a: 13). Employment generation is also limited by the capital-intensive nature of the sector, a problem exacerbated by the growing use of surface mining technologies, which has constrained employment opportunities in the sector and increased expatriate staff quotas (Akabzaa, 2009). Moreover, local officials often lack the capacity to accurately monitor the output and capital expenditures of multinational mining companies, allowing firms to manipulate their tax obligations and minimize the royalties paid to national governments and mining-affected communities (ibid.: 46). The World Bank's *Africa's Pulse* reported in 2012 that strong economic growth in resource-rich countries had "failed to make a significant dent on their poverty levels," most often due to a failure by governments and multinational companies to reinvest resource revenues into health, education and employment creation services (Tran, 2012). Hence, while successful in attracting increased foreign investment, the liberalized mining regimes adopted across Africa since the 1980s have displayed key shortfalls in their ability to meet the development challenges of the continent. The lack of capacity on the part of African states to monitor and enforce natural resource management regulations, limited benefits for local employment and pro-poor economic growth at the community level, and a perceived lack of transparency in resource revenue management, have prompted calls for stronger natural resource governance strategies.

## EMERGENCE OF A FOURTH GENERATION? NATURAL RESOURCE GOVERNANCE IN THE TWENTY-FIRST CENTURY

Provoked by these developmental problems, a new wave of natural resource governance initiatives — what might be called a "fourth generation" — has emerged in recent years. These campaigns focus on transparency and accountability, not only among host governments, but also with investing partners and private companies. The launch of the Global Mining Initiative in 1998, spearheaded by a consortium of mining company executives, marked the beginning of this new approach. The International Council on Mining and Metals' (ICMM) Mining, Minerals and Sustainable Development project, for example, represents an effort by the industry to introduce guidelines and codes of practice — such as health, environmental and transparency standards, as well as required contributions to social and economic development in host communities — that are voluntarily adopted by their members. The Extractive Industries Transparency Initiative (EITI), the Publish What You Pay campaign and the Natural Resource Charter pursue similar objectives, encouraging the full publication and verification of company payments made to governments and the revenues accrued from oil, gas and mining activities. These alternative accountability mechanisms are driven by a host of heterogeneous actors, including corporations and state governments, but also regional organizations and civil society groups at both the domestic and international level.[1] Some cover a broad spectrum of social and environmental issues, while others target specific themes, such as labour practices, corruption, corporate governance, human rights, environmental impact and protection, and compliance reporting. For extractive companies, the adoption of voluntary corporate social responsibility (CSR) codes as a supplement to national regulatory schemes allows them to secure a "social license to operate"[2] in affected communities, and to avoid additional government regulation in the future. Schemes such as the Kimberley Process, discussed in the next chapter in this volume, provide both rewards and punishments in the form of certification for compliance and sanctions for non-compliance. Similarly, the International Finance Corporation (IFC) conditions the disbursement of funds on compliance with the IFC's Performance Standards, a requirement that has bolstered the norm of seeking free, prior and informed consent[3] from local communities for projects with significant social and environmental impacts.

These good governance initiatives have attracted widespread support for their potential to minimize environmental and social harms by encouraging responsibility and transparency among private sector mining companies operating in developing countries. They are, however, also clearly problematic. Observers worry that mining companies are "blue washing" their operations, signing on to non-binding international compacts in order to give a positive public image to unsound practices (Nwete, 2007: 313). Meanwhile, the type of financial flows covered by the EITI and other reporting schemes remains limited; for instance, these rules usually do not affect bilateral loans, permitting donor countries to lend money to companies that may collude with officials in resource-rich countries without public scrutiny. These voluntary codes and performance standards also complicate questions of legal responsibility and legitimacy, with many regulatory functions transferred to either the transnational legal arena or to contractual agreements between companies and specific communities (Campbell, 2010: 214). Ultimately, without sufficient state capacity and political will to enforce good governance norms and corporate behaviour, industry self-regulation alone appears unlikely to guarantee broad-based benefits from natural resource extraction.

## CANADA AND NATURAL RESOURCE GOVERNANCE IN AFRICA

Canadian-owned mining companies have been at the forefront of foreign investment and exploration in Africa since the early 1990s, with assets on the continent representing the second-largest regional bloc (the largest being Latin America) for Canadian mining investment, at over CDN$23.6 billion (Government of Canada, 2011a).[4] Behind the financial services industry, the energy and metallic minerals sector comprises the largest component of

Canadian direct investment abroad, with over CDN$14 billion annually in mining investment in Africa. Mining companies registered on Canadian stock exchanges are present in over 35 African countries, representing the largest source of investment in the sector behind Australia, China, South Africa and India. Most of this investment in concentrated in eight countries: South Africa (25.6 percent), the DRC (17.8 percent), Madagascar (13.8 percent), Zambia (9.9 percent), Tanzania (9.5 percent), Ghana (6.5 percent), Burkina Faso (4.7 percent) and Mauritania (3 percent) (ibid.).

As Canadian mining companies increasingly operate in high-risk countries across Africa, the associated reputational and social license risks concerning human rights and indigenous rights have become more salient. In response to the growing awareness of the negative impacts of mining operations abroad, particularly in African states with low domestic governance capacity, both mining corporations and the Canadian government have made attempts to improve the industry's public image through the adoption of CSR codes and participation in natural resource governance initiatives. According to a 2009 report by the Canadian Centre for the Study of Resource Conflict (CCSRC), 78 percent of Canadian mining firms with publicly available annual reports included a formal CSR policy to mitigate environmental and social disruptions and provide monetary compensation to groups affected by mining operations (CCSRC, 2009). The IFC's Performance Standards have also been incorporated within the mandate of the Canadian extractive industry's Office of the Corporate Social Responsibility Counsellor.

Nevertheless, these measures are often overshadowed by persistent reports of human rights violations and government corruption in countries hosting Canadian mining operations. In 2009, a report commissioned by the Prospectors and Developers Association of Canada labelled Canadian corporations among the worst violators of social and environmental rights,[5] adding that "the Canadian mining and exploration community needs to shift its current strategy if it is to improve its relationships with communities, governments, civil society and risk mitigation operations" (Whittington, 2010).

Following the lead of US and European lawmakers, Canadian legislators and civil society groups have attempted to strengthen government oversight of foreign operations by Canadian mining firms through Bill C-300.[6] The legislation sought to implement "eligibility criteria" for political and financial support provided to extractive firms by the Canadian government, including the adoption of the IFC's Performance Standards, and create a complaints mechanism to permit investigations into a company's compliance with CSR guidelines. However, opponents of the legislation in the Canadian mining industry lobbied successfully against the bill, defeated in the House of Commons by a vote of 140 to 134 in October 2010.

This legislative decision has not precluded the Canadian government from pursuing alternative natural resource governance initiatives, however. In November 2012, the government announced the creation of the Canadian International Institute for Extractives and Development (CIIED) to be co-established by the University of British Columbia and Simon Fraser University in British Columbia. The institute is mandated to coordinate resource-sector governance and technical capacity building in developing countries. Moreover, the Government of Canada is co-financing a number of CSR projects with Canadian mining companies Rio Tinto Alcan, IAMGOLD and Barrick Gold in Ghana, Burkina Faso and Peru as part of the government's Corporate Social Responsibility Strategy for the Canadian International Extractive Sector.[7] The Burkina Faso project — a CDN$7.5 million deal between IAMGOLD, the Canadian International Development Agency (CIDA) and the private NGO, Plan Canada — aims to provide job skills training for thousands of adolescents in two regions of the country (Government of Canada, 2011b). Critics contend that this type of public-private cooperation in the mining sector amounts to public subsidization of corporate CSR policies, and that foreign aid budgets are being inappropriately used to benefit highly profitable mining companies. The Canadian NGO MiningWatch, for instance, has expressed concern that the government's technical assistance in regulatory and legal reforms in the natural resources sector has involved insufficient input from local civil society groups, dismissing proposals such as bans on open-pit mining, community-consultation requirements, and increased taxes and royalties (MiningWatch Canada, 2012). Advocates, however, maintain that these initiatives will better direct international aid funds towards building legal and financial frameworks in partner countries that encourage responsible investment in extractive sectors, leading to greater economic development. Moreover, mining companies argue that partnering with experienced public and private development NGOs will deliver more effective results than trying to carry out CSR programs alone.

Hence, in contrast to fourth generation initiatives calling for stronger oversight and legal accountability for international mining firms, it appears likely that Canada's role in shaping natural resource governance regimes in the African mining sector will continue to focus on greater public-private integration as a means of promoting responsible resource extraction and economic development. New initiatives such as the CIIED, as well as the Government of Canada's growing collaboration with mining companies in African countries, signals a preference for working collaboratively with the mining industry, alongside civil society groups, to provide technical assistance and best practices for reforming Africa's extractive sector. While it is too early to assess the effectiveness of these projects, viewed optimistically, it represents a "socially responsible capitalism" that recognizes private sector involvement as indispensable for addressing Africa's development challenges.

## FUTURE TRENDS AND POLICY CHALLENGES IN AFRICA'S MINERALS SECTOR

Looking forward, what are the major trends shaping natural resource investment and governance in Africa's future? One major development is the prominence of investment from emerging economies, particularly the BRICS. Since 2000, China has been particularly active in establishing a series of resource-backed deals in which dams, power plants and other infrastructure projects are exchanged for rights to mining exploration and development. In 2010, trade flows between Africa and BRIC countries (excluding South Africa) were approximately US$150 billion, with US$60 billion in foreign direct investment stock in the continent, the majority concentrated in natural resources. These figures are projected to increase threefold in the next half decade (Gaunt, 2010).

The involvement of the BRICS in Africa's extractive sector is both a potential advantage and risk for the continent. On the plus side, increased competition for mineral resource access can increase the negotiating power available to host governments seeking to maximize local revenues; in some cases leading to developing countries' enterprises outbidding historically dominant Western firms (Prichard, 2009). This has been the situation with China's relationship with Angola, whereby the former has received significant exploratory and production rights in return for a multi-billion dollar aid package to promote construction and expansion of infrastructure (Botchway, 2011). Similar loans have been proposed for Nigeria (in 2008) and the DRC (in 2007), which would provide China with access to large deposits of natural resources to fuel its growing demand. At the same time, however, serious criticisms of these growing economic ties have been raised. Resource investments popularly perceived as "land grabs," poor labour standards in mining operations, the importation of foreign workers and a lack of accountability in government budgets have provoked tensions between civil society groups, African governments and foreign investors. In Zambia, popular outcry against the poor labour standards of China's copper mining operations following the death of several dozen workers in 2007 prompted the Zambian government to openly criticize Chinese business practices and even make threats concerning future mining contracts.

Another key development is that with higher profits registered by companies operating in Africa's minerals sector, governments are facing heightened pressure to legislate more equitable revenue-sharing codes and adopt a larger developmental role for the state. Observers have noted a growing trend towards "resource nationalism" across Africa, with at least 11 countries recently deciding to review their mining contracts in light of demands for social regulation of the private sector (Campbell, 2010). This reflects a growing concern that African states may require a significant broadening of policy space — space restricted by previous generations of mining codes — to ensure a positive developmental role for mining, including the integration of mining activities into other sectors, such as industrial policies (ibid.: 213). South Africa, for example, banned the export of unprocessed chromium to China in 2007 after it placed tariffs on these mineral imports. Governments have also begun using higher tariffs and royalties on license approvals as a means to recover from the recent global economic crisis (Deloitte, 2010). This was seen in 2011, when Guinea conducted a revision of its national mining codes, empowering government officials to impose a tarriff up to 35 percent on revenues from foreign extractive operations. The AfDB has also recently reported that countries like Burkina Faso, Ghana, Mali and South Africa have increased royalty rates in their mining codes above the average rate of three percent (Gajigo, Mutambatsere and Ndiaye, 2012b).

How can policy makers respond to these challenges and maximize the positive developmental role of the extractive industry? First and foremost, contractual arrangements between host governments, local communities and mining corporations must be created in a transparent manner in accordance with established mining codes, rather than through secret and individually negotiated deals. Corruption and patronage in the contracting and licensing of mining concessions impede efficient tax administration and undermine the popular legitimacy of foreign-owned mining operations. Yet even policy mechanisms like the EITI, which explicitly target transparency, are unlikely to reduce rent-seeking behaviour without more fundamental institutional changes in African countries, including respect for the rule-of-law, independent judiciary and legal systems, and an informed and engaged citizenry (Hilson and Maconachie, 2009: 58). The Canadian government and Canadian mining corporations must recognize the long-term value of investing in local technical capacity and adhering to the regulatory regimes of host governments. The Government of Canada, already bilaterally supporting the implementation of EITI reporting protocols in Tanzania and Mozambique, should likewise focus development assistance on improving auditing and accounting capacity among local administrators and civil society organizations. Increased transparency and accountability alone, however, may be insufficient for African states to engage in further positive development. Many African governments are simultaneously locking themselves into bilateral treaties that protect the interests of foreign investors and restrict the scope for public policy making (UNCTAD, 2007, quoted in Campbell, 2010: 213). International donor strategies focussed on increased private sector participation, typified by Canada's recent approach, are also being scrutinized for continuing to restrict the policy space available to developing countries to pursue aggressive socio-economic development and pro-poor growth (Kindoray and Reilly-King, 2013). The outstanding question is whether fourth generation mining codes in Africa can provide an effective avenue for policy implementation. While hope exists for the establishment of concrete and enforceable legislative protections and legal frameworks for corporations operating internationally, progress remains limited by a lack of clarity over who assumes the role of enforcement agent: the host state, with potentially ineffective political, institutional and legal structures, or the country in which the corporation is permanently headquartered? Perhaps what is required is not a further proliferation of legal codes and regulations, but a re-imaging of those we already have and a refocussing of efforts on leveraging natural resources to create broad-based economic opportunities. This will ensure that while demands for extractives are met, it is done in a manner that increases local development, protects populations, reduces harm to the environment and promotes a sustainable future for generations to come.

## ENDNOTES

[1]   ICMM members include major mining firms Barrick, BHP Billiton, Anglo American, Rio Tinto, Goldcorp, and Inmet. Other organizations involved in ICMM activities include the World Bank, United Nations Conference on Trade and Development (UNCTAD), the International Union for Conservation of Nature and the International Labor Organization. Among non-governmental groups (NGOs), groups such as the Enough Project, MiningWatch and Global Witness have been instrumental in pushing for transparency initiatives.

[2]   A social license to operate takes place in the event when a mining project is seen as having the ongoing approval and broad acceptance of society to conduct its activities.

[3]   It is the responsibility of governments and private sector actors to ensure local communities have the ability to negotiate on equitable terms and retain the right to withhold consent for an activity, program or policy. See S. Bass et al. (2003), *Prior Informed Consent and Mining: Promoting the Sustainable Development of Local Communities*, Washington, DC: Environmental Law Institute; and R. Goodland (2004), "Free, and Prior Informed Consent and the World Bank Group," *Sustainable Development Law and Policy* IV, no. 2: 66–74.

[4]   In 2010, Canadian mining assets abroad were predominantly concentrated in Latin America and the Caribbean (47 percent), Africa (21 percent) and the United States (11 percent) (Government of Canada, 2011a).

[5]   The report stated that 34 percent of the 171 companies identified in incidents in the mining and exploration sector globally in the decade prior to 2009 were Canadian.

[6]   The Corporate Accountability for the Activities of Mining, Oil or Gas Corporations in Developing Countries Act.

[7]   The Canadian government's formally announced CSR strategy, "Building the Canadian Advantage: A CSR Strategy for the International Extractive

Sector" is designed to serve as a comprehensive strategy on CSR for Canadian firms operating abroad in the extractive sector. It is informed by the national round tables of industry and civil society stakeholders in 2006, as well as the recommendations of the 2005 Standing Committee on Foreign Affairs and International Trade report, *Mining in Developing Countries — Corporate Social Responsibility* (Government of Canada, 2011b).

## WORKS CITED

Akabzaa, Thomas (2009). "Mining in Ghana: Implications for National Economic Development and Poverty Reduction." In *Mining in Africa: Regulation and Development,* edited by Bonnie Campbell. Pages 25–65. New York, NY: Pluto Press.

Aykut, D. and S. Sayek (2007). "The Role of the Sectoral Composition of Foreign Direct Investment on Growth." In *Do Multinationals Feed Local Development and Growth?*, edited by L. Piscitello and G. Santangelo. Amsterdam: Elsevier.

Botchway, Francis N. (ed.) (2011). *Natural Resource Investment and Africa's Development.* Cheltenham: Edward Elgar Publishing Limited.

Butler, Paula (2004). "Tanzania: Liberalisation of Investment and the Mining Sector Analysis of the Content and Certain Implications of the Tanzania 1998 Mining Act." In *Regulating Mining in Africa: For Whose Benefit?*, edited by Bonnie Campbell. Pages 67–80. Discussion Paper 26. Uppsala, Sweden: Nordic Africa Institute.

Campbell, Bonnie (2010). "Revisiting the Reform Process of African Mining Regimes." *Canadian Journal of Development Studies* 30, nos. 1-2: 197–217.

Campbell, Bonnie (ed.) (2004). *Regulating Mining in Africa: For Whose Benefit?* Discussion Paper 26. Uppsala, Sweden: Nordic Africa Institute.

———— (2009). *Mining in Africa: Regulation and Development.* New York, NY: Pluto Press.

CCSRC (2009). "Corporate Social Responsibility: Movements and Footprints of Canadian Mining and Exploration Firms in the Developing World." October. Available at: www.miningwatch.ca/sites/miningwatch.ca/files/CSR_Movements_and_Footprints.pdf.

Deloitte (2010). *Tracking the Trends 2011: The Top 10 Issues Mining Companies Will Face in the Coming Year.* Canada: Deloitte.

Gajigo, O., E. Mutambatsere and G. Ndiaye (2012a). *Gold Mining in Africa: Maximizing Economic Returns for Countries.* AfDB Working Paper Series no. 147.

———— (2012b). "Royalty Rates in African Mining Revisited: Evidence from Gold Mining." *Africa Economic Brief* 3, no. 6.

Gaunt, J. (2010). "Building BRICS in Africa." *Reuters News.* November 23. Available at: http://blogs.reuters.com/macroscope/2010/11/23/building-brics-in-africa/.

Government of Canada (2011a). "Canada's Mining Assets Abroad Information Bulletin, February 2011." Natural Resources Canada. Available at: www.nrcan.gc.ca/minerals-metals/publications-reports/3086.

———— (2011b). "Minister Oda announces initiatives to increase the benefits of natural resource management for people in Africa and South America." CIDA. September 29. Available at: www.acdi-cida.gc.ca/acdi-cida/ACDI-CIDA.nsf/eng/CAR-929105317-KGD.

Hilson, Gavid and Roy Maconachie (2009). "'Good Governance' and the Extractive Industries in Sub-Saharan Africa." *Mineral Processing and Extractive Metallurgy Review* 30, no. 1: 52–100.

IMF (2012). *Regional Economic Outlook: Sub-Saharan Africa: Sustaining Growth amid Global Uncertainty.* World Economic and Financial Surveys. Washington, DC. Available at: www.imf.org/external/pubs/ft/reo/2012/afr/eng/sreo0412.htm.

Kindoray, Shannon and Fraser Reilly-King (2013). *Investing in the Business of Development: Bilateral Donor Approaches to Engaging the Private Sector.* The North-South Institute. January 10.

Labonne, B. (2002). "Harnessing mining for poverty reduction, especially in Africa." *Natural Resources Forum* 26, no. 1: 69–73.

MiningWatch Canada (2012). "Canada's Development Aid Dollars at Odds with Communities." November 26. Available at: www.miningwatch.ca/article/canada-s-development-aid-dollars-odds-communities.

Nwete, Bede (2007). "Corporate Social Responsibility and Transparency in the Development of Energy and Mining Projects in Emerging Markets: Is Soft Law the Answer?" *German Law Journal* 8, no. 4: 311–340.

Prichard, Wilson (2009). "The Minerals Boom in Sub-Saharan Africa: Continuity, Change and Prospects for Development." In *The New Scramble for Africa? Imperialism, Investment and Development,* edited by H. Melber and R. Southall. Durban: KwaZulu-Natal Press.

Ross, Michael (2012). *The Oil Curse: How Petroleum Wealth Shapes the Development of Nations.* Princeton: Princeton University Press.

Roxburgh, Charles et al. (2010). *Lions on the Move: The Progress and Potential of African Economies.* McKinsey Global Institute.

Sarrasin, Bruno (2004). "Madagascar: A Mining Industry Caught Between Environment and Development." In *Regulating Mining in Africa: For Whose Benefit?*, edited by Bonnie Campbell. Pages 53–66. Discussion Paper 26. Uppsala, Sweden: Nordic Africa Institute.

Tran, Mark (2012). "Africa's mineral wealth hardly denting poverty levels, says World Bank." *The Guardian,* October 5.

Tsui, Kevin K. (2011). "More Oil, Less Democracy: Evidence from Worldwide Crude Oil Discoveries." *The Economic Journal* 121, no. 551: 89–116.

UNCTAD (2007). *World Investment Report 2007.* Geneva: UNCTAD.

Whittington, L. (2010). "Canadian Mining Firms Worst for Environment, Rights: Report." *The Toronto Star*, October 19. Available at: www.thestar.com/news/canada/article/877438--canadian-mining-firms-worst-for-environment-rights-report.

# Blood Diamonds:
# Canada, Africa and Some Object
# Lessons in Global Governance

Ian Smillie

•  •  •  •  •  •  •  •  •  •  •  •  •  •  •  •  •  •  •

## INTRODUCTION

When Chuck Fipke and his partner Stewart Blusson hit pay dirt in the
Barren Lands of Canada's Northwest Territories at the end of 1991, they
could hardly imagine that their diamond find would make them rich beyond
imagination, or that it would link Canada inextricably in the years ahead with
a curse that diamonds were about to inflict upon countries halfway across the
globe.

Over the next two decades, as it became the world's third-largest diamond
producing country, Canada would lead the battle against blood diamonds
at the United Nations. A Canadian non-governmental organization (NGO)
would take the fight to the heart of the diamond industry. Canadians would
help design the first global regulatory system for rough diamonds, and another
Ottawa-based NGO would coax funding from Tiffany, Cartier and De Beers
in order to improve the lot of a million and a half artisanal diggers at the
source of the diamond pipeline in Africa and South America.

## CONFLICT DIAMONDS[1]

Blood diamonds, or "conflict diamonds," began to trickle and then to flood out of Angola around the same time as Fipke and Blusson made their find in Canada. The breakdown in 1992 of a fragile peace agreement between Angola's government and the rebel movement, União Nacional para a Independência Total de Angola (UNITA), marked a return to the war that had flared off and on since independence in 1975. Now, however, with an end to the Cold War and the absence of great power backing, the government turned to oil for its strength, and UNITA turned to the country's vast diamond resources. During the 1990s, more than half a million Angolans died in this conflict and, in the process, UNITA exchanged around US$4 billion worth of diamonds for the weapons it needed to prosecute its war (Global Witness, 1998: 3).

Far to the north, Charles Taylor was also fighting a resource-fuelled war in his effort to take power in Liberia. Timber became his first export — tropical hardwood from Liberia's virgin forests to feed voracious timber appetites in Europe and China. Liberia had no diamonds to speak of, but neighbouring Sierra Leone produced some of the best and most sought-after gem-quality diamonds in the world. In 1991, Taylor began to support a ragtag gang of disaffected Sierra Leoneans, led by a former army corporal he had met at Muammar Gadhafi's infamous training camp for terrorists near Benghazi, and soon Foday Sankoh was the leader of the grandly named Revolutionary United Front (RUF). In return for weapons, training and a safe haven in Liberia, Sankoh and his RUF invaded Sierra Leone's alluvial diamond fields and carried their tribute back to Taylor. They cleared the diamond areas of unwanted people and authority, using a tactic improvised by King Leopold a hundred years earlier in the Congo. They cut the hands and feet off women, children and men as a means of sending a message: If you get in our way, this is what will happen to you.

In February 1994, Robert Kaplan wrote about Sierra Leone in *The Atlantic,* and US President Clinton passed it around the White House as required reading. The article was called "The Coming Anarchy," and it is worthy of attention because it so badly missed the point of what was going on in Sierra Leone and other parts of the Africa Kaplan knew.

Sierra Leone is a microcosm of what is occurring, albeit in a more tempered and gradual manner, throughout West Africa and much of the underdeveloped world: the withering away of central governments, the rise of tribal and regional domains, the unchecked spread of disease, and the growing pervasiveness of war. West Africa is reverting to the Africa of the Victorian atlas. It consists now of a series of coastal trading posts, such as Freetown and Conakry, and an interior that, owing to violence, volatility, and disease, is again becoming, as Graham Greene once observed, "blank" and "unexplored..." It is Thomas Malthus, the philosopher of demographic doomsday, who is now the prophet of West Africa's future. And West Africa's future, eventually, will also be that of most of the rest of the world. (Kaplan, 1994)

What Kaplan failed to see was that the RUF in Sierra Leone, UNITA in Angola and other diamond-seeking armies in Liberia, the Democratic Republic of the Congo (DRC) and Côte d'Ivoire were not in it for the blood sport. Their objective was power, and terror — easier than conventional fighting — was the preferred tactic. Plunder, favoured by armies since Greek and Roman times, was the fuel on which these armies, such as they were, ran. And diamonds — with a higher value-to-weight ratio than almost any other substance on earth, completely unregulated and managed by an industry that had, at its fringes, become dangerously infected by money laundering, tax evasion and criminality — were an epic disaster waiting to happen.

## CANADA AT THE UNITED NATIONS

In June 1998, the United Nations added the export of unofficial diamonds to a growing list of unrequited sanctions against UNITA, to no evident avail. At the end of that year, a British NGO, Global Witness, produced a scathing report detailing the role of diamonds in fuelling the Angolan catastrophe. A year later, in January 1999, Canada began a two-year term as a temporary member of the UN Security Council, accepting the Chairmanship of the Angolan Sanctions Committee. UN sanctions up to then had been little more than a fig leaf for a variety of failed UN efforts, and for the evacuation of its peacekeeping forces. Canada's Ambassador to the United Nations, Robert

Fowler, took a new approach: he created an independent "panel of experts" to examine the relationship between weapons, oil and diamonds. Fowler was no armchair diplomat, and his panel eschewed standard UN diplomacy. It travelled to more than three dozen countries, interviewing heads of state and diamond industry executives. It worked with NGOs, law enforcement agencies and informers to uncover the murky underworld of the diamond trade. When its report appeared in March 2000, it provided detailed evidence of the link between diamonds and armed conflict in Angola, and for the first time in a UN report, it named sitting African heads of state as sanctions-busting traffickers in weapons and diamonds.[2]

Three month earlier, the Canadian NGO, PAC, had also produced a report on diamonds, this one detailing diamond-related violence in Sierra Leone, the link to Liberia's then-President, Charles Taylor, and the careless ambivalence of the world's diamond industry (Smillie, Gberie and Hazelton, 2000). PAC showed, among other things, that Belgium and its diamond industry were importing hundreds of millions of dollars' worth of diamonds every year from Liberia, a country that at the best of times had produced only a fraction of that amount.

NGO reports are one thing, but Security Council reports are another. When the UN report by Robert Fowler corroborated everything the NGOs had said, the world took note, and a campaign to halt the flow of conflict diamonds began.

## KIMBERLEY[3]

There are many villains in the story of conflict diamonds, but there are heroes as well, many of them African. One is South Africa's then Minister for Minerals and Energy, Phumzile Mlambo-Ngcuka. In May 2000, she called together industry leaders, concerned NGOs and governments to see whether a solution could be found. The minister had strong backing from Botswana and Namibia, where well-managed diamond industries were important to economic development. The meeting was held in the town of Kimberley, where South African diamonds had been discovered in the 1860s, and it became the first in a series of meetings that came to be called the "Kimberley Process."

By the end of 2002, in just over two years, the Kimberley Process had hammered out an international regulatory system for rough diamonds. As such things go, the KPCS is probably unique: there is no treaty, no ratification system and no UN involvement beyond general encouragement. Moreover, it is voluntary, and yet it aims to cover all of the world's rough diamonds. It is voluntary in the sense that governments join of their own volition, but if they do join, they must meet a series of minimum standards. They are required, for example, to pass legislation conforming to KPCS requirements; they must institute a series of internal controls with an auditable tracking system for rough diamonds and they must guarantee that each shipment of diamonds can be tracked back to the place where the diamonds were mined, or in the case of re-export, to the point of import. No diamonds may be exported by a member state to a non-KPCS member, and no diamonds may be imported by a Kimberley Process member state from a non-member. These latter provisions, endorsed by the World Trade Organization, mean that while technically voluntary, the KPCS is absolutely compulsory for any country with a legitimate diamond business. As of November 2012, 82 countries, including all members of the European Union, were represented in the Kimberley Process.

As a model of global governance, the KPCS was unique in other ways. The negotiations and the subsequent meetings, working groups and monitoring missions all included members of both civil society and industry. These participants take part in all deliberations and have the power to block consensus. As important, and putting the lie to Robert Kaplan's thesis, African governments played and continue to play a key role in the development and management of the Kimberley Process. Although Britain and Canada were staunch supporters from the outset, there was never any question of North or South in the Kimberley Process, and there was none of the paternalism that is found in the aid paradigm. All member countries are equal, and Namibia plays as big a role as China; Angola and Ghana have as much to say, and with as much authority, as Canada and Russia.

## THE DEVELOPMENT IMPERATIVE[4]

Much has been made by casual observers of the difference between Botswana and Sierra Leone. Botswana, with a history of democracy and good governance, has benefitted enormously from its diamond wealth; Sierra Leone, prone to coups and corruption, has not. There is, however, another difference. Botswana's diamonds come from deep, capital-intensive mines that have very small surface footprints and are relatively simple to police. In Sierra Leone, and all the other countries that suffered from conflict diamonds, the gems are alluvial in nature, close to the surface and scattered over hundreds of square miles. Hard to police and easy to exploit, these diamonds are as resistant to new laws and regulations as they were to older ones dealing with theft, smuggling and tax evasion. While good policing is essential, there is another imperative. Illicit alluvial diamond mining is not a get-rich-quick enterprise. It is dirty, difficult and dangerous. There are as many as 1.5 million artisanal diamond diggers in Africa and South America, a large proportion of them outside the formal economy, few of them earning much more than a dollar a day.[5]

To bring this kind of diamond mining — which accounts for 15 percent of the world's gem diamonds — into the ambit of the formal sector, a different approach is required. Here we have a *development* problem, one that requires development solutions.

When it became clear that many of the state members of the Kimberley Process were unwilling to add a development agenda to the KPCS regulatory framework, a new initiative began, spearheaded by PAC, Global Witness and De Beers. The irony of civil society and industry — antagonists in the early days of the conflict diamond campaign — joining together around a development agenda is perhaps not as odd as it might appear. Industry had been caught flat-footed by the conflict diamond issue, and now here was another problem at the heart of the diamond business, one that cried out for attention in an industry whose product is sold on the basis of love and beauty.

An exploratory meeting was held in London in January 2005, with the idea of paralleling the Kimberley Process: interested governments, industry and civil society would come together to tackle the development issues that lay at the root, not just of conflict diamonds, but of the economic and social disarray in the alluvial diamond fields of more than a dozen African and South American countries. What became the foundational meeting of the DDI was held later that year in Ghana, and the new organization, incorporated with charitable status in both the United States and Canada, received its first start-up grants from the Government of Sweden and The Tiffany and Co. Foundation.

Headquartered in Ottawa, the DDI has avoided the controversy around NGOs working with the extractive sector in two ways. First, it did not back unwittingly into agreements with mining companies around a corporate social responsibility agenda. Instead, the DDI actively sought out relevant companies. The DDI *wants* the diamond industry, from mining through to the retail sector, to be involved in the effort, to take responsibility, to help fund it and to be involved in its governance. The DDI guards its independence carefully, however, and its support from industry is unearmarked, with no connection to any specific corporate interest along the diamond pipeline. As a development NGO, the DDI's main funders are, and will probably remain traditional donor agencies, but success has brought a new source of financial support: African governments. Ably led by two African-Canadians, the DDI is probably one of the very few international NGOs that has ever received unearmarked financial contributions from African governments, testimony to the organization's growing success in developing a fair trade diamond system, its registration of 100,000 artisanal diggers in the DRC in a single year[6] and its new approach to human rights in the diamond fields of Africa.

## THE DARK SIDE OF THE MOON

This version of a nicely rounded regulatory system and a complementary development initiative is not the whole story. If it were, it would seem almost too good to be true, an exemplary model of inclusive global governance brought to bear on a calamity of horrific proportions. When the ink dried at the end of 2002 on the KPCS, a number of areas still needed attention and would be developed as the years passed. But when it came to serious issues — issues of non-compliance, examples of countries where the rules were not enforced — the Kimberley Process stumbled over the political potholes that confound many agreements. One shortcoming in the agreement stood out above all others: all decisions were to be taken by consensus, and consensus meant unanimity. If just one government disagreed with a proposed way forward, nothing would happen.

This seemingly tiny flaw has played out with disastrous results for KPCS effectiveness and credibility. All of Venezuela's diamonds are smuggled out of the country (and into others) under the somnolent gaze of the Kimberley Process. This is not because industry, civil society and most governments think nothing should be done. It is because a small handful of Venezuela's friends have blocked consensus, allowing politics to trump conflict prevention, common sense and the well-being of the industry that the KPCS was designed to protect. There is more: internal controls in half a dozen member states are virtually non-existent. Government-sponsored murder, human rights abuse and corruption in Zimbabwe's diamond fields occasioned much Kimberley Process sound and fury, but no action or comeuppance worthy of mention.

## IMPORTANCE OF THE BLOOD DIAMOND ISSUE TO CANADA[7]

Some argue that the diamond wars are over, so what does it matter? It matters in several ways, not least to Canadians who each make, through their taxes, a contribution to the UN peacekeeping bills in Liberia, Côte d'Ivoire and the DRC — some CDN$2 billion in 2012-2013 alone. The danger of renewed violence notwithstanding, there is no question of this industry returning to where it was in the 1990s. In the post-9/11 world, $5 or $10 billion worth of rough diamonds cannot be allowed back into their old, unregulated ways. Governments are much more concerned than they once were about money laundering, drugs and guns, and are unlikely to allow such an obvious cash substitute back onto unwatched streets.

Because diamonds are important to the economies of many of Canada's northern communities, Canadians have a long-term interest in the commercial *bona fides* of diamonds. And because Canada is a major international player in other extractive industries, it has much to gain from making this multi-stakeholder initiative work, in its own right and as a possible model where other minerals and other kinds of conflict are concerned. The development challenge is another area for potential Canadian leadership, not in promoting the narrow commercial interests of Canadian mining firms, but in finding solutions to generic development issues, such as the problems of artisanal miners.

The Kimberley Process is being pushed from within and without to reform itself, to use the tools it has to bite down on non-compliance, smuggling and diamond-related violence. If it cannot, or will not, before long other instruments will undoubtedly come into play: tough, unilateral diamond regulations in the United States, for example, where almost half of the world's gem diamonds are sold every year. The multilateral Financial Action Task Force, which deals with money laundering and terrorist financing, is already turning its attention to diamonds, as are consumers who increasingly ask jewellers for "ethical" diamonds.

As a model for global governance, the Kimberley Process is an example of what can be done and what should not be done. Canada has been ably represented in the best of the effort, and has played a constructive role throughout — at the United Nations, in the creation, management and efforts to reform the KPCS, in its support for civil society and the development agenda. But this is an African story, and African governments and civil society have played their role as well. The diamond fields of Africa are still volatile and many questions remain. The bleak portrait described by Robert Kaplan in 1994 has been altered with new, fresh colours, and more positive images of the way things can and, perhaps, will be. The challenge, where diamonds are concerned, is to keep moving in that direction.

## ENDNOTES

[1]  A great deal of information on conflict diamonds can be found on the Partnership Africa Canada (PAC) website, available at: www.pacweb.org.

[2]  The "Fowler Report" is available at: www.un.org/News/dh/latest/angolareport_eng.htm.

[3]  The Kimberley Process, the Kimberley Process Certification Scheme (KPCS) and any information relating to these in this section are described at www.kimberleyprocess.com/.

[4]  The development challenge, and all related material in this section, is well described in material on the Diamond Development Initiative (DDI) website, available at: www.ddiglobal.org.

[5]  See: www.ddiglobal.org/pages/issues.php.

[6]  Details on DDI projects can be found on its general website, noted above. Details of its registration project can be found on a dedicated website at: www.ddidrc.org/eng/index.php.

7    A more extensive discussion of the issues raised in this chapter can be found in Ian Smillie (2010), *Blood on the Stone: Greed, Corruption and War in the Global Diamond Trade*, Anthem Press: London.

## WORKS CITED

Global Witness (1998). *A Rough Trade*. London.

Kaplan, Robert D. (1994). "The Coming Anarchy: How Scarcity, Crime, Overpopulation, Tribalism, and Disease are Rapidly Destroying the Social Fabric of Our Planet." *The Atlantic*, February 1.

Smillie, Ian, Lansana Gberie and Ralph Hazelton (2000). *The Heart of the Matter: Sierra Leone, Diamonds and Human Security*. Ottawa: PAC.

# Part Four:
# Development and Health

# Canadian Aid to Africa

## Stephen Brown

• • • • • • • • • • • • • • • • • •

## INTRODUCTION

Africa is the greatest recipient of Canadian foreign aid. Canada provided more official development assistance (ODA) to Africa than to any other region in every year from 1980 to 2011, with only one exception (assistance to Asia in 2005). In 2010-2011, 38 percent of Canadian international assistance went to Africa and six of the top 10 recipients were in Sub-Saharan Africa, namely Ethiopia, Tanzania, Mozambique, Ghana, Mali, Sudan and Senegal (Canadian International Development Agency [CIDA], 2012b: 5). The Canadian government has, however, never developed a clearly defined policy or strategy for assistance to Africa. Instead, CIDA's allocation of aid flows has been combined with sporadic initiatives to form de facto approaches to aid.[1]

This chapter describes the main trends in Canadian ODA to Africa over the past 50 years, analyzes underlying motivations, in particular over the past decade, and considers the impact of aid. After decades of waxing and waning, the future of aggregate financial flows to Africa is unclear. There are strong indications, however, that the modalities of aid to Africa are changing, increasingly emphasizing commercial self-interest. This suggests that the types of African countries receiving assistance will change, with greater priority given to countries with natural resources that are of interest to Canadian companies, as will the specific sectors that the Canadian government supports within recipient countries in Africa. It is difficult to pinpoint the impact of Canadian aid to date; however, the new emphasis is likely to reduce aid's contributions to poverty reduction.

## AID TRENDS

This section traces the main trends in Canadian aid to Africa, highlighting the shifts in emphasis.[2] Figure 1 illustrates the aid levels to the three main recipient regions — Africa, the Americas and Asia — from 1960 to 2011. It illustrates the changing priority placed on Africa, as well as the sometimes very high level of aid that is not categorized as going to a specific region.

Throughout the 1960s, as can be noted in the figure, Canada provided the majority of its ODA to Asia. Over the following two decades, the volume of aid to Africa began to grow exponentially, from less than US$200 million in 1970 to over US$900 million per year in 1988 and 1989. In order to promote Canadian national unity, the government carefully balanced its contributions to anglophone and francophone Africa. In 1986, CIDA launched a special "Africa 2000" fund, designed to run for 15 years. This period, under the leadership of Prime Ministers Pierre Trudeau (Liberal) and Brian Mulroney (Progressive Conservative), was a veritable golden age for aid to Africa — and not just from Canada. The continent attracted considerable international attention, in part because of famine and the struggle against apartheid. Western donors also spent considerable resources in support of structural adjustment programs — and sometimes trying to mitigate their ravages.

After 1993, however, Western aid levels in general and Canadian aid to Africa in particular entered into a steep decline. With the end of the Cold War and the diminishing strategic importance of Africa, as well as severe fiscal deficits and the onset of aid fatigue, Africa lost its appeal in donor capitals. Canadian aid to the region fell below US$400 million in 2000, less than half the average annual amount provided between 1982 and 1992.

Rather suddenly in 2001, the trend reversed itself. The Millennium Development Goals, a set of eight objectives established as part of the United Nations Millennium Declaration in 2000, epitomized the recognition that urgent action was required to fight poverty, while the terrorist attacks on September 11, 2001 reminded donors that conditions abroad could have important repercussions for their national security. In Canada, Liberal Prime

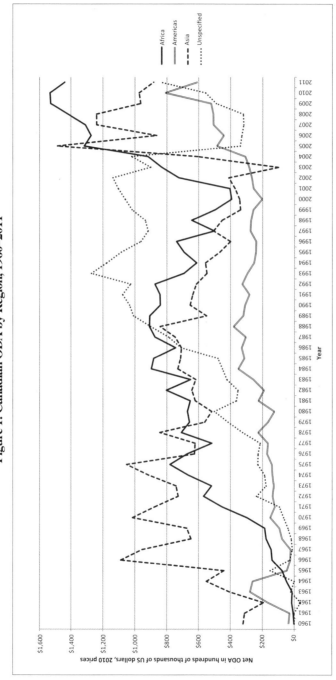

**Figure 1: Canadian ODA by Region, 1960–2011**

Africa
Americas
Asia
Unspecified

Net ODA in hundreds of thousands of US dollars, 2010 prices

Year

Source: OECD, 2013.

Minister Jean Chrétien entered the final years of his political career and, having presided over draconian cuts in aid to Africa, sought to improve his legacy through a few special initiatives. For instance, at the 2002 Group of Eight (G8) summit he hosted in Kananaskis, Alberta, Chrétien gave African development an important place on the agenda, announcing eight percent annual increases in Canadian ODA, of which half would go to Africa, as well as a five-year, CDN$500 million Canada Fund for Africa, which included CDN$100 million to support private sector investment. Also in 2002, CIDA issued a policy statement that emphasized a focus on low-income countries, especially those in Africa, as well as the importance of the private sector. Soon after, CIDA identified nine countries of focus, including six in Africa.

After Chrétien's retirement in 2003, his successor Paul Martin continued to increase aid and focus on Africa. As a final "legacy project," the Liberal government passed the Jean Chrétien Pledge to Africa Act in 2004, which aimed to facilitate the shipment of life-saving generic pharmaceuticals to developing countries. The process that drug manufacturers must go through is, however, so onerous that the law has had almost no impact: since 2004, it has facilitated only two shipments of one medication to one country by one company. Opposition-led efforts to improve the legislation in 2011 and 2012 both failed.

The Martin government's 2005 international policy statement further enshrined its commitment to Africa, promising to double aid to the continent, also stressing the importance of the private sector. CIDA announced the addition of new countries of focus — 14 out of the total of 25 were in Africa. However, the government also emphasized the importance of providing increased aid to "failed and fragile states," in particular Afghanistan, Iraq and Haiti, which were in other regions of the world.

Since Prime Minister Stephen Harper was first elected in 2006, the Canadian government has been sending out confusing and often contradictory signals on its commitment to African development. David Black (2012) describes the Conservative government's approach as a combination of indifference and idiosyncrasy. In 2007, Harper announced a shift in emphasis from Africa to the Americas. In 2009, CIDA's new list of countries of focus added Sudan but dropped the eight African countries that had been included only four years earlier, leaving only seven African countries on the list of 20. Many observers condemned Canada for "turning its back" on Africa (Halliday, 2009).

However, such statements were overblown: The government continued to increase its ODA flows to the continent, reaching an all-time high of US$1.5 billion in 2010. It also met the Martin government's commitment to double aid to Africa between 2003-2004 and 2008-2009, albeit by recalculating the base amount.

It is not clear if this upward trend will continue. The government does not make public its projected aid levels and the sustained increase in spending in Africa could be the result of already-approved projects continuing their activities as foreseen. Disbursements for 2011 decreased by 2.4 percent from the previous year, but this does not necessarily mark the beginning of a new downward trend. In fact, the government's Maternal, Newborn and Child Health Initiative (MNCH), announced at the Muskoka G8 Summit in 2010, is likely to provide additional assistance to Africa, where needs are the greatest (see discussion in the chapter by David R. Black). In addition, the renewed emphasis on Canadian commercial interests, discussed below, could prompt the Canadian government to allocate additional funds where Canadian companies are active, especially in the extractive sector. Still, the 2012 federal budget cut CIDA's funding; the agency subsequently announced it would end bilateral aid to five African countries and reduce the amounts provided to three of the seven remaining African countries of concentration.[3]

Finally, a word of caution about aid statistics calculated on a regional basis. Confusingly, ODA statistics show large increases in the percentage of aid to Africa, the Americas and Asia during the period 2000–2010. When the overall budget is growing, dollar flows to all regions can increase simultaneously. However, how can the share of all major regions simultaneously increase? It was not achieved through significant aid cuts to the other two regions, Europe and Oceania, which were, in any case, quite small, but rather by reallocation from a residual "unspecified" category. Thus, aid was redistributed from a generic category (US$1.1 billion in 2000, 39 percent of total, down to US$320 million or 6 percent in 2008) to the regions. As a result, the recorded increase in aid to Africa (as well as the two other major regions) could, in large part, be due to a change in accounting practices, rather than solely the allocation of additional funds. The data are, unfortunately, too imprecise to be able to track the regional trends with great accuracy.

## UNDERLYING MOTIVATIONS

Having traced the trends in Canadian aid to Africa, this chapter now attempts to track the underlying motivations. It is perforce a speculative exercise, as no official documents set out the "real" reason Canada provides aid or adopts new policy initiatives. It also runs the danger of reifying CIDA or the Canadian government as a unitary — and self-conscious — actor that is capable of rational reasoning. Nonetheless, from government officials' statements and official documents, one can often deduce rationales and from them identify motivations.

Canadian aid has always been underpinned by a discomfiting mix of motivations. During the Cold War, geostrategic interests fundamentally shaped Canadian aid, beginning with the Canadian government's assistance to Southern Asia under the Colombo Plan in the 1950s. Security is an important factor in the post-Cold War dispensation as well, especially in the fight against terrorism, best illustrated by the size of Canadian aid to Afghanistan and its focus on Kandahar province while Canadian troops were stationed there. Other foreign policy interests, including commercial ones, have long influenced aid destination and modalities. The desire for prestige is also an important — if understudied — motivation, be it among donor peers or the Canadian electorate. Still, altruism, or what Cranford Pratt (2000) calls "humane internationalism," has also greatly contributed to foreign aid (and motivated CIDA employees). Self-interest and selflessness can also overlap when generosity and "doing the right thing" can be in Canada's long-term interest, for instance, in creating a stable and prosperous world.

In the past, the Canadian government often "moved with the crowd" when it came to aid to Africa (Black, Thérien and Clark, 1996). It followed and sometimes contributed to international trends, but was also influenced by domestic factors. When Western donors as a whole turned their attention to Africa, so did Canada, on occasion taking a leading role. When donors' interest waned, for example, in the 1990s, Canada cut its aid more radically than the average (Brown, 2008). Chrétien's emphasis on African development in his final years in government was part of an international trend, but it was also motivated — as mentioned above — by a desire for a positive legacy.

Martin continued in the same direction, as did the Harper government in its first few years in power, probably more out of inertia than design. Under

CIDA Minister Josée Verner, Canada's aid policies seemed increasingly motivated by a desire for prestige, not personal as in Chrétien's case, but national, especially in Afghanistan (Brown, 2011). The Muskoka Initiative on MNCH seemed born from the desire for a high-profile "announceable" at the Canadian-chaired G8 summit, rather than a well thought-out strategy.

After Bev Oda replaced Verner as minister of international cooperation in 2007, commercial interests loomed larger. The shift in focus from low-income African countries to middle-income ones in the Americas, especially in places where Canada had important trade and investment ties (such as Peru and Colombia), was a concrete manifestation of that new trend. It also marked the end of Canada's alignment with the consensus on Western aid priorities and the forging of a more independent, self-interested approach. Tellingly, the official criteria for selecting CIDA's 20 countries of focus in 2009 included "alignment with Canada's foreign policy" (CIDA, 2012a). Although that had always been a de facto consideration, it was the first time CIDA officially stated it.

Canadian aid policies have increasingly aligned with the interest of the Canadian extractive industry. In 2011, CIDA announced its funding of three partnerships between Canadian non-governmental organizations (NGOs) and mining companies, with two of the three projects taking place in African countries (Ghana and Burkina Faso). CIDA funds would be managed by the NGOs and not the private companies; however, at least one of the projects in Africa can be interpreted as providing indirect subsidies for the companies, since public funds will help the private company obtain and maintain the consent of mining-affected communities by providing them with social and economic benefits. These activities would not take place if the communities did not host Canadian mining operations.

In 2012, the House of Commons Standing Committee on Foreign Affairs and International Development issued a report that praised these types of partnerships, recommending that more CIDA funds be set aside to support work with the Canadian private sector. Soon after its release, newly appointed CIDA Minister Julian Fantino (2012) publicly emphasized the importance of the Canadian private sector in poverty reduction, emphasizing the benefits for Canadian companies' bottom lines. Among the various rationales for public-private partnerships, he also "said CIDA's work with mining companies would help them compete on the international stage" (Mackrael, 2012a), thereby contradicting the government's claim that foreign aid funds would not be subsidizing Canadian companies — a practice that could be illegal under the 2008 ODA Accountability Act, which specifies that aid must focus on poverty reduction, but falls within the mandate of other government bodies, such as the Department of Foreign Affairs and International Trade (DFAIT) and Export Development Canada. Moreover, Fantino's (2012) repeated use of the term "mutual benefit" — for instance, he stated that "CIDA is working to help the Canadian mining, oil and gas sector to partner in development with local governments and NGOs for mutual benefit" — mirrors the Chinese government's justification for its bundling of aid, trade and investment in Africa (and elsewhere).

Past experience, however, has shown that actively targeting partnerships with a donor's private sector and working in natural resource extraction are rarely effective measures for reducing poverty in developing countries. For instance, between 1975 and 2005, CIDA's own Industrial Cooperation Program "disbursed over [CDN]$1.1 billion in support of Canadian private sector initiatives in developing countries" (CIDA, 2007: 8). An internal evaluation found that only 15.5 percent of its projects from 1997 to 2002 had actually been implemented (ibid.: 13).[4] A recent report by the World Bank, an institution known for its support of the private sector, recognized that few benefits of natural resource wealth actually flow down to the poor (2012: 19-20).

Although the amounts currently allocated through partnerships with Canadian companies are relatively small, the government has signalled on several occasions that it will increasingly use ODA funds to fund the Canadian private sector's activities. Given the lack of evidence that this is an effective use of aid money, the government's motivation can be attributed to commercial self-interest — this is not completely new, as can be seen from the repeated emphasis on the role of the private sector since 2002, mentioned above. However, the Harper government seems more serious about taking additional concrete initiatives further than the Chrétien or Martin governments and is linking Canadian geographic priorities to Canadian corporate interests to an extent not seen for decades. Fantino has stated that "we have a duty and a responsibility to ensure that Canadian interests are promoted" and that "Canadians are entitled to derive a benefit" (Mackrael, 2012b). Such a perspective is at odds with the Western consensus on aid effectiveness, which is why Canada and most other Western donors have ceased tying the provision of goods and services to their own country. Even before Fantino replaced Oda as CIDA minister, a review of Canada's aid program by other Western donors criticized the Canadian government for this approach, reminding it that "there should be no confusion between development objectives and the promotion of commercial interests" (OECD, 2012: 11).

## IMPACT

This chapter now turns to the question of the impact of Canadian aid to Africa. Though tempting, no sweeping generalizations can be made on assistance that not only goes to 54 countries, but that takes on very different forms, such as humanitarian assistance, food aid, capacity building, strengthening governance and support to civil society. Moreover, not all forms of progress can be reliably measured (for instance, women's empowerment or the rule of law) and, even when they can, the problem of attribution remains. For example, how to tell what share of economic growth or improved primary school enrollment can be credited to Canadian aid, let alone foreign aid as a whole?

The government has never undertaken a comprehensive review of its aid programming in Africa. The Standing Senate Committee on Foreign Affairs and International Trade, however, did study Canada's contributions to economic development in Sub-Saharan Africa. Its deeply flawed report summarized the record as "40 years of failure" (Government of Canada, 2007; see critique in Brown, 2007). Given the progress across numerous socio-economic indicators, it is not clear that development has flat-out failed, even if results are often inadequate. In addition, it is unclear whether Canada's aid specifically has failed. Given that Canadian ODA historically constitutes only between 1.3 percent and 3.5 percent of annual global aid flows to Africa (OECD, 2013), why should the alleged lack of results be attributable to Canada? It could be that Canadian aid was highly effective, but other countries' far less so.

An underlying problem with the Senate report and the Harper government's current emphasis on short-term visible results is that they are based on an outmoded understanding of development assistance. Politicians and journalists generally want to be able to see stand-alone projects that can be identified as Canadian-supported. However, decades of development work have demonstrated that such isolated projects have very limited impact. Rather than focussing on things that can "fly the Canadian flag," aid is generally more effective when it supports recipient government-led programs, which usually involve pooled funding, often with other donors. Such programs are definitely less "photogenic," but it does not follow that their impact is any lesser. Politicians would do development a service if they would stop promising voters to account for every nickel of Canadian aid through visibly demonstrable results over the course of three to five years, and instead educate themselves and the public on the benefits of a longer-term vision that focusses more on benefits for recipients and less on brownie points for individual donors.

The inherent difficulties of demonstrating aid effectiveness combine with an innate suspicion of foreign aid within the Conservative Party (Black, 2012) to help predispose its members to cutting CIDA's budget and redirecting what remains towards meeting narrowly defined Canadian interests, in particular those of the private sector. It is likely that Canadian aid to Africa will suffer as a result, in quality if not necessarily in quantity. This could also reallocate aid among African countries or among sectors within specific countries, in line with the interests of Canadian companies, rather than development criteria.

## CONCLUSION

Canadian aid policy to Africa does not follow a grand strategy. Rather, it comprises disparate initiatives that respond to different imperatives and motivations. In his final years in power, Liberal Prime Minister Chrétien reversed almost a decade of neglect and made Africa a priority, as did his successor Paul Martin. The Conservative government of Stephen Harper has shifted rhetorical emphasis to the Americas, but aid flows to Africa have not yet declined. This could be because approved projects take years to wind down, or because the new initiative on MNCH has provided new funds to African programs.

A clearer trend is the increase in self-interest underpinning Canadian aid, especially regarding the role of the Canadian private sector in development assistance and expressed in its fullest in CIDA's recent alliances with Canadian mining companies and the promise of more public-private partnerships. While touted as a way of achieving mutual benefit, including greater impact in poverty reduction, there is little reason to believe that poor Africans will benefit significantly. Instead, the new emphasis could well lead to a geographical reallocation within Africa of the shrinking aid budget in line with individual countries' appeal to the Canadian extractive industry — and hamper, rather than enhance, Canadian aid's effectiveness at reducing poverty. DFAIT's recently announced takeover of CIDA is likely to accelerate the rise of self-interest in Canadian assistance to Africa.

## Acknowledgements

The author is grateful to Esref Aksu, workshop participants and the editors for helpful suggestions.

## ENDNOTES

[1] In its March 2013 federal budget, the government announced that it planned to merge CIDA with DFAIT to form one super-ministry, the Department of Foreign Affairs, Trade and Development. For a detailed analysis of what constitutes Canadian aid policy, see Molly den Heyer (2012), "Untangling Canadian Aid Policy: International Agreements, CIDA's Policies and Micro-policy Negotiations in Tanzania," In *Struggling for Effectiveness: CIDA and Canadian Foreign Aid,* edited by Stephen Brown. Pages 186–216. Montreal and Kingston: McGill-Queen's University Press.

[2] This section draws on David R. Morrison (1998), *Aid and Ebb Tide: A History of CIDA and Canadian Development Assistance*, Waterloo, Ontario: Wilfrid Laurier University Press, and the author's previous discussion of trends in Canadian aid to Africa (see Brown, 2008). All figures, unless specified otherwise, are taken from the Organisation for Economic Co-operation and Development (OECD) (2013) and expressed in US dollars, based on data provided by CIDA to the OECD. Constant 2010 dollars are used to enhance comparability.

[3] According to *Embassy*, Canada will no longer provide bilateral aid to Malawi, Niger, Rwanda, Zambia and Zimbabwe, selected due to "high

operating costs" for those specific programs. Canada will also cut its assistance to Ethiopia, Mozambique and Tanzania (Shane, 2012: 8).

4    The program was transferred from CIDA to DFAIT in 2009. It was suspended in 2012, pending a police investigation of financial irregularities. See James Munson (2012), "Past failure not deterring CIDA minister from business partnership model," *iPolitics*, December 4, available at: www.ipolitics.ca/2012/12/04/past-failure-not-deterring-cida-minister-from-business-partnership-model.

## WORKS CITED

Black, David (2012). "Between Indifference and Idiosyncrasy: The Conservatives and Canadian Aid to Africa." In *Struggling for Effectiveness: CIDA and Canadian Foreign Aid*, edited by Stephen Brown. Pages 246–268. Montreal and Kingston: McGill-Queen's University Press.

Black, David R. and Jean-Philippe Thérien with Andrew Clark (1996). "Moving with the crowd: Canadian aid to Africa." *International Journal* 51, no. 2.

Brown, Stephen (2007). "Le rapport du Sénat sur l'aide canadienne à l'Afrique: une analyse à rejeter." *Le Multilatéral* 1, no. 3.

——— (2008). "L'aide publique canadienne à l'Afrique: vers un nouvel âge d'or ?" In *L'aide canadienne au développement*, edited by François Audet, Marie-Eve Desrosiers and Stéphane Roussel. Pages 267–290. Montréal: Presses de l'Université de Montréal.

——— (2011). "Aid Effectiveness and the Framing of New Canadian Aid Initiatives." In *Readings in Canadian Foreign Policy: Classic Debates and New Ideas*, 2nd edition, edited by Duane Bratt and Christopher J. Kukucha. Pages 469–486. Don Mills, ON: Oxford University Press.

CIDA (2007). *Executive Report on the Evaluation of the CIDA Industrial Cooperation (CIDA-INC) Program*. Gatineau, Canada: CIDA Evaluation Division.

———— (2012a). "Aid Effectiveness Agenda." June 21. Available at: www. acdi-cida.gc.ca/acdi-cida/ACDI-CIDA.nsf/eng/FRA-825105226-KFT.

———— (2012b). *Statistical Report on International Assistance, Fiscal Year 2010–2011*. Gatineau, Canada: CIDA.

Fantino, Julian (2012). "Minister Fantino's Keynote Address to the Economic Club of Canada titled 'Reducing Poverty — Building Tomorrow's Markets.'" November 23. Available at: www.acdi-cida.gc.ca/acdi-cida/ ACDI-CIDA.nsf/eng/NAT-1123135713-Q8T.

Government of Canada (2007). *Overcoming 40 Years of Failure: A New Road Map for Sub-Saharan Africa*. Ottawa: Senate of Canada, Standing Senate Committee on Foreign Affairs and International Trade.

Halliday, Anthony (2009). "Canada is Turning its Back on the Poorest of Africa." *The Globe and Mail*, April 3. Available at: www. theglobeandmail.com/commentary/canada-is-turning-its-back-on-the-poorest-of-africa/article4189464.

Mackrael, Kim (2012a). "Canada's Foreign Aid doesn't Exist to Keep NGOs Afloat, Fantino says." *The Globe and Mail*, November 28. Available at: www.theglobeandmail.com/news/politics/canadas-foreign-aid-doesnt-exist-to-keep-ngos-afloat-fantino-says/article5751774.

———— (2012b). "Fantino defends CIDA's corporate shift." *The Globe and Mail*, December 3. Available at: www.theglobeandmail.com/news/ politics/fantino-defends-cidas-corporate-shift/article5950443.

OECD (2012). *Canada: Development Assistance Committee (DAC) Peer Review 2012*. Paris: OECD.

———— (2013). Query Wizard for International Development Statistics. Available at: http://stats.oecd.org/qwids.

Pratt, Cranford (2000). "Alleviating Global Poverty or Enhancing Security: Competing Rationales for Canadian Development Assistance." In *Transforming Development: Foreign Aid for a Changing World*, edited by Jim Freedman. Pages 37–59. Toronto: University of Toronto Press.

Shane, Kristen (2012). "Countries hit by aid cuts sympathetic, disappointed." *Embassy*, June 6.

World Bank (2012). *Africa's Pulse*, vol. 6. Washington, DC: World Bank. Available at: http://siteresources.worldbank.org/INTAFRICA/Resources/Africas-Pulse-brochure_Vol6.pdf.

# The Role and Influence of Non-traditional Aid Providers in Africa: Implications for Canada

Bill Morton

• • • • • • • • • • • • • • • • • •

## INTRODUCTION

The last 10 years have seen unprecedented change in the number and type of actors providing development assistance. This includes a large group, often labelled as new or emerging donors — but referred to here as "non-traditional providers" of aid (NTPs).[1] Middle-income countries and emerging economies constitute a large part of this group, the most active of which include Brazil, Chile, China, Colombia, Egypt, India, Malaysia, Mexico, South Africa, Thailand and Venezuela (Zimmerman and Smith, 2011). The stronger role of these players in the provision of aid, and within the development cooperation system as a whole, means that the traditional Organisation for Economic Co-operation and Development (OECD) donors no longer have free reign over decisions on aid norms and principles; instead, these must be arrived at with other governments that have become increasingly powerful and influential. This amounts to a major change in what is referred to as the "global aid architecture."

Reflecting these broad changes, the nature of aid and development cooperation in Africa has also changed dramatically in the last 10 years. Brazil, India, China and South Africa are among the most important new players. Overall, they provide a relatively low proportion of total development assistance to Africa; however, to dismiss them on this basis is a mistake. Their significance is not so much about the amount of aid they provide, but about *how* they provide it. In most respects, this is markedly different to the way OECD donors have traditionally provided aid.

NTPs' different delivery of aid, and the new types of aid-related relationships they are establishing with African countries, has the potential to redefine the nature of development cooperation in Africa. At the same time, NTPs' provision of development assistance cannot be separated from a range of other complex motives that are concerned with their pursuit of broader economic, strategic and foreign policy objectives, and with the overall intent of positioning themselves as important actors on the African continent. So far, however, traditional donors, including Canada, have been slow to recognize the implications of these moves. This paper considers these issues in two parts. The first part provides an overview of NTPs in Africa, including the nature of their engagement, with a focus on China and Brazil, while the second considers the implications of this engagement and how Canada should respond.

## PART ONE

## Non-traditional Aid Providers in Africa

NTPs' provision of aid globally and in Africa differs from the approaches undertaken by traditional donors in a number of significant ways. First and foremost is their rejection of the typical "donor-recipient" terminology, in particular the notion that their provision of aid makes them "donors," and that the countries they provide it to should be seen as "recipients" (Zimmerman and Smith, 2011). Instead, NTPs see their engagement in terms of a broader concept understood as South-South cooperation (SSC), which involves the promotion of political, technical and economic cooperation among developing countries that are pursuing common development goals (ibid.).

The development cooperation aspect of this process is sometimes described as South-South development cooperation (SSDC). There is now considerable enthusiasm among participants in SSDC, in particular regarding its comparative advantages over North-South (N-S) cooperation. Most notably, SSDC participants view the process not as a "vertical" N-S transaction, but as a "horizontal partnership" that is part of a mutually beneficial arrangement for both parties (ibid.), and that is more equal than the traditional donor-recipient relationship.

Participants in SSDC refer to a host of other advantages that set it apart from N-S cooperation, including: it is usually guided by principles of respect for national sovereignty and non-interference; it is not subject to political or governance conditionalities; and it is based on mutual respect, solidarity and common experience of development challenges. When the cooperation involves a transfer of financial resources, the process is often seen as more predictable, faster and with lower transaction costs than N-S aid, and therefore as better value for money (Morton, 2010; United Nations, 2010).

Some countries view SSDC as "re-defining the parameters of development cooperation" (Morton, 2010). Such claims regarding SSDC reflect these countries' enthusiasm and backing for this type of cooperation, and indicate that within the context of current dialogue on development cooperation and the increasingly active role of SSDC providers, such views cannot be dismissed. They provide a clear challenge to dominant N-S modes of cooperation.

NTPs' engagement in Africa draws on many of the above characteristics of SSDC. This applies to the BRICS (Brazil, Russia, India, China, South Africa), which are key NTPs in Africa. The following section explores the main features of these actors' development assistance, and other involvement in Africa, focussing on Brazil and China.

## Brazil's Development Cooperation in Africa: An Expanding Program

Brazil's development cooperation has increased substantially over the last decade, in particular in the last half. Total whole-of-government development cooperation doubled between 2005 and 2009 (Zimmerman and Smith, 2011), and Technical, Scientific and Technological Cooperation tripled during this period (Institute of Applied Economic Research [IPEA]/The Brazilian Cooperation Agency [ABC], 2011). As well as in its traditional geographic focus in Latin America and the Caribbean, there has been substantial growth in Brazil's development cooperation with Africa over the last decade. This has occurred, in particular, in Lusophone countries, but also in other countries such as Ghana. About 55 percent of disbursements by ABC are now made for programs in Africa (Ramero, 2012).[2]

Brazil's development cooperation approach in Africa reflects many of the characteristics of SSC. Its cooperation is "motivated by a feeling of solidarity with its Africa partners" and is part of its "moral obligation" towards Africa (Stolte, 2012: 11-12; IPEA/ABC, 2011) In particular, Brazil's support for cooperation programs has little to do with traditional Northern models, but instead draws on Brazil's own experience in successfully overcoming development challenges, much of it over the last decade. Thus, its support for poverty reduction, food security and anti-hunger projects in Africa all draw on Brazil's own poverty reduction and anti-hunger experience, including its transition from a net food importer in the 1970s to becoming the third-largest global food exporter, and its success in lifting 30 million people out of poverty in less than a decade (Stolte, 2012).

## Brazil's Other Interests[3]

At the same time, however, solidarity with Africa and the principles of SSC are by no means the only drivers of Brazil's engagement in Africa. Economic and foreign policy motives are clearly strong factors, and Brazil's development cooperation is intricately bound up with these broader motives. Brazil has significantly increased its economic engagement with Africa over the last decade. Like other emerging economies, this has occurred primarily in the natural resource and construction sector. While Brazil-Africa trade has increased overall, trade with resource-rich African countries has increased in particular. Oil continues to dominate Brazil's imports from Africa, making up 85 percent of the total in 2011 (Stolte, 2012).

As a result, Brazil's trade (and associated development cooperation) interest in Africa has been characterized as predominantly associated with its need for oil to meet the energy needs of its growing economy. However, as major oil discoveries in 2007-2008 begin to show results and Brazil transitions from dependency on foreign oil imports, its longer-term commercial interests in Africa's growing economies are more likely to be in their potential consumer markets for Brazilian goods and services. Brazil's development cooperation engagements are also likely to be connected to these interests. However, its engagement in Africa goes beyond a one-dimensional motivation based on securing economic and commercial objectives. Instead, it is part of a broader strategy of positioning itself on the global — as well as African — political and economic arena. Its international cooperation program with Africa is one vital part of this, which operates to serve both its economic and foreign policy objectives, as well as genuine development and "solidarity" objectives (Stolte, 2012).

## China's Development Cooperation

China has a long history in international cooperation and in the provision of aid. There is no definitive information on the volume of Chinese aid.[4] Nevertheless, China's foreign aid has likely increased substantially in recent years: according to its foreign aid policy, China's budgeted foreign aid increased by nearly 30 percent a year between 2004 and 2009 (The People's Republic of China, 2011; Provost; 2011).

Historically, the bulk of Chinese aid has been directed to Asian countries, particularly North Korea and Vietnam. At the same time, Africa has always been a key recipient, and cooperation has increased substantially over the last decade. Deborah Bräutigam estimates that China's aid to Africa in 2008 was US$1.4 billion, "making China one of Africa's main bilateral donors, but by no means the largest" (Bräutigam, 2010: 27). According to China's 2011 foreign aid policy, 45.7 percent of China's foreign aid went to Africa in 2009 (The People's Republic of China, 2011).

While the vast majority of China's foreign aid is negotiated on a bilateral, country-to-country basis, the overall parameters for its increasing cooperation within Africa — on aid and in other areas — is driven by a series of ministerial conferences under the Forum on Africa-China Cooperation (FOCAC) that began in 2004. This provides China's and African governments with a high-level platform to establish cooperation relationships and agreements, and also provides a measure of public profile for their joint activities. As well as setting out a wide range of principles for cooperation, at the 5th Ministerial Conference in 2012, China announced it would provide US$20 billion in new loans to Africa over the next three years — thus doubling the commitment made at the previous conference. This is intended to mainly support the development of infrastructure, agriculture, manufacturing and development of small- and medium-sized enterprises (FOCAC, 2012, Huang, 2012).

## Chinese Aid and SSC

Like Brazil, China's engagement in Africa has strong and long-standing foundations in the principles of SSC. Its "Eight Principles for China's Aid to Foreign Countries" — which dates back to 1964 — highlights equality and mutual benefit, respect for sovereignty, recipient self-reliance and independent economic development, and provision of quality technical expertise (Bräutigam, 2010: 29). Drawing strongly on these principles, China's 2006 Africa policy refers to a "new type of strategic partnership with Africa," which will be based on "political equality and mutual trust, economic win-win cooperation and cultural exchange" (The People's Republic of China, 2006). The policy states that it will gradually increase assistance to African nations "with no political strings attached" and also cites principles for the provision of aid that include "sincerity, friendship and equality... mutual benefit, reciprocity and common prosperity...mutual support and close coordination" (ibid.). China's 2011 foreign aid policy perhaps states the case most clearly: "as development remains an arduous and long-standing task, China's foreign aid falls into the category of south-south cooperation and is mutual help between developing countries" (The People's Republic of China, 2011).

## China's Other Interests

Like Brazil, China's engagement is also strongly driven by economic and foreign policy motives. Much has been made of this, with suggestions that China is motivated solely by money, access to raw materials and international politics (Naím, 2007), and that its drive for resources, mixed as it is with the provision of aid, represents a new type of colonialism (Sharife, 2009). Others refute these assertions, arguing that China is no more motivated by political and economic motivations than other providers of development assistance, the DAC donors included (Bräutigam, 2010; Dreher and Fuchs, 2011).[5]

These debates are ongoing. What is not in dispute is the increasing scale and reach of China's economic, commercial and strategic, as well as development cooperation engagement in Africa. Between 2005 and 2010, about 14 percent of China's outward investment occurred in Sub-Saharan Africa (*The Economist,* 2011). Trade between China and Africa increased exponentially during the first decade of the 2000s: China's exports to Sub-Saharan Africa increased from $6.89 billion in 2003 to $53.32 billion in 2011, and its imports increased from $6.43 billion to $59.94 billion over the same period (Burges, 2012). While China made up less than five percent of Africa's trade at the start of the 2000s, it had tripled by the end of the decade to almost 16 percent, and in 2009, China's share of African trade went past that of the United States (Reisen and Stijns, 2011). To feed its oil imports, China has invested in refinery projects throughout Africa and has also invested heavily in a wide range of infrastructure projects, many of them "prestige" projects such as stadiums, conference halls and government buildings that have high public visibility (Bräutigam, 2010).

## PART TWO

## Responding to the NTPs: Implications for Canada

NTPs and the SSDC approaches they follow offer African governments a greater range of choices: not only in terms of *who* they receive aid from, but equally important, in terms of *how* they receive aid. Governments will most likely welcome this expansion of choice. There is also good reason to expect they will prefer particular aspects of SSDC over traditional N-S cooperation. These include the horizontal, mutually beneficial, more equal partnerships that SSDC offers; its promise of non-interference; and some of its practical aspects related to aid delivery and management.

Overall, however, it may be that African governments will not only prefer and welcome these aspects of aid provision, but that they will increasingly be in a position to start to demand them. As the Overseas Development Institute (ODI) points out, "The growth in the variety of providers of development assistance, particularly the non-traditional, is helping strengthen the negotiating power of governments" (Greenhill, Prizzon and Rogerson, 2013: ix). Recipient countries that can choose between a greater range of providers — particularly countries that can take advantage of increasing growth opportunities and that have a stronger political and economic base — will be in a much better position to more strongly set the terms and conditions for their receipt of aid. This includes doing so with established, traditional donor countries (ibid.).

All of these factors — African governments' choice from a greater range of providers, their increased negotiating power, and their increased ability to set the terms for the receipt of aid — throw out a clear challenge for traditional providers, including for Canada. Canada needs to work out how to respond in this new context. This involves assessing what the new SSDC principles and approaches mean for its own provision of aid, for its relationships with African countries and for how it delivers aid to them. In particular, Canada must determine to what extent it is prepared to change the ways it currently provides aid.

Identifying the areas in which Canada may need to change its aid provision is a long-term proposition and is somewhat speculative. There are, however, at least three possible areas where Canada can respond to the challenge set by the NTPs.

## Reforming the Mechanics of Aid Delivery

African governments may increasingly want traditional donors, such as Canada, to provide aid that includes some of the practical advantages of aid delivered through SSDC approaches. Key among these is greater predictability and greater speed in the delivery of funds and projects: two aspects which are central to increasing the efficiency of donor-side delivery of aid, and to decreasing recipient-side transaction costs involved in its receipt and management.

The need for improvements in these aspects of aid delivery and management comes as no surprise. Improving the predictability of aid has been a persistent theme throughout the last decade of official OECD DAC-led efforts to improve aid effectiveness. While the speed of aid delivery has not featured in these processes, it has nevertheless been part of the consideration for improving aid effectiveness. ODI's study of the implications of NTPs found that speed was a key priority for recipient governments — and that non-DAC donors scored well in this area (Greenhill, Prizzon and Rogerson, 2013).

For Canada, improving the speed and predictability of its aid delivery should be among the easier changes it can make to match NTPs' performance and SSDC approaches. Speed and predictability are procedural issues to do with the "mechanics" of aid delivery that require reform of the Canadian

International Development Agency's (CIDA's) and other government departments' business practices and administrative processes. Previous experience suggests, however, that improvement will be more difficult than one might expect. Canada has struggled for years to increase the predictability of its aid: the 2012 OECD-led peer review identified this as a particular weakness of Canada's aid, and an area that has compromised alignment with countries' planning and budgeting systems (OECD DAC, 2012). Improving the speed of project approval and implementation is an even greater problem. In 2009, a project required on average 43 months to get project approval (Office of the Auditor General of Canada, 2009). While there appears to have been some improvement (OECD DAC, 2012), Canada is still likely to perform slower than the NTPs in this area.

## Reforming the Aid Relationship

The second area that Canada will need to rethink in order to adjust to the increasing role and influence of the NTPs is potentially more difficult than making changes in the speed and predictability of aid delivery. This concerns the type of aid relationship it engages in with African governments, and in particular the terms and conditions it attaches to its provision of aid. The challenge here is that by following SSDC principles, NTPs engage in aid relationships with partner governments that are differentiated from traditional donor-recipient aid relationships in a number of key respects, including that that they are "horizontal" and more equal, and that they follow the principle of non-interference.

For Canada, and other traditional donors, engaging in a more equal relationship suggests they need to be more prepared to "let go" once they provide aid to partner governments. It involves moving away from the types of principal-agent, or donor-recipient notions that have persisted within the development cooperation system. In particular, it means a greater willingness to provide aid with fewer conditionalities, and to allow partner countries to more fully control the use of aid that is provided to them.

There are two issues that are central to allowing partner countries greater control over the aid they receive, both of which have also been important aspects of official aid effectiveness processes: strengthening the alignment of aid with partner country priorities, and (as a result), supporting greater country ownership over aid.

The 2013 ODI study demonstrates the importance of ownership and alignment to partner countries, and that they may prefer NTPs because of the different approaches they take on these issues. NTPs were popular with governments because of their non-interference in government policy and limited conditionality, with Ethiopia placing a particularly strong emphasis on the importance of ownership (Greenhill, Prizzon and Rogerson, 2013). Sectoral alignment was emphasized as a key priority by governments, and NTPs were "better aligned with government priorities because of their focus on infrastructure, energy and growth-promoting sectors" (ibid.: 27).

Canada, however, is already struggling to address alignment and ownership. As Brown (2012) notes, Canada has performed poorly on alignment: the monitoring report on the Paris Declaration found that Canada's alignment with national priorities in 32 countries declined between 2005 and 2010. Since alignment is one of the main ways donors can support country ownership of aid, Canada's poor performance on alignment also compromises its support for country ownership.

A key way that Canada could more effectively support ownership is through the provision of general budgetary support (GBS). GBS gives partner governments greater direct control of aid and allows governments to use it across the general range of budget programs and expenditure — rather than its use being conditioned on the donor's sectoral or political priorities. Country-level experience, however, suggests GBS is highly problematic for Canada. A whole range of obstacles means it is generally underused as a tool for supporting ownership, even when circumstances support it. This is starkly illustrated in Tanzania, one of CIDA's focus countries (den Heyer, 2012). CIDA staff who wanted to use GBS as a funding mechanism encountered a range of administrative and corporate management roadblocks: restrictions under the Federal Accountability Act, terms and conditions set by the Treasury Board and decision-making delays within CIDA resulting from senior management personnel changes (ibid.).

## Owning Up to Mutual Benefit and Self-interest

The third — and most difficult — area where Canada may need to change its approach in order to respond to the greater role of NTPs also relates to the provider-recipient aid relationship and concerns the issue of mutual benefit. Mutual benefit is key to SSDC principles, including their foundation in a more equal aid relationship, and the premise that both the provider and recipient of aid will, either directly or indirectly, gain something out of the transaction. This implies an acceptance that the provider has more than a purely altruistic motive for the provision of aid, and that there is at least some measure of self-interest involved. As we have seen, China and Brazil's development cooperation is clearly premised on mutual benefit and on a broader "package" of engagement in Africa, based around economic and strategic interests as well as the provision of aid. Hence, China's open acknowledgement that its engagement in Africa will be based on "economic win-win cooperation" (The People's Republic of China, 2006).

OECD donors have traditionally premised their development cooperation programs on the objective of poverty reduction. They have maintained this as the primary motivation for their aid programs in their public rhetoric, and, in some cases (as Canada has done), through enshrining the objective in law. However, it is widely accepted that OECD donor aid programs have always also been motivated by an element of self-interest, and that they are based on political, commercial and strategic as well as poverty reduction objectives. But donors have been reticent about admitting to these mixed motives, partly as a result of public pressure to delink the provision of aid from non-poverty reduction objectives.

Nevertheless, self-interest has been a growing part of the Canadian aid program over the last 10 years. CIDA has admitted that self-interest is a motivation for its provision of aid and for choosing priority recipient countries (Brown, 2012). In 2012, in one of his first speeches as the new minister for international cooperation, Julian Fantino indicated that Canada's aid will more directly promote its economic interests overseas (Mackrael, 2012). This was presented in terms of the government's move towards a greater emphasis on the private sector and development, including promoting a greater role for the Canadian private sector (Fantino, 2012).

A key focus for this new emphasis, unsurprisingly, is the mining and natural resources extractives sector in Africa. Fantino's announcement follows CIDA funding approval in 2011 for partnerships between three mining companies and Canadian non-governmental organizations (NGOs), including in Ghana and Burkina Faso. His speech makes CIDA's emphasis on self-interest and the mining sector more explicit, stating that partnering between CIDA and the Canadian mining and extractives sector represents "a huge opportunity for both Canada and developing countries" (Fantino, 2012).

An increasing focus on self-interest and economic objectives in the aid program reflects Canada's increasing preoccupation with Africa as a destination for broader economic interests, in particular in terms of trade and investment. In this respect, Canada is following the lead of not only the NTPs, but of other developed countries, all of which are getting on board Africa's potential for growth and development. There are strong signs that Canada's engagement in poor African developing countries will increasingly include an emphasis on trade and investment, and that they will be pursued with African governments concurrently with the development cooperation aspects of engagement.

This was evident, for example, in 2012, when Prime Minister Stephen Harper launched a new package of cooperation with Tanzania. The announcement included funding for two new Maternal, Newborn and Child Health projects funded through the aid program (Harper, 2012). At the same time, however — and with an eye closely on Canada's economic interests — Harper also announced the signing of a new Foreign Investment Promotion and Protection Agreement (FIPPA), noting that Tanzania is an "economic growth leader in Sub-Saharan Africa" and that two-way trade between Canada and Tanzania increased more than 40 percent between 2007 and 2012 (ibid.). The FIPPA would, amongst other things "increase investor confidence and make it easier for Canadian companies to do business in Tanzania" (ibid.). Referring to the particularly strong potential for resource development in Tanzania, Harper also announced that Canada had agreed on measures to support its management of these resources (Harper, 2012).

These moves demonstrate how Canada's aid program objectives exist alongside a broader set of objectives for engagement in Africa. In this respect, Canada reflects some aspects of the NTPs own approach to engagement in Africa: a greater acknowledgement of multiple objectives for engagement (including that development cooperation occurs alongside trade and investment objectives); an underlying element of self-interest; and an expectation of mutual, rather than one-sided, benefit from aid and other arrangements.

While Canada's mirroring of the NTPs' approach to mutual benefit is almost certainly unintentional, it could, in itself, be a good thing. Rather than obfuscating the provision of aid behind the veneer of altruism, part of a more transparent and mature aid relationship may involve traditional donors now more clearly declaring their self-interest, more openly stating that they have multiple objectives for providing aid and that they, too, expect mutual benefit from their provision of aid.

The risk here, however, is between more open acknowledgement that aid is part of a package of broader motives, and the increased use and expenditure of aid to serve those objectives. Canada's ODA Accountability Act rightly determines that aid must be used only for poverty reduction objectives. It is inevitable that Canada — as it is doing now in countries such as Tanzania, and as donors have always done — will bring to its engagement in Africa other objectives alongside those encapsulated within its aid programs. If, however, Canada starts to divert aid to pay for the promotion of these other objectives, then the aid program will slide incontrovertibly off track — and will also have violated the ODA Accountability Act. While Minister Fantino (2012) asserts that "CIDA does not subsidize Canadian companies," the very close association of the aid program with Canadian private sector interests — as well as its move towards funding NGOs to work with mining companies — could be seen as moving precariously close to the edge of a slippery slope, one which leads towards the diversion of aid funds towards other objectives that have more to do with self-interest than with poverty reduction.

## CONCLUSION

Canada has its work cut out for itself to respond to the greater role and influence of the NTPs in the global aid architecture and in Africa, and to the challenges these providers pose through their engagement in development cooperation that is differentiated from traditional N-S cooperation. To determine a way forward, Canada must first answer a range of related and fundamental questions. Overall, what is its aid program trying to achieve? How does it balance poverty reduction objectives with self-interest? How does it balance multiple motives in its engagement with developing countries? And in Africa, in the next decade or so, how will it balance development cooperation with trade and investment priorities? In relation to the NTPs in Africa, the more specific question is: will Canada find itself competing for the attention of partner governments, who may prefer the more predictable, faster aid that NTPs supply within a more equal relationship and with less-conditioned terms? From the vantage point of stronger negotiating positions, African governments may make stronger demands on Canada to follow the lead of the NTPs in these areas.

These are questions that now face all of traditional donors. So far, however, there is no public evidence that Canada is taking steps to answer them, or that it has even thought about what the NTPs mean for its own engagement in Africa. This failure to address fundamental questions is symptomatic of a larger problem: the broader policy and analytical malaise that affects the Canadian aid program as a whole. As the OECD has pointed out, Canada's program lacks an overarching framework for its development cooperation (OECD DAC, 2012). It also lacks any strategic framework for its engagement in Africa. Unless Canada can articulate an overall vision and set of principles for the Canadian aid program and a coherent strategy for Africa, its engagement in African countries, including its responses to the NTPs, are likely continue to be ad hoc and directionless. If China can set out both a foreign aid policy and an Africa policy, Canada can as well.

## ENDNOTES

[1] There is no consensus on how to classify or name this group of countries. Countries such as China and Brazil reject the term "donor," and point out that they have been providing development assistance for decades. The use of NTP has been selected here, and is drawn from the terminology used by Greenhill, Prizzon and Rogerson, 2013.

[2] The above section drawn from Zimmerman and Smith, 2011; IPEA/ABC, 2011; and Ramero, 2012.

[3] This section draws strongly on Stolte, 2012.

[4] China does not subscribe to official OECD Development Assistance Committee (DAC) definitions of what constitutes official development assistance (ODA). Some commentators suggest that China considers its foreign aid spending a state secret. See, for example, J. Weston, Caitlin Campbell and Katherine Koleski (2011), "China's Foreign Assistance in Review: Implications for the United States," US-China Economic and Security Review Commission Backgrounder,

available at: www.uscc.gov/researchpapers/2011/9_1_%202011_
ChinasForeignAssistanceinReview.pdf.

[5] See also the chapter by Stephen Brown.


# WORKS CITED

Bräutigam, Deborah (2010). "China, Africa and the International Aid Architecture." Africa Development Bank Group Working Paper Series No. 107. Available at: www.afdb.org/fileadmin/uploads/afdb/Documents/ Publications/WORKING%20107%20%20PDF%20E33.pdf.

Brown, S. (2012). "Canadian Aid Enters the Twenty-First Century." In *Struggling for Effectiveness: CIDA and Canadian Foreign Aid,* edited by S. Brown. Montreal: McGill-Queens University Press.

Burges, S. (2012). "Developing from the South: South-South Cooperation in the Global Development Game." *Austral: Brazilian Journal of Strategy & International Relations* 1, no. 2: 225–249.

Den Heyer, M. (2012). "Untangling Canadian Aid Policy." In *Struggling for Effectiveness: CIDA and Canadian Foreign Aid*, edited by S. Brown. Montreal: McGill-Queens University Press.

Dreher, Axel and Andreas Fuchs (2011). "Rogue Aid? The Determinants of China's Aid Allocation." Courant Research Centre PEG Discussion Paper No. 93. Available at: http://ncgg.princeton.edu/IPES/2011/papers/ F1120_rm3.pdf.

Fantino, Julian (2012). "Reducing Poverty — Building Tomorrow's Markets." Minister Fantino's keynote address to the Economic Club of Canada, November 23. Toronto, Ontario. Available at: www.acdi-cida.gc.ca/acdi-cida/ACDI-CIDA.nsf/eng/NAT-1123135713-Q8T.

FOCAC (2012). "The Fifth Ministerial Conference on the Forum on China-Africa Cooperation Beijing Action Plan (2013-2015)." Available at: www.focac.org/eng/ltda/dwjbzjjhys/t954620.htm.

Government of the People's Republic of China (2006). "China's African Policy." Available at: www.fmprc.gov.cn/eng/zxxx/t230615.htm.

———— (2011). "China's Foreign Aid: Foreign Aid Policy." Available at: http://news.xinhuanet.com/english2010/china/2011-04/21/c_13839683. htm.

Greenhill, R., A. Prizzon and Andrew Rogerson (2013). "The Age of Choice: Developing Countries in the New Aid Landscape: A Synthesis Report." Overseas Development Institute Working Paper Issue 364. Available at: www.odi.org.uk/publications/7163-age-choice-developing-countries-new-aid-landscape.

Harper, Stephen (2012). "PM Announces Development Initiatives in Tanzania," news release, October 4. Available at: www.pm.gc.ca/eng/media.asp?category=1&featureId=6&pageId=26&id=5069.

Huang, Carol (2012). "China Doubles Loans to Africa to $20 billion", Agence France Presse, 19 July. Available at: www.google.com/hostednews/afp/article/ALeqM5i1zQLP3uv9eO_87y_JivBPXhmZ6w?docId=CNG.562 73701c9b896ee29f7bca5955dcb4a.171.

IPEA/ABC (2011). *Brazilian Cooperation for Development : 2005-2009.* Available at: http://api.ning.com/files/eJz*iuu91W9QU UwVGXxLlxghZj*0EdBVVvuL4zmY4LOGZgIsIgI*O1pfQz R75Am03DPdDY9TK2sWqP3SmCEv0HoNU0Pn3etN/Book_ brazilian_cooperationWEB.pdf.

Mackrael, Kim (2012). "CIDA, Private Sector Partnering Scheme Concerns Aid Workers." *The Globe and Mail,* November 24.

Morton, Bill (2010). "Bogota High Level Event on South Cooperation: Record of Meeting" (unpublished).

Naím, Moisès (2007). "Rogue Aid." *Foreign Policy* 159: 95-96.

OECD DAC (2012). "Canada: Development Assistance Committee (DAC) Peer Review 2012." OECD. Available at: www.oecd.org/dac/peerreviewsofdacmembers/canadapeerreview2012.pdf.

Office of the Auditor General of Canada (2009). *Report of the Auditor General of Canada to the House of Commons, Ottawa, Government of Canada.*

Provost, Claire (2011). "China Publishes First Report on Foreign Aid Policy." *The Guardian,* April 28. Available at: www.guardian.co.uk/global-development/2011/apr/28/china-foreign-aid-policy-report.

Ramero, Simon (2012). "Brazil Gains Business and Influence as it Offers Aid and Loans in Africa." *New York Times,* August 7. Available at: www.nytimes.com/2012/08/08/world/americas/brazil-gains-in-reaching-out-to-africa.html?_r=0.

Reisen, H. and Jean-Philippe Stijns (2011). "Emerging Partners Create Policy Space for Africa." *Vox,* July 12. Available at: www.voxeu.org/article/how-emerging-donors-are-creating-policy-space-africa.

Sharife, Khadija (2009). "China's New Colonialism." *Foreign Policy,* September 25. Available at: www.foreignpolicy.com/articles/2009/09/25/chinas_new_colonialism?page=0,1&wp_login_redirect=0.

Stolte, C. (2012). "Brazil in Africa: Just Another BRICS Country Seeking Resources?" Chatham House Briefing Paper. Available at: www.chathamhouse.org/publications/papers/view/186957.

*The Economist* (2011). "The Chinese in Africa: Trying to Pull Together." April 20. Available at: www.economist.com/node/18586448.

United Nations (2010). *World Economic and Social Survey 2010, Retooling Global Development.* Available at: www.un.org/en/development/desa/policy/wess/wess_archive/2010wess.pdf.

Zimmerman, Felix and Kimberley Smith (2011). "More Actors, More Money More Ideas for International Development Cooperation." *Journal of International Development* 23: 722–738.

# Canadian CSOs and Africa: The End of an Era?

Betty Plewes and Brian Tomlinson

• • • • • • • • • • • • • • • • • • •

The engagement of Canadian non-governmental organizations (NGOs) or civil society organizations (CSOs)[1] in African development began in a concerted way in the 1960s.[2] The roots of this citizen engagement lie in the decades of Canadian churches' overseas missionary work, the expansion of the mandate of refugee and relief organizations created to assist in the reconstruction of post-war Europe and the internationalization of a long tradition of voluntary action in Canada. The political space and optimism created by decolonization in many African countries and the United Nations' designation of the 1960s as the "Decade of Development" provided the impetus for many new organizations and initiatives to address poverty and "underdevelopment" in the "Third World."

This engagement evolved into many diverse and rich development encounters between Canadian CSOs and their African counterparts over the next 50 years. But today, many Canadian CSOs are at a crossroads. The relationships and assumptions that shaped the CSOs' involvement since the early 1960s have been badly shaken, and they face a series of challenges that they are responding to in different ways. This chapter explores some of the main factors driving the evolution of the Canadian CSO community and sets out five main trends for CSOs since 2000. The evolution and resolution of these trends will shape future directions for Canadian CSOs as they redefine their roles and relationships, and in some cases their very existence, in reaction to this dramatically different political context.

The 1960s represented the coming of age of the Canadian voluntary development community. Secular Canadian agencies, such as CUSO/SUCO[3] and Operation Crossroads Africa were established, and Canadian branches of foreign organizations, such as CARE and Foster Parents Plan (now Plan Canada), which had established affiliates in Canada as fundraising branches, became more independent. Some, such as Oxfam Canada and Save the Children Canada created organizational paths distinct from their parent bodies (Brodhead and Herbert-Copley, 1988: 18). In parallel, many of the mainstream churches adopted more liberal conceptions of mission, dramatically transforming partnerships with churches in Africa to work on issues of social justice and development (Brouwer, 2010).

In 1968, the Canadian government established the Canadian International Development Agency (CIDA) with a dedicated NGO division whose mandate was to promote citizen participation in development activities. Canada became one of the first donor countries to support civil society partnerships and pioneered policies and approaches that were copied by other donors, some many decades later. Another innovation within CIDA was the creation of the Public Participation Program to support citizens' groups in public education and advocacy in Canada. With financial support from CIDA and its members, the Canadian Council for International Cooperation (CCIC) was also created in 1968 to facilitate inter-agency cooperation.

Canada's international CSO community is composed of about 800 mainly small- and medium-sized organizations, along with a few larger ones. Of the 270 Canadian CSOs funded by CIDA in 2010, two-thirds (180 CSOs) had programs in Africa.[4] The larger NGOs, such as CARE, World Vision and Oxfam are increasingly integrated within their family of international NGOs (INGOs).

Since the early 1960s, Canadian organizations have evolved from a service-oriented focus to take on more diverse roles and activities supporting African development. They have provided hundreds of millions of dollars of financial support — from small grants to local women's organizations, to multi-year, multi-million-dollar democracy-promotion, agriculture and health initiatives — and developed a wide variety of partnerships. Key individuals at Canadian CSOs have carried out pioneering work to influence governments and corporations through "track two" diplomacy in Ethiopia and Somalia, creating multilateral policies for the preservation of traditional seeds and in the control of blood diamonds. They have contributed to international efforts, such as the International Campaign to Ban Landmines, the Jubilee Debt Campaign to cancel unpayable debts and the coming into force of the UN Small Arms Treaty. Canadian organizations' responses to the 1980s famine in Ethiopia and following the war in Biafra in the late 1960s are perhaps the best-known examples of Canadian CSOs' humanitarian work in Africa. This is a role which has increasingly defined the public image of a number of large CSOs today. For several decades, however, Canadian grassroots organizations, churches and traditional CSOs were involved in Canadian education action campaigns, policy advocacy and played a significant role in material support in solidarity with the liberation struggles in Southern/South Africa (Hope, 2011). Such humanitarian work has increasingly defined the public image of a number of large CSOs today.

Canadians who volunteer overseas make not only direct contributions to African development, but also stimulate greater attention to Africa on their return to Canada. Of the approximately 65,000 Canadian volunteers who worked overseas between 1960 and 2005, between 40 and 50 percent went to Africa (CIDA, 2005: 18). The experience profoundly affected many of them, leading them to a new political awareness of the causes of global poverty and inequality. Some returned with a desire to find ways to address these issues in Canada through the creation of new organizations, development education programs and solidarity campaigns (Brodhead and Herbert-Copley, 1988: 4). Some former volunteers went to work for CIDA, where they had a strong influence over growing agency partnerships with Canadian CSOs.

Because there are few other institutional sources of funding for Canadian CSOs, government funding for those working internationally has been crucial to the development of a robust and innovative community. This development was due, in no small measure, to the relative flexibility and responsiveness of this funding in the 1960s, 1970s and 1980s. It is important to recognize, however, that these resources have always been matched by substantial amounts raised mainly from the Canadian public. In 2007, the CCIC estimated that Canadians were contributing more than CDN$750 million to these efforts. In 2010, another estimate, based on figures from Revenue Canada, put these contributions at about CDN$1.5 billion.[5] The INGOs have always raised significant Canadian private resources for development and humanitarian assistance in emergencies, as well as CIDA funding.[6] These agencies rely heavily on fundraising in two main areas: humanitarian assistance and child sponsorship. Consistently, over 50 percent of privately fundraised dollars in Canada for international cooperation go to child sponsorship organizations. This has made these organizations less dependent on CIDA than the smaller and medium-sized organizations that do not use the same fundraising strategies.

The Canadian government's political interest in Africa waxed and waned over the three decades from 1980 to 2010. While the 1984 Ethiopian crisis precipitated a high level of government leadership and involvement, the 1990s became a "lost decade" for Canada's relationships with Sub-Saharan Africa, with declining aid contributions in these years symbolizing the trend.

Despite these changing and challenging dynamics with the Canadian government, Canadian CSOs sought to maintain and strengthen long-standing partnerships for local development efforts across the African continent. The deep cuts in the 1995 federal budget, however, dramatically affected their capacities to sustain partnerships at previous levels and to engage with the Canadian public and political system. This led to a collective questioning on the part of CSOs involved in Africa about the most effective ways to work with African counterparts, the impact of their development programming in Africa and the decline in official Canadian policy interest in Africa. These questions led to the creation of the CCIC's Working Group, the Africa-Canada Forum, to explore alternatives and promote renewed policy focus on development issues in Africa at the end of the 1990s (CCIC, 2006).

The 2000s opened with renewed attention by both the Canadian government and civil society to African development. Not only did aid to the region increase dramatically, the 2002 Group of Eight (G8) Kananaskis Summit launched the G8 Africa Action Plan. The plan focussed on improving peace and security, access to medicine for those affected by HIV/AIDS and working with the African Union to improve governance. These initiatives were extended in the 2005 Gleneagles summit, which focussed on Africa and a commitment to double aid for the continent. Canadian CSOs were strongly present and influenced the agenda of Kananaskis (ibis.), and millions petitioned Group of Seven leaders through the 2005 global civil society campaign to "make poverty history." Canada's 2010 G8 profiled the Muskoka Initiative, promising

CDN$1.1 billion in new resources over five years to improve maternal and child health, much of which would be directed to Africa. During this decade, the value of annual CIDA disbursements to Africa through Canadian CSOs grew by more than 75 percent, from CDN$129 million in 2000 to CDN$229 million in 2010.[7]

The 2000s ended, however, with a Conservative government whose growing foreign policy emphasis is on Canadian extractive resource industries in Africa, and infrastructural development related to energy, power generation and mining. The Harper government also has a different vision of civil society and sees a very limited role for CSOs in policy dialogue and advocacy (Siddiqui, 2012). As a result, these new policy emphases have been accompanied by an almost complete marginalization of Canadian CSOs, in both government aid programs and in policy engagement. Fundamental changes to CIDA's long-standing funding arrangements for CSOs (now almost exclusively a call-for-proposal mechanism) will have deep and lasting impacts on the scale, capacities and nature of Canadian CSOs' collaboration with their long-term counterparts in Africa (CCIC, 2012).[8] These funding mechanisms favour large organizations that are capable of putting together multiple proposals in response to different CIDA calls and criteria.

Rather than seeing CSOs as independent development actors, the Harper government has moved to a much more instrumental approach towards CSOs, using selected organizations to implement government-determined priorities. Several CSOs who critiqued CIDA policy have had their funding cut or eliminated.[9] On the other hand, a number of other government-selected CSOs, such as CARE Canada, Plan Canada and World Vision, have been funded to form strategic partnerships with mining companies or in maternal and child health.[10]

CSOs in Canada have responded in a variety of ways. Some, mainly the larger organizations, are willing to play a more instrumental role in program delivery, while others, particularly those that are smaller or more oriented towards advocacy and solidarity, have been increasingly alienated from the government. Both approaches are generating a lot of debate within the CSO and broader community.

## KEY TRENDS AND CHALLENGES FOR FUTURE CSO ROLES IN AFRICA

Government relations and policies have a critical impact on CSO work. But in the past decade, there has also been an increasing critical reflection on their roles in Africa. How can they work and collaborate more effectively with African partners for development outcomes among poor and marginalized peoples? In this regard, CSOs have not shied away from self-criticism and change. They have acknowledged the need to significantly improve their transparency and means for accountability to key stakeholders, the need to improve coordination and to address their limited record in promoting gender equality and women's rights in their work, among other areas of concern.

In the past three years, these concerns and reflections have come together in a self-reflective global CSO-led process to examine their roles and effectiveness as actors in development.[11] Canadian CSOs have taken up this agenda for improving their practices, both as individual organizations and through their participation in the ongoing work of the CCIC and several parallel provincial councils. How these trends are resolved will affect future development roles for Canadian CSOs.

## The Evolution of INGOs and the Challenge of Local Ownership

The increasingly dominant role played by the large INGOs, both in Canada and globally, has already been noted. With the growth of highly sophisticated South-led CSOs throughout the developing world, there are increasing tensions between international CSOs and INGOs. The international organizations may command large resources, but they are often reluctant to permit greater local control over setting priorities for the deployment of these resources.

Some INGOs, such as Oxfam and Save the Children, have a longer experience with African CSO partnerships. Nevertheless, they share the concern that they may be crowding out local organizations as they compete for donor resources and take advantage of their "brand recognition." Some of the largest INGOs, such as World Vision, have "localized" their presence in many African countries, with local boards and staff overseeing their programs and priorities. Canadian development organizations are well aware of both the growing challenges and also respect the essential importance of structuring equitable local partnerships in their future relationships with African counterparts. But what conditions need to change within Canadian CSOs, and with respect to funding partners, to make more equitable structuring a reality?

## Withering Canadian CSO Policy Engagement in Africa and in Canada

In the last 20 years, Canadian CSOs have played an important role in promoting policy options in many areas: supporting gender equality, legitimizing the concept of citizens' diplomacy, developing principles of constructive roles in conflict resolution and reconstruction, and advocating for aid policies that focus on poverty reduction. Today, however, there is considerably reduced space and capacity for CSO policy engagement. In addition to budget reductions, there is a chill on policy and advocacy activities within the CSO community. It is clear from public statements that CIDA's recent ministers looks unfavourably on organizations that do policy and advocacy work, especially in areas that are controversial for the current government or when advocacy efforts are critical of current policies.[12]

In a globalized world, Canadian CSOs involved in international development have an obligation to directly engage Canadians on Canadian foreign policy issues. What conditions are required for CSOs to create new ways that connect Canadians with compounding crises in global food production, the impacts of climate change, and widening global inequalities and marginalization of billions of poor people in developing countries?

## Declining Engagement by Canadians with International CSOs in Their Communities

Canadian CSOs have played crucial roles in strengthening global awareness and a sense of global citizenship among Canadians. But over the past 15 years, funding cuts have closed many Canadian CSOs' regional offices. Canadian members of INGOs have focussed on highly sophisticated fundraising campaigns for global INGO programs and centralized campaigning models for public engagement.

Canadian churches have played a crucial and invaluable role in bringing to the attention of Canadians issues such as the debt crisis, food security, the impact of HIV/AIDS and the right to health, and corporate responsibility in the context of African conflicts. These organizations have also suffered serious setbacks, not only because of government budget cuts to organizations like KAIROS and Development and Peace, but also a changing demographic and diminishing church membership.

With a declining presence across the country and limited membership involvement beyond funding, many CSOs have a diminished ability to mobilize and sustain large numbers of people in support of policy changes. Recreating the energy and depth of engagement of Canadians found from earlier anti-apartheid or Jubilee campaigns on issues of importance to Africa, such as climate change or human rights, is difficult to sustain (Hope, 2011).

All of this notwithstanding, African civil society organizations are looking to Canadian counterparts to put greater attention and resources into addressing Canadian and global policies affecting African development options. The transfer of charitable financial resources is no longer a sufficient response. In the current Canadian political climate, CSOs need to find new ways to work more closely together, involving African counterparts, in the education and organization of Canadians in their communities to understand the implications of current Canadian policies.

## Creating Greater Impact through Partnership and Collaboration

Because of the small size of many Canadian CSOs and their relatively limited resources, there has always been a tendency for them to rely on the growing African-led CSO community to implement projects, more than other CSOs in the North. Canadian CSOs have also found ways to work together. For example, Partnership Africa Canada supported the strengthening of African civil society organizations; Solidarité Canada Sahel focussed on issues of desertification; and Cocomo brought together organizations working in Mozambique, but is now managed by a Mozambican board of directors. This kind of collaboration is perhaps what needs to happen more in the years ahead: large numbers of CSOs all working independently is simply unsustainable in the current funding climate. Long-term partnerships between African and Canadian CSOs are challenged by arbitrary cuts in their resources due to CIDA's episodic call-for-proposal mechanism (CCIC, 2012). How will Canadian CSOs, either acting alone or in concert with other

CSOs, effectively work with African counterparts around shared goals, with more limited resources?

## From Humanitarian Assistance to Reconstruction

Since the great African famine emergency of the 1980s, humanitarian action has figured prominently in the Canadian CSO response to African crises and conflicts. Humanitarian assistance and food aid made more than 20 percent of CIDA disbursements for CSOs working in Africa in 2010, a proportion that is likely considerably higher for some CSOs when their private fundraised money is included. These resources have been concentrated in fewer than 10 large Canadian CSOs and INGOs, which have become increasingly sophisticated in identifying their brand and international network with the capacity for effective and immediate humanitarian engagement.

This is important, but these organizations are well aware that longer-term commitments are required that bridge the gap between on-the-ground emergency response and building local capacities in conflict affected situations for sustained development, social protection and good governance, whether through local CSOs or local government. They have been developing programs that respond to these needs, but because of media exposure, it is often easier to raise public and government funds for the immediate emergency than for the longer-term reconstruction and peace building.

## CONCLUSIONS

The engagement between African and Canadian CSOs has evolved substantially over the last five decades. They created early models of partnership and developed important campaigns that have influenced Canadian and international policies. They have worked with the Canadian public and government on human rights, small arms, and trade and investment issues, which are essential for making progress on poverty and inequality in Africa.

But the context for civil society in both Africa and Canada, as noted in other chapters in this volume, is changing. Canadian government interest in Africa has become primarily focussed on Canadian trade and less on the promotion of human rights, poverty reduction and sustainable development.

In this context, focussed CSO partnerships with African counterparts are as relevant and as needed as at any time over the past 40 years.

The CSO relationship with the Canadian government, which was once collaborative, responsive and flexible, has been severely damaged under the Harper government. But the challenge for Canadian CSOs is broader than this. The ways that Canadian CSOs deal with other significant trends, such as the demands for greater CSO accountability and transparency, the internationalization of Canadian NGOs in INGO families, the effectiveness of CSO interventions in development change, and the change in their evolution as organizations (often influenced by government policies) will also affect their relevance to African civil society counterparts.

CSOs remain highly relevant to the development outcomes for poor and marginalized people in Africa. The challenge now is to create new and innovative opportunities for Canadians to engage with their government on development policy questions, involving the knowledge of African counterparts on critical issues such as extractive investment, food security and climate change, through building support for alternative policy proposals. In partnership with African civil society and governments, Canadian CSOs can, and must, continue to contribute to piloting — and, where appropriate, scaling-up — people-centred development alternatives. This work must be accomplished with fewer government resources and will require reorganizing to work more effectively in consortia, networks and partnerships in Canada and abroad.

As Tetteh Hormeku-Ajei of the Third World Network observed recently,[13] Canadian and African CSOs are at a crossroads. Many of the issues that CSOs have been working on for more than four decades are becoming more sharply drawn. The challenge is to identify how to redefine CSO roles and relationships in a highly dynamic political context. Perhaps it is time to implement his proposal for an *indaba*,[14] bringing Africans and Canadians together to discuss an African vision for civil society, drawing on the best experiences over these past four decades.

# ENDNOTES

[1]    While the term NGO is commonly used to describe not-for-profit organizations, this chapter uses the more inclusive term CSO. Churches

and trade unions, for example, do not consider themselves to be NGOs in that they are constituency-based organizations.

2    The historical account of the roles and highlights of Canadian CSOs in development is largely unwritten. The account in this chapter, and the issues subsequently identified, has been informed by existing documentation set out in the Works Cited, as well as 10 interviews with key informants with a long-standing experience with Canadian CSOs, conducted by one of the authors in December 2012, and the experience of the authors themselves, who have been engaged in various capacities with Canadian CSOs since the 1960s. Of particular importance for documenting the early history is Brodhead and Herbert-Copley, 1988.

3    The original organization was called CUSO/SUCO. It split in 1980 and created two separate organizations: one is now called CUSO International and the other SUCO.

4    Authors' calculations from CIDA's Historical Projects Dataset, available at: www.acdi-cida.gc.ca/acdi-cida/ACDI-CIDA.nsf/eng/CAR-1128144934-R9J.

5    Authors' calculations, based on a database created by Mark Blumberg, partner at Blumberg Segal LLP, Barristers and Solicitors.

6    In 2010, six INGO families (Save the Children, Oxfam, CARE, World Vision, Plan International and ActionAid) had a global combined revenue of US$8.3 billion, up 50 percent from 2005. In Canada, these same INGOs (excluding ActionAid, which does not work in Canada) had combined revenues of CDN$604.8 million (authors' calculations, based on a review of the organizations' most recent Canadian annual reports).

7    Authors' calculations, based on CIDA's Historical Project Dataset, available at: www.acdi-cida.gc.ca/acdi-cida/ACDI-CIDA.nsf/eng/CAR-1128144934-R9J .

8    As of January 2013, there has been no general call-for-proposals from CIDA's Partnerships with Canadians Branch for more than a year. The impact on small- and medium-sized organizations, their existence and the scale of their operations will have deepened considerably since the CCIC survey in early 2012.

9    Of particular note, KAIROS, the CCIC, the Mennonite Central Committee, Rights and Democracy and the Canadian Catholic Organization for Development and Peace have had their funding cut. For a detailed list

of Canadian civil society organizations affected by government policy-oriented cuts see Voices-Voix, available at: http://voices-voix.ca/en/facts/attacks-on-organizations. See also Plewes, 2010; Pearl Eliadis, Nikki Skuce and Fraser Reilly-King (forthcoming 2013), "Silencing Voices and Dissent in Canada," In *2012 State of Civil Society Report,* available at: www.civicus.org; and G. Caplan (2012), "The Harper Government, Women's Rights and the Cost of Speaking Out." *The Globe and Mail,* August 23, available at: http://m.theglobeandmail.com/news/politics/second-reading/the-harper-government-womens-rights-and-the-cost-of-speaking-out/article1314268/?service=mobile.

[10] The proposed merger of CIDA's mandate relating to development cooperation with the Ministry of Foreign Affairs and International Trade was announced after the completion of this chapter. The impacts for civil society and for Africa are unknown at this point, but are deeply concerning for sustaining a focus in Canadian foreign policy on poverty reduction, human rights and social justice in Africa. For more information and initial CSO reactions to the proposed merger, see AidWatch Canada and CCIC's "Budget 2013: Implications for Canadian ODA," available at: www.ccic.ca/_files/en/what_we_do/2013_03_27_Analysis_Budget_2013.pdf.

[11] The outcome of this process has been a CSO commitment to the Istanbul Principles for CSO Development Effectiveness. See the reports of the Open Forum consultations, the Istanbul Principles and the International Framework on the Open Forum's website, www.cso-effectiveness.org, and CSO Effectiveness Wiki, available at: http://wiki.cso-effectiveness.org/.

[12] In 2010, Canada's then-Minister for International Cooperation, Bev Oda, stated in the House of Commons that only "NGO organizations and partners that are actually feeding children who are starving" deserve support. Or, as John Baird put it, when talking about funding for women's groups, "We want less talk and more action" (quoted in Plewes, 2010). In December 2009, at a conference in Jerusalem, Canadian Minister of Citizenship, Immigration and Multiculturalism Jason Kenney (falsely) accused KAIROS of being an anti-Semitic organization and promoting an economic boycott of Israel, giving this as the reason for the cut to its funding. Subsequent documents released under an Access to Information request from CIDA indicated that the agency highly valued the quality

of KAIROS's work and had recommended the organization for further funding, which was refused by the Minister with the famous insertion of "not" into the approval document.

13   Remarks made during the Africa-Canada Forum round table discussion "Africa's Renaissance: A Critical Discussion," held October 31, 2012, at Carleton University. For details see: www.ccic.ca/_files/en/working_ groups/2012_10_ACF_HI_IAS_%20roundtable.pdf.

14   An *indaba* is a council at which indigenous peoples of Southern Africa meet to discuss important issues.

## WORKS CITED

Brodhead, T. and B. Herbert-Copley (1988). Bridges of Hope? Canadian Voluntary Agencies and the Third World, Ottawa: The North South Institute. Available at http://idl-bnc.idrc.ca/dspace/ bitstream/10625/9490/1/78025.pdf.

Brouwer, R. C. (2010). "When Missions Became Development: Ironies of 'NGOization' in Mainstream Churches in the 1960s." *The Canadian Historical Review* 91, no. 4: 661–693.

CCIC (2006). "Challenging Afro-Pessimism: The Africa Canada Forum Story." Available at: www.ccic.ca/_files/en/what_we_do/002_capacity_ bldg_stories_afc.pdf.

——— (2012). Putting Partnership Back at the Heart of Development: Canadian Civil Society Experience with CIDA's Call-for-Proposal Mechanism, Partnerships with Canadians Branch: An Analysis of Survey Results. February. Joint CCIC with the Inter-Council Network of Provincial/Regional Councils for International Cooperation. Available at: www.ccic.ca/_files/en/what_we_do/2012_03_Survey_Report_e.pdf.

CIDA (2005). The Power of Volunteering: A Review of the Canadian Volunteer Cooperation Program. Final Report, March. CIDA. Available at www. acdi-cida.gc.ca/inet/images.nsf/vLUImages/Performancereview6/$file/ VCP%20English%20Final.pdf.

Hope, K. (2011). "In Search of Solidarity: International Solidarity Work between Canada and South Africa 1975–2010." Ph.D. dissertation. University of Oxford, United Kingdom. Available at: www3.sympatico. ca/dindar/cahp/kofi/InSearchOfSolidarity.pdf.

Plewes, B. (2010). "Aiding Symptoms Not Causes." *The Mark,* June 16. Available at: www.themarknews.com/articles/1701-aiding-symptoms-not-causes/#.UT-urxl8vdB.

Siddiqui, H. (2012). "Prime Minister Harper Muzzles Diplomats and Foreign Agencies." *The Toronto Star,* April 7. Available at: www.thestar.com/ opinion/editorialopinion/2012/04/07/prime_minister_harper_muzzles_ diplomats_and_foreign_agencies.html.

# Canada and the
# African Development Bank

## Bruce Montador

• • • • • • • • • • • • • • • • • •

The African Development Bank (AfDB) is important for African countries, politically as well as financially. It is an institution where Canada played a significant role historically, and which could provide an avenue for greater Canadian engagement with the continent as its development accelerates.

## THE HISTORY OF THE AfDB

The AfDB was founded by 35 African countries in 1964 — just after the Inter-American Development Bank (IADB) and before the Asian Development Bank (ADB). These regional development banks (RDBs) support the growth of their members and regions through borrowing based on their pooled credit and lending at market rates. An early realization, however, that very poor countries needed concessional finance, such as interest-free loans and later actual grants, led the AfDB and developed countries (with Canada in a lead role) to create the African Development Fund (AfDF) in 1972 to provide such assistance, primarily through donor contributions.

After a modest start, a combination of poor management and imprudent lending to countries that could not manage the resulting debt put the AfDB in financial difficulty. In 1982, AfDF donors took 33 percent of the capital and joined the AfDB board of directors, where they had not previously been represented, with six of the 18 executive director (ED) positions.[1] In 1995, as problems continued, the donors' shareholding was increased to 40 percent. Canada took a disproportionately large share of the non-regional capital in 1982, and has maintained that position since, holding nearly four percent of the total capital, on a par with France and tied for fourth among non-regional shareholders.

In 1995, the problems were quite severe. Negotiations for an AfDF replenishment had not been completed and the AfDB was downgraded by Standard & Poor's. As a condition of their additional support, non-regional shareholders insisted on improving internal governance and lending policies. A new AfDB president, Omar Kabbaj of Morocco, was elected that year. A former banker, Kabbaj improved the Bank's finances, obtained the confidence of donors for two AfDF replenishments and saw the AfDB's AAA rating restored in 2003.

Since 2005, current AfDB President Donald Kaberuka, an economist and former Rwandan finance minister, has sought to make the AfDB a key player on the continent, an objective supported by donors. Kaberuka reorganized the AfDB to put countries in the "driver's seat" by paying more attention to their views — particularly those of AfDF recipients, whose wishes had often been ignored. He also promised greater focus in programming. A strong AfDF replenishment in 2007 showed solid donor support.

The AfDB, the only major RDB to have been downgraded, also had to move from Abidjan to Tunis in 2003 because of political unrest in Côte d'Ivoire. The AfDB faces another handicap: Africa has few middle-income countries to borrow on commercial terms. Such lending allows the AfDB to build up reserves and financial capacity from retained earnings.[2] The primary middle-income customers were, until recently, North African countries. Since the 2008 financial crisis, Southern African middle-income countries have also become more regular customers. The handicap from AfDB's small size is increased because it covers so many countries (now 54); transactions are smaller on average, so overhead costs are higher.

## WHAT DOES THE AfDB DO?

Kaberuka promised more focussed programming because of concern that the AfDB was copying the range of the World Bank, but without adequate resources. He appointed a high-level panel to assess the AfDB's future, co-chaired by former Canadian Prime Minister Paul Martin and former President Joaquim Chissano of Mozambique. Reflecting the panel's 2007 report, the AfDB's "Medium-Term Strategy" emphasized four key areas: infrastructure, private sector development, governance and higher education/science and technology. The AfDB concentrated on the first two. Infrastructure has always been central to its efforts, and its development importance is once again better recognized. For Africa, regionally integrating infrastructure is critical, particularly given the many landlocked countries.

Sustainable economic development also requires solid private sector growth. The AfDB's efforts to encourage analytic work and strengthen the business environment have seen limited progress. But a third pillar of the AfDB's work, catalytic financing of the private sector, saw spectacular growth early in Kaberuka's presidency. AfDB private-sector financing expanded rapidly because of Africa's better prospects and the limited demand for AfDB loans from middle-income African countries. (Private sector lending, like that to middle-income countries, uses borrowed funds and can earn profits that build up the Bank's capital.) These operations become catalytic when, for example, they attract other investors, because the AfDB's presence provides political "cover." Power generation through public-private partnerships can also be transformative, given chronic problems from electricity shortages.

## THE AFRICAN VIEW

Despite the important non-regional shareholding, the AfDB remains an "African" institution. The RMCs take pride in the AfDB's achievements and its AAA rating (which they want to protect), worry about excessive influence from non-regional member countries and staff, and think of the AfDB as an instrument of pan-African ambitions; indeed, the AfDB's Articles of Agreement make regional integration a prime objective. Success on this front has been limited, but the AfDB is addressing the issue more actively than in the past.[3]

A second, more recent illustration of these pan-African ambitions is the work that the AfDB undertook with the United Nations Economic Commission for Africa and the African Union (AU) Commission to ensure that African views were systematically taken into account as the G20 began to operate at the leaders' level to tackle the problems created (or made apparent by) the financial and economic crises that began in 2008.

A third example of the aspirations African countries have for the AfDB is in climate change programming. Outside Africa, most attention is on climate change mitigation, for which fairly clear choice metrics exist to choose among investments (amount of $CO_2$ equivalent avoided for a given amount invested). In Africa, such programming will necessarily be largely for adaptation, and it is far from obvious how one should allocate funds between, for example, drought-proofing seeds and flood-proofing roads. The AU thus asked potential donors (implicitly) that all climate change funding for Africa be administered — though not necessarily programmed — by the AfDB to avoid leaving such political decisions in the hands of either the World Bank or donors; however, this seems unlikely to happen.

## THE DONOR PERSPECTIVE AND THE MULTILATERAL DEVELOPMENT SYSTEM

While a country's shareholding in the AfDB determines its formal position at the AfDB, its "burden share" with the AfDF is, in practice, just as important. There is no link between shareholding and burden share: for example, the United Kingdom holds less than half of Canada's share of the AfDB's capital, but it is the AfDF's largest donor, providing more than double Canada's contribution. As a result, the United Kingdom has substantial informal influence despite a small shareholding and no permanent ED position.

Until the early 1990s, Canada, as a major non-regional shareholder, was also a major contributor to triennial AfDF replenishments, at times in second or third place. That position proved impossible to sustain, however, as replenishments, initially very small, grew faster than Canada's aid budget, and the Canadian International Development Agency (CIDA) could not sustain the same burden share. Canada now ranks a still respectable sixth among donors, with its burden share about five percent of the donors' total contributions.

Canada, like other donors, provides aid both bilaterally and multilaterally, with multilateral aid ensuring donor coordination and harmonization. Regional banks like the AfDB are usually looked at in conjunction with the World Bank. These multilateral development banks (MDBs) are important sources of official finance, both funds raised in capital markets, and from donor contributions for low-income countries and global public goods through vehicles like the AfDF and the International Development Association (IDA) at the World Bank. However, MDB financing is small, relative to foreign direct investment (FDI) or remittances from migrant workers or emigrants, and, even for non-resource-rich developing countries, typically relative to their own resources.

The MDBs provide knowledge as well as financial assistance. Over the years, the World Bank has been at the centre of debates about development, although its recommendations (and those of the International Monetary Fund [IMF]) have often been controversial. The local character of the RDBs makes them natural sources of regionally specific approaches to broader IMF and World Bank prescriptions, which can be important in making the institutions' advice palatable to developing countries. The AfDB, being relatively small as noted earlier, has not been able to grow its knowledge capacity as much as the other RDBs, and probably faces an even greater diversity of challenges. It needs to strengthen its skills in this area.

Canada has tended to "punch above its weight" at the RDBs, with permanent ED positions at each bank, as the United States and Japan have, but as leading European donors do not. Canadian support for the RDBs' activities is helped by the bureaucratic relationship. The primary and budgetary responsibility lies with Canada's Minister for International Cooperation, who heads CIDA, but the AfDB governor representing Canada is the Minister of Foreign Affairs and the alternate governor is a senior Finance Department official.[4] With each department having other links to Canada's foreign aid activity, this relatively unusual arrangement provides more interdepartmental support than might be expected.

Canada thus plays a somewhat greater role in AfDF replenishments than as a donor overall. The AfDF receives Canada's third-largest core contribution to a multilateral institution — currently CDN$108.5 million of the total of CDN$1,277.9 million of its core contributions for multilateral institutions for 2010-2011[5] — after the finance department's CDN$435.5 million contribution to the IDA and CIDA's CDN$150 million contribution to the Global Fund to Fight AIDS, Tuberculosis and Malaria, both heavily Africa-oriented. As a recent report from the Center for Global Development (CGD) indicates, however, the MDB concessional funds may create challenges for donors in the next 10 to 15 years. Many non-African (and some African) IDA beneficiaries should "graduate" from a need for concessional assistance, so the IDA will look much like the AfDF. The report suggests options that include differing sectoral concentrations in Africa (broadly consistent with the AfDB's present focus), with the IDA targeting the poor in middle-income countries (CGD, 2012).

## CANADA'S ROLE AT AND WITH THE AfDB

Canada is an active donor at the AfDB, although its AfDF burden share is below earlier levels. Since the Canadian ED also represents several other countries (China, Korea and Kuwait), the "weight" of the Canadian chair is significant.

The Canadian chair has generally worked more to strengthen the AfDB than to protect specific Canadian interests.[6] Initially, its attention was on ensuring financial accountability, but that has broadened to include the effectiveness and results of the Bank and the Fund's programming. Canada's support of the AfDB's continent-wide coverage shows continued concern for Africa as a whole, even as Canada's bilateral programming targets fewer countries, to ensure sufficient size for lower administrative costs and real impact. Moreover, the AfDB's attention to infrastructure tackles a vital area beyond the reach of CIDA's budget.

Canadian EDs' willingness to take an AfDB-wide perspective has enhanced their impact. In the 1990s, Canada accepted China in its group — China became a shareholder in 1985, but had no constituency. Later, Canadian EDs helped foster discussions between China and the AfDB, although it would be wrong to overemphasize this: China has not played a big role at the AfDB; its African relationships are primarily bilateral. The EDs have also helped strengthen Korea's links with the AfDB and persuaded its constituency to accept Turkey as a member, when none of the other groups would do so. However, Turkey has yet to finalize its membership.

In various AfDB fora, Canada plays its traditional role of honest broker, between the US and European chairs, between non-regional and regional shareholders and between AfDB management and its board. If a single Canadian decision strengthened its reputation with the AfDB and its regional shareholders, it was the 2009 offer of temporary callable capital, in the middle of the financial crisis, when the AfDB's vital role for middle-income regional shareholders was under threat. This offer allowed the AfDB's "non-concessional" window to keep operating. The AfDB can only borrow up to the total pledges by shareholders rated A- and above. When middle-income countries turned to the AfDB as private sector lenders stepped back, it rapidly ran out of room to borrow and thus to lend. Canada offered additional callable capital equal to twice its existing commitment. Canada's role is not huge, but, with existing capital largely committed, the tripling of its pledge (only high-quality pledges, of which Canada provides about 10 percent, can back AfDB borrowings) greatly increased the AfDB's capacity for the coming year. Between 2009 and 2010, AfDB shareholders negotiated a general capital increase, tripling the authorized capital and allowing Canada to switch its temporary pledge into support for the permanent capital increase.[7]

Canada's AfDB involvement is led by CIDA, whose minister is responsible for the financial relationship, notably the AfDF contribution. CIDA also provides two other types of support. The Canadian Trust Fund helps strengthen specific administrative and programming areas, while multi-donor thematic trust funds tackle specific challenges. Two of these funds build on initiatives launched by the 2002 Canada Fund for Africa: the Infrastructure Project Preparation Facility for regionally integrating projects and the African Water Facility. More recently, CIDA launched an Aid for Trade Trust Fund with the AfDB to help strengthen African countries' world trade links.[8]

Despite solid links with the AfDB Group, Canada and CIDA have not built on the relationship. No Canadian minister attended an annual meeting between 2003 and 2010. It is particularly regrettable that the unprecedented recent five-year period without a change in minister did not lead to a stronger relationship.[9] In all the RDBs, there is a risk that Canada gets lost between the Europeans, who typically work in concert among themselves and often take joint positions, and the United States, who remains a very large player despite a proportionately modest role at the RDBs. There have been few senior Canadians at the AfDB, although Canadians make up the third-largest group of non-regionals among AfDB employees after the French and the Americans. Many are African-Canadians and the number of Canadian citizens is even larger, because of staff members with dual citizenship who register at the AfDB under their African nationality. Other African staff members are Canadian-educated and many employees' children study in Canada.

Canadian civil society frequently voices concern about the IMF and World Bank, which non-governmental organizations often view as imposing inappropriate Western standards on developing countries, yet it seldom notices the regional banks, whose policy prescriptions are similar. RDBs' regional "ownership" seems to provide some protection from accusations of outside interference.

Canadian private investment in Africa is concentrated in the mining sector, where the AfDB is not that active: viable projects seldom lack financing. On occasion, the AfDB funds mining projects with broader goals. At Ambatovy in Madagascar, it helped Sherritt Mining of Canada and its partners to develop a major nickel and cobalt deposit, which has begun operations despite continued political turmoil in the country. Export Development Canada and, to a limited extent, some Canadian pension funds, are now co-financing with the AfDB on some projects. Much of the AfDB's private sector work seeks to bolster the still-limited African financial sector. One Canadian firm, Développement International Desjardins, is partnering with the AfDB to transfer the concept of small business financing centres to anglophone eastern and southern Africa. The Desjardins Group developed this model in Canada and had already successfully adapted it to francophone West Africa.

Most AfDB procurement is for civil works and goods, areas where Canadian firms seldom bid. Canadian firms are quite successful, however, in consulting services, including supervision contracts for construction; in fact, Canada is usually first or second among suppliers. While individual contracts are not large, they have created an important link between Canada and the AfDB and have allowed many mid-sized consultancies to become known in Africa and to bid successfully for work with national governments.

## THE OUTLOOK

Can the AfDB sustain the strong growth it has enjoyed since Kaberuka took office? The recent rise in lending to middle-income countries, reversing an earlier shift to borrowing in private markets, may be sustained if continued risk aversion by private lenders discourages emerging African countries from relying on them too heavily, and as more countries, such as Angola, Ghana and Cape Verde, reach middle-income status. The recent expansion in private sector operations will slow, partly because risk-management concerns limit the expansion of private-sector operations in low-income countries, despite donor requests during the capital increase negotiations. Finally, the AfDF concessional window will face challenges as donor countries' economies constrain aid budgets and thus replenishment size. Despite talk about emerging donors, only Korea showed much upward flexibility during the 2010 AfDF negotiations, which already reflected budget pressures on traditional donors and produced a small increase from 2007.

The AfDB's growth has strengthened its knowledge acquisition and provision of advice to RMC governments; however, this should be more clearly focussed. There is no point in trying to replicate the role of the IMF for Africa — already cited as a problem in the mid-1990s (English and Mule, 1996: 10). The AfDB needs to tackle issues central to its mandate, notably regional integration, to which many coastal countries give only lip service. Proper analytic work could identify the benefits for them as well as for the landlocked countries. A second area is private-sector development, particularly in its governance dimension. The AfDB should not leave the calculation and promotion of "Doing Business" indicators to the World Bank, because its advice risks being seen as intended to make Africa safe for OECD companies, when African business faces still greater handicaps. The AfDB is better placed to convince RMC governments of the gains from improved governance.

The AfDB would like to attract new donors, such as Australia or Singapore, and to encourage more involvement from existing ones, such as China, India, Brazil and Korea. However, unless (other) existing shareholders cede their relative importance and absolute access to board positions, it may be difficult to accomplish. Canada might want to be proactive in working with the AfDB and its constituency, encouraging China, in particular, to do more with it. However, this could have implications for Canada's role on the board. Canada's permanent ED position, much-prized in official Ottawa, could be at risk.[10] Maintaining it will be easier if Canada once again shows more than simply a "steady as she goes" approach to the AfDB.

The AfDB will replace its 2008–2012 "Medium-Term Strategy" with a ten-year strategy. Concerns provoked by the Arab Spring have suggested inclusive growth as a goal, but infrastructure — particularly for regional integration — governance and private sector development remain important. Regional integration should be a key Canadian objective: a fragmented Africa will grow more slowly than needed and thus delay the continent's ability to attain true emerging market status. However, private sector development is the main opportunity for Canadian collaboration.

CIDA sees the private sector as a motor for growth. A recent report by the Standing Committee on Foreign Affairs and International Development calls on CIDA to "pursue appropriate public-private partnerships" including with "multilateral development agencies, and developing country governments," which it could do with the AfDB (Government of Canada, 2012: 99). Private sector, in this context, often refers to mining, which seldom needs financial support from either the AfDB or CIDA. However, power projects, including hydro, often need support, and Africa's growing middle class also provides opportunities for private sector growth. Moreover, the regulatory framework for resource development could be an area for joint work by Canada and the AfDB to improve African countries' abilities to manage resource boom and bust cycles, building on recent announcements of additional funding by CIDA for the Extractive Industries Transparency Initiative at the World Bank and a new Canadian International Institute for Extractive Industries and Development in Vancouver, developed by a partnership between the University of British Columbia, Simon Fraser University and the Ecole Polytechnique de Montreal. The AfDB has the potential for greater credibility with African interlocutors.

## CONCLUSION

The AfDB must further strengthen its capacity to deliver both programming results and regionally sensitive development knowledge. Much will depend on a possible return to Abidjan. Over 80 percent of the AfDB's staff members were recruited after the 2003 relocation to Tunis, but how many among them would accept a move to Abidjan? Political pressures for the move are growing, fuelled by recent unrest in Tunisia, but concerns about the unstable situation in Côte d'Ivoire remain. Early clarity about the future would be good, but a second emergency move would not. The AfDB's greater decentralization may make the headquarters decision less critical. The new Regional Resource Centres (in Nairobi and Pretoria, so far) provide other places to work, as will the growing country offices.

The AfDB is an important multilateral partner for Canada and CIDA. The offer of temporary callable capital showed that Canada was there for Africa and the AfDB when it counted. Stronger ongoing engagement with the AfDB would allow Canada to signal its continued interest in the continent as a whole, notwithstanding more focussed bilateral assistance. To date, Canada has done little to build on its past contributions and current common interests. With renewed interest in Africa's economic prospects, such a (re)engagement would be timely. All channels for supporting Africa are important, but the AfDB offers the potential for the continent-wide political engagement that has been lacking.

## ENDNOTES

1   In fact, the AfDF has a separate board from the AfDB, reflecting the bigger donor role at the AfDF. Canada has sensibly encouraged efforts to merge the AfDB and AfDF boards, in order to increase regional member countries' (RMCs') "ownership" of the AfDF.

2   The IADB and, to a lesser extent, the ADB are much larger (in absolute terms, and relative to the World Bank in their regions) than the AfDB, reflecting in part their greater capacity for internal growth.

3   For a history of the AfDB to the mid-1990s, see English and Mule, 1996.

4   The March 2013 federal budget proposes merging the Department of Foreign Affairs and International Trade with CIDA into a new department. It also seeks to introduce legislation to clarify aspects of the new department's mandate, particularly with respect to development. Exactly how the new department will manage relations with the AfDB will probably only be decided as the new structures are created and the government gets experience with their operation.

5   Core funding is defined by the Organisation for Economic Co-operation and Development's (OECD's) Development Assistance Committee as unearmarked contributions to multilateral institutions. It is the only type of funding the committee calls multilateral assistance.

6    Canadian procurement at the AfDB is the responsibility of the Department of Foreign Affairs and International Trade, and the Embassy in Abidjan or Tunis, rather than the Canadian ED. The record is reasonably positive.

7    With the capital increase, the board expanded to 20, to allow South Africa a permanent ED position without eliminating another African chair, while non-regional chairs increased to seven. Non-regionals remain "under-represented," with 35 percent of seats and 40 percent of shares.

8    At the Francophonie Summit in Ouagadougou in 2008, Canada contributed to the Rural Water Supply and Sanitation Initiative, an existing multi-donor trust fund.

9    Minister Oda did attend the 2011 Annual Meeting, but there was no follow up.

10   Canada has a majority of constituency shares at the AfDB and the ADB; however the permanent Canadian possession of the ED positions reflects agreements among shareholders; other AfDB constituencies rotate the ED position even when one country has a majority. Canada could see its role contested in the future, for example, by a China more active at the AfDB. (At the IADB, Canada does not represent other countries so naturally has the ED post.)

## WORKS CITED

CGD (2012). *Soft Lending without Poor Countries: Recommendations for a New IDA.* Available at: www.cgdev.org/sites/default/files/1426547_file_Moss_IDA_FINAL_web.pdf.

English, E. Philip and Harris M. Mule (1996). *The Multilateral Development Banks: Volume 1, The African Development Bank.* Boulder: Lynne Rienner Publishers.

Government of Canada (2012). *Driving Inclusive Economic Growth: The Role of the Private Sector in International Development.* Report of the Standing Committee on Foreign Affairs and International Development. November. Available at: www.parl.gc.ca/HousePublications/Publication.aspx?DocId=5732913.

# The Muskoka Initiative and the Politics of Fence-mending with Africa

David R. Black

• • • • • • • • • • • • • • • • • • •

## INTRODUCTION

The Stephen Harper government's disposition towards Africa during its first four years in office was distant and disinterested. While it did not abandon Africa, as some commentators have suggested, its policies drifted forward on the momentum of decisions taken by previous Liberal governments, while new priorities (including Latin America and, latterly, Asia) gradually came into focus. The symbolic nadir of this growing policy distance came with the announcement in February 2009 of a new list of 20 "countries of focus" for Canadian bilateral aid that dropped eight of 14 African bilateral partners designated as core priorities only four years previously.[1] Strikingly, there was no consultation with affected governments or other interested "stakeholders" prior to the announcement of this decision.

By early 2010 however, there were tentative signs of a course correction, including meetings with African heads-of-mission in Ottawa and ministerial visits to Africa.[2] The most significant indicator of a revised approach, however, was Prime Minister Harper's announcement at the World Economic Forum (WEF) in Davos, Switzerland in late January 2010, that his government would launch an initiative at the Muskoka Group of Eight (G8) Summit to inject new funds and momentum in support of Millennium Development Goals (MDGs) 4 and 5, committing signatories to:

- reduce by two-thirds the under-five mortality rate between 1990 and 2015 (MDG 4);
- in the same period, reduce by three-quarters the maternal mortality ratio (MDG 5a); and
- achieve universal access to reproductive health by 2015 (MDG 5b).

While none of these goals focus specifically on Africa, the highest incidences of maternal, newborn and child mortality and morbidity continue to be heavily concentrated in the continent, with "an African woman's lifetime risk of dying from pregnancy-related causes [being] 100 times higher than that of a woman in a developed country" (World Health Organization [WHO] and United Nations Children's Fund [UNICEF], 2012). Similarly, when the details of Canada's commitment to the "Muskoka Initiative" (MI) came into focus in November 2010, 80 percent of funds under the MI were designated for Africa, with seven of 10 priority countries located in the continent.[3] Thus, the hallmark initiative of the Muskoka G8 Summit was (like most G8 summits of the previous decade) African-centric, though not exclusively focussed on Africa.

How are we to understand the Harper government's decision to focus on Maternal, Newborn and Child Health (MNCH) as the centrepiece of its aid policy in the context of the cautious beginnings of a re-engagement with Africa? To what extent can the MI be expected to have the sort of catalytic effect on international efforts to improve MNCH that government representatives posit?[4]

This chapter argues that the MI must be understood, in part, as an effort to refresh and recast the ethical identity of the (Conservative-led) Canadian state, and that it was, indeed, a "good" initiative. Its ability to shape international outcomes and improve MNCH prospects has been significantly diminished, however, by three key factors: the flawed process by which it was introduced and operationalized; its disconnection from an appropriately gendered analysis of the relative lack of progress on MNCH issues; and its inconsistency with broader changes to Canadian aid policy that have reduced the government's ability to address the structural conditions within which MNCH deficiencies persist. Together, these weaknesses reflect the ongoing failure of Canadian policies in Africa, specifically in the domain of health, to take a sufficiently long-term and coordinated approach to the challenges faced.

## MNCH, AFRICA AND THE PURSUIT OF THE "GOOD STATE"[5]

In the run-up to the Muskoka G8 Summit, there are a number of reasons why a focus on MNCH made sense. In the broadest terms, every summit host has sought to cast an ethical gloss on its meeting by promoting initiatives on one or more particular issue or cause, through which the G8 can project an image of enlightened global leadership. For example, Canada's previous summit was anchored by then-Prime Minister Jean Chrétien's advocacy of the Africa Action Plan.[6] Many causes have, like MNCH, been health-focussed, though with results typically failing to live up to expectations (Guebert, 2010; Kirton and Guebert, 2009). As the Harper government launched its campaign for a non-permanent seat on the UN Security Council, it was faced with the need to regain some of the diplomatic capital lost through its perceived indifference towards African governments and concerns during the previous four years. While no government, and particularly this one, is inclined towards overt public policy reversals, the MNCH initiative offered an indirect means of demonstrating renewed interest in the well-being of the African continent and its people.

At a deeper level, governments and the politicians that lead them must articulate a sense of ethical purpose for the state they lead. This is an imperative the Harper government has struggled with, since the issues it has chosen to represent as ethical identifiers (such as support for Israel, the war in Afghanistan or the promotion of religious freedom) have been domestically divisive. In contrast, an emphasis on "saving the lives of women and children" could reasonably be expected to garner more broadly based support. Moreover, an emphasis on ameliorating the plight of some of the most powerless people on the most marginalized continent reflected a time-honoured approach to defining a sense of moral purpose for the Canadian state.

Julia Gallagher, in her analysis of the sustained preoccupation with Africa evinced by the UK government of former Prime Minister Tony Blair, argues that partly *because of* the British public's widespread indifference to the continent, British policy in Africa could be plausibly portrayed as selfless and virtuous. Africa, and African issues, thus worked as a source of self-idealization and a means of defining Britain as a good state: "From Britain, the work in Africa looks very clearly good...disinterested...unifying, and differentiating" (Gallagher, 2011: 108). The paradox, of course, is that this portrayal requires that the "African other," and its long-standing linkages with the United Kingdom, be virtually drained of historical and political context. It results in a flat, de-politicized view of a rich, varied and contradictory continent and relationship.

Canada's state leaders have had a comparable tendency to define the Canadian self with reference to the distant and dimly understood African other. Edward Akuffo (2012) discusses the way in which Africa has served as an anchor for Canada's "moral identity." I argue that African issues have formed the basis of a "serial morality tale" in Canadian foreign policy (Black, 2010). Initially, the Harper government either discounted or dismissed this role, in part because it viewed Africa as being a Liberal priority from which it was keen to distinguish itself (Black, 2012b). With the MNCH initiative, however, it found a focus that captured much of the same potential for moral self-definition through engagement with a category of subjects — poor women, newborns and children — that for the most part does not audibly 'speak for itself,' and could be portrayed as "beyond politics" (Toycen, 2010). In doing so, Canada also found an indirect way to begin mending fences with Africa.

One should not be too cynical in this portrayal. There are ways in which MNCH was indeed a "good issue," not only because of its potential to do good by improving the life prospects for millions of women and children, but because it was an issue on which there was a clear need for donor state leadership, which Canada was relatively well positioned to provide.[7] While international mobilization on MNCH issues has been evident since the late 1980s, especially among international and non-governmental organizations,[8] MDGs 4 and 5 remained the most off track of the eight MDGs when the government's initiative was launched in 2010. As noted in *Countdown 2015: Maternal, Newborn & Child Survival: Building a Future for Women and Children: The 2012 Report*, despite some progress on both objectives, 287,000 maternal deaths still occurred in 2010 and only nine of 75 "countdown countries"[15] were on track to meet MDG 5a (WHO and UNICEF, 2012: 1–3). Similarly, 7.6 million children under five years of age still died in 2010, and only 23 of 75 countries were on track to meet MDG 4 (ibid.). Indeed, one of the architects of the MDGs, Jan Vandemoortele, argues that MDG 5 on maternal mortality was a particularly ambitious and even unrealistic target: "A big exception [to the achievability of the MDGs] is the target for maternal mortality. No evidence can be found to show that a reduction by three-quarters by 2015 is feasible at the global level. It seems that this particular target was set at random, more as a noble intention than as a realistic objective" (2011: 14). Yet a range of evidence-based interventions have clearly demonstrated that advances can be made.[9] Thus, high profile leadership from a developed G8 country like Canada — with a strong tradition of activism on gender and development issues, and a high level of capacity and expertise on maternal and child health issues — was both plausible and arguably necessary to address this looming failure. In this sense, the focus of the MI was ambitious but well chosen. Regrettably, the full potential of this Initiative has been undermined in three significant ways.

## PROCESS ISSUES

Canadian leadership aspirations on MNCH have been constrained by a paucity of followership. As noted by Guebert (2010), Canada's commitment of CDN$1.1 billion over five years in new money at the Huntsville G8 Summit was "disproportionate" — that is, relatively much higher than most other G8 members — with the United Kingdom being the only other G8 member to match it proportionately. The total of US$7.3 billion committed at the summit (with contributions from a number of non-G8 donors, including the Gates Foundation) fell far short of the US$30 billion estimated as necessary to meet MDGs 4 and 5 by 2015. Moreover, the G8 Information Centre's *Deauville Compliance Report* (Aidid et al., 2012) found that a year later, in 2011, only four of nine G8 members were meeting their relatively modest targets — and two of these, Russia and the European Union, had made the most modest initial commitments among the group.

There are many reasons for this relative lack of commitment and coordination, not least the ongoing travails of member-states' economies in the wake of the 2008 global financial crisis, as well as the diminishing salience of the G8 itself. In addition, however, the process by which the MI was launched and promoted effectively truncated opportunities to leverage the MI among other international actors, and delayed the operationalization of Canada's own commitment. These process problems were, in turn, predictable results of the excessively secretive and centralized policy approach that has prevailed in the Conservatives' Ottawa.

In short, the MI was launched at the WEF in Davos a mere five months prior to the summit, providing limited time to mobilize support from other governments and organizations. It suffered throughout its promotion over the next several months from uncertain focus and controversial mixed messages over whether or not it would support reproductive care and safe abortions.[10] Canada's own sizeable commitment was not formally announced until shortly before the Muskoka summit in late June, minimizing the possibilities for leadership by example. The uncertainty and mixed messages over reproductive and safe abortion funding (discussed further in the next section) indicated the lack of thought given to planning the MI. It was not widely discussed within CIDA prior to its launch, leaving officers in the field scrambling to respond. The broad outlines of Canada's own response were only clarified in November 2010, including a CDN$75 million Muskoka Initiative Partnership Fund to solicit MNCH project proposals from Canadian non-state actors. The Canadian Network on MNCH, involving a wide range of non-state actors along with CIDA, was launched in November 2011, with modest funding of CDN$1.8 million over three years finally confirmed in October 2012. Agreement on robust indicators to measure impact of MI funded efforts on MNCH outcomes remains elusive.[11]

In sum, and without discounting the commitment of those working to bring the MI to fruition inside and outside CIDA, the government's constricted approach to policy making and CIDA's legendary problems of transparent and timely decision making[12] combined to constrain the impact and influence of the MI, within and beyond Canada. Situating the MI in relation to the broader history of Canadian involvement in global health, it is consistent with an ongoing pattern of periodic, interesting and promising initiatives,[13] but within an overall approach that has been fragmented, reactive and lacking in strategic vision (Percival and Blouin, 2009: 4).

## GENDER ISSUES

If the Harper government thought MNCH was an issue beyond politics, this proved a significant miscalculation. Its championing of maternal health, while simultaneously prevaricating on funding for family planning[14] and later confirming that government funds would not be used to support safe, legal abortions, plunged it directly into the fraught arena of reproductive rights and gender equality. As the *Countdown* report notes, 22 million unsafe abortions (half of all induced abortions) occur globally each year, resulting in the deaths of 47,000 women and temporary or permanent disability of five million more (WHO and UNICEF, 2012). Furthermore, it is estimated that "75% of unsafe abortions could be avoided if the need for family planning were fully met" (ibid.: 19). Consequently, a comprehensive approach to dealing with maternal mortality and morbidity must ultimately get to grips with both family planning and abortion rights. The Harper government's refusal to allow safe abortion funding as part of its own contribution to the MI placed it at odds with the US and UK governments in the G8 context, and with gender rights advocates at home (Carrier and Tiessen, 2012: 184–186).

The government's approach was aligned with its own socially conservative political base, but against the preferences of the majority of Canadians. Haussman and Mills (2012) note that following the 2011 election, 102 of 166 members of the Conservative caucus in Parliament were publicly identified as "pro-life," but the prime minister and cabinet were too politically attuned to the preferences of the majority of Canadians to support a re-opening of the "abortion question" domestically. As a result, Carrier and Tiessen (2012) conclude that the MI reflected a form of "hypocritical internationalism," imposing value preferences on poor women in developing countries that the government was not prepared to impose at home.

This is not a straightforward issue, since as Haussman and Mills (2012) observe, the government's approach was also broadly aligned with the dominant, deeply hesitant, approach to abortion rights that had evolved internationally over the previous two decades. Given that abortion was illegal or heavily restricted in the majority of *Countdown* countries, it was still possible to achieve substantial advances for maternal health without directly engaging the issue of abortion.

The broader issue within which this controversy should be situated, however, is the government's diminished commitment to a gendered analytical approach in its aid policy. Carrier and Tiessen (2012: 187-188) point out that the government now favours the language of "equality of women and men" over the more far-reaching "gender equality." While the distinction may seem semantic, this new language reflects a more practical, rather than strategic, approach to gender issues. For many years, CIDA was widely regarded as an international leader on gender analysis and issues, and continues to assert that "equality of women and men" is an important cross-cutting issue. Yet failure to understand and address MNCH issues as a manifestation of pervasive social structures of gender inequality is to fail to get at the underpinnings of this issue. After all, the very fact that progress on maternal and child health has lagged behind all other MDGs needs to be understood as a manifestation of gender inequality. Targeted, technocratic interventions that do not address these deeper political conditions are likely to prove unsustainable.

## MNCH AND THE REFORM OF CANADIAN AID POLICY

The conceptual disembedding of MNCH from structures of gender inequality is related to the broader disconnect between the hallmark MI, on the one hand, and wider reforms, refocussing and reductions to development assistance on the other. The starting point for this analysis is the strong correlation of poor maternal and child health outcomes with high levels of poverty, and the fact that MNCH "[p]rogress has been much slower, and inequities in coverage much wider, for skilled birth attendants at birth and other interventions that require a strong health system" (WHO and UNICEF, 2012: 1). In other words, the greatest obstacles to progress on MDGs 4 and 5 are firmly linked to poverty, inequality and weaknesses in health systems that are, in turn, a manifestation of weak governance. These are all (or should be) key foci of "traditional" development assistance writ large. In this context, Canada's relatively small and declining aid program, and its mounting emphasis on private sector-led economic growth as the key to development,[16] is inconsistent with the conditions necessary to improve MNCH outcomes where they are weakest.

Beginning in 2008, the government launched a series of reforms designed to make CIDA and Canadian aid more "effective" and "accountable."[17] These involved greater concentration of bilateral aid in a smaller number of countries of focus — proportionately fewer of them African and more of them middle income — and revised and streamlined thematic priorities. While these changes are not necessarily undesirable, the uncertainties and instability they generate can compromise aid effectiveness in the short to medium term. The federal government's precipitous decision to fold CIDA into the Department of Foreign Affairs and International Trade, announced in the March 2013 federal budget, may ultimately produce some process improvements, but the most likely outcome in the medium term is an *increased* burden of administrative demands, along with a growing emphasis on deploying aid to serve Canadian "interests."

With regard to Africa and MNCH, the government's decision making on countries of focus has generated several inconsistencies that undermine the connections between its MI-linked programming and bilateral programming more broadly. For example Kenya — a country making progress on reproductive health — was dropped as a bilateral country of focus in 2009 (Haussman and Mills, 2012: 11). Malawi — a country widely regarded as making advances on governance and development as well as MNCH — was dropped as a country of focus in 2009, but then added to the list of MNCH focus countries in November 2010. Nigeria — a country notorious for high levels of corruption and inequality, but an emerging economic priority for the Government of Canada — was never on the list of bilateral focus countries, but was added as an MNCH focus country in 2010. These disconnects between bilateral aid programming and MNCH programming raise questions about the impact and sustainability of the latter. If improved MNCH outcomes depend fundamentally on sustained health-system strengthening, for example, strictly time-bound MI contributions in Malawi and Nigeria can hardly be expected to have a durable impact in the absence of ongoing development partnerships.

More broadly, it is hard to square the hallmark prioritization of MNCH, accompanied by stable medium-term funding, with the severe cuts to aid spending as a whole announced in the past two federal budgets. These cuts are projected to total 7.6 percent in actual dollar amounts between 2011-

2012 and 2014-2015, resulting in an estimated decline in aid as a percentage of gross national income from an already desultory 0.34 percent in 2010 to 0.25 percent in 2015 (Canadian Council for International Cooperation [CCIC], 2012). The private sector-led growth promoted by the government, while widely welcomed, is characteristically accompanied by growing inequalities. Particularly when concentrated in the extractive sector, it has often exacerbated, rather than improved, governance problems. Thus, the changes and cuts made to the aid program as a whole tend to work *against* the conditions for improvements in MNCH provision, particularly for the poorest and most marginalized people and communities. While the MI will have run its course by 2015, when the government's five-year funding commitment ends, the longer-term impact of real cuts to aid spending, and a growing emphasis within this reduced aid "envelope" on private sector-led economic growth and partnerships, will be gathering momentum in ways that are likely to compromise gains in maternal and child health for the most vulnerable.

## CONCLUSION

The MI remains, in principle, an admirable undertaking with particular relevance for the women and children of Africa. Many dedicated people have been mobilized in the effort to bring it to life. Yet the process by which it has been implemented, as well as the wider changes in the aid program within which it is embedded, have compromised its potential impact and sustainability. The risk is that, disarticulated from wider government policies, it will float free as a niche or boutique initiative, partially obscuring more pervasive changes in Canadian policy that limit its reach, effectiveness and longer-term results.

## ENDNOTES

[1]   The countries cut were long-time Commonwealth and Francophonie partners: Benin, Burkina Faso, Cameroon, Kenya, Malawi, Niger, Rwanda and Zambia. See Black, 2012a.

[2]   See Black, 2012b.

3    These included Malawi, which was cut as a focus country in 2009, and Nigeria, which was not on either the 2005 or 2009 list. The other six (Ethiopia, Ghana, Mali, Mozambique, Tanzania and Sudan) were already Canadian International Development Agency (CIDA) countries of focus. See CIDA (2012), "Maternal, Newborn and Child Health," available at: www.acdi-cida.gc.ca/acdi-cida/ACDI-CIDA.nsf/En/FRA-127113657-MH7.

4    See, for example, John Baird (2012), "Address by Minister Baird at Montreal Council on Foreign Relations Luncheon," address, September 14, Montreal, Quebec.

5    The idea of the "good state" is adapted from Gallagher, 2011. It is elaborated below.

6    See Robert Fowler (2003), "Canadian Leadership and the Kananaskis G8 Summit: Towards a less Self-Centred Canadian Foreign Policy," In *Canada Among Nations 2003: Coping with the American Colossus,* edited by David Carment, Fen Osler Hampson and Norman Hillmer, Pages 219–241, Don Mills: Oxford University Press Canada.

7    See Steven Hoffman (2012), "Foreign Aid Should Reflect Canada's Priorities: Equality, Democracy, Health," *The Globe and Mail,* November 26, available at: www.theglobeandmail.com/commentary/foreign-aid-should-reflect-canadas-priorities-equality-democracy-health/article5661021/.

8    See Haussman and Mills, 2012.

9    The *Countdown* report notes that maternal deaths have declined from 543,000 in 1990 to 287,000 in 2010 (WHO and UNICEF, 2012).

10    See Avinash Gavai (2010), "How the Rest of the G8 stacks up on Contraceptives, Abortion," *Embassy,* March 31.

11    Interview with Canadian Network on MNCH participant, confidential, January 2013.

12    See Molly den Heyer (2012), "Untangling Canadian Aid Policy: International Agreements, CIDA's Policies, and Micro-Policy Negotiations in Tanzania," In *Struggling for Effectiveness,* edited by Stephen Brown, Pages 186–216, Montreal and Kingston: McGill-Queen's University Press.

13    See the chapter by Dr. Victor Neufeld.

14  It was finally clarified by the Prime Minister that Canada would be prepared to fund organizations that supported family planning.

15  "Countdown countries" are a group of 75 countries that collectively account for 95 percent of maternal and child deaths.

16  See CIDA (2012), "Speaking Notes for the Honourable Julian Fantino Minister of International Cooperation for the Economic Club of Canada 'Reducing Poverty – Building Tomorrow's Markets,'" speaking notes, November 23, Toronto, Ontario.

17  See Stephen Brown (2012), "Aid Effectiveness and the Framing of New Canadian Aid Initiatives," In *Struggling for Effectiveness,* edited by Stephen Brown, Pages 79–107, Montreal and Kingston: McGill-Queen's University Press.

## WORKS CITED

Aidid, Abdi et al. (2012). *2011 Deauville G8 Summit Final Compliance Report.* Available at: www.g8.utoronto.ca/evaluations/2011compliance-final/index.html.

Akuffo, Edward Ansah (2012). *Canadian Foreign Policy in Africa: Regional Approaches to Peace, Security, and Development.* Farnham, Surrey: Ashgate Press.

Black, David R. (2010). "'Africa' as Serial Morality Tale in Canadian Foreign Policy." Paper presented to the annual meeting of the Canadian Association of African Studies, Carleton University, Ottawa, May.

———— (2012a). "Between Indifference and Idiosyncrasy: The Conservatives and Canadian Aid to Africa." In *Struggling for Effectiveness,* edited by Stephen Brown. Pages 246–268. Montreal and Kingston: McGill-Queen's University Press.

———— (2012b). "The Harper Government, Africa Policy, and the Relative Decline of Human Internationalism." In *Canada in the World, Internationalism in Canadian Foreign Policy,* edited by Claire Turenne Sjolander and Heather Smith. Pages 217–237. Don Mills: Oxford University Press Canada.

Carrier, Krystel and Rebecca Tiessen (2012). "Women and Children First: Maternal Health and the Silencing of Gender in Canadian Foreign Policy." In *Canada in the World, Internationalism in Canadian Foreign Policy,* edited by Claire Turenne Sjolander and Heather Smith. Pages 183–199. Don Mills: Oxford University Press Canada.

CCIC (2012). CCIC Analysis of Budget 2012. Available at: www.ccic.ca/_files/en/what_we_do/2012_08_CCIC_Initial_Analysis_Budget_2012.pdf.

Gallagher, Julia (2011). *Britain and Africa under Blair: In Pursuit of the Good State.* Manchester: Manchester Unversity Press.

Guebert, Jenilee (2010). "What happened to the Maternal and Child Health Initiative at the 2010 G8 Muskoka Summit?" Toronto: G8 Information Centre, June 29.

Haussman, Melissa and Lisa Mills (2012). "Doing the North American Two-Step on a Global Stage: Canada, its G8 Muskoka Initiative and Safe Abortion Funding." In *How Ottawa Spends 2012-13: The Harper Majority, Budget Cuts, and the New Opposition,* edited by G. Bruce Doern and Christopher Stoney. Montreal and Kingston: McGill-Queen's University Press.

Kirton, John and Jenilee Guebert (2009). "Canada's G8 Global Health Diplomacy: Lessons for 2010." *Canadian Foreign Policy* 15, no. 3, 85-105.

Percival, Valerie and Chantal Blouin (2009). "Canada, Global Health, and Foreign Policy: Muddling through is not Good Enough." *Canadian Foreign Policy* 15, no. 3, 1–9.

Toycen, Dave (2010). "Maternal, Child Health Go Beyond Politics." *Embassy,* September 22.

Vandemoortele, Jan (2011). "If Not the Millennium Development Goals, Then What?" *Third World Quarterly* 32, no. 1, 9–25.

WHO and UNICEF (2012). *Countdown 2015: Maternal, Newborn & Child Survival: Building a Future for Women and Children: The 2012 Report.* Washington, DC: Communications Development Incorporated.

# A Stronger Role for Canada in Health Research in Africa

Dr. Victor Neufeld

●  ●  ●  ●  ●  ●  ●  ●  ●  ●  ●  ●  ●  ●  ●  ●  ●

## INTRODUCTION

This chapter places Canada's contribution to health research in Africa within the broader context of health research for development, as it has evolved over the past 25 years, specifically describing important developments since 2000. The final section presents some challenges for Canada to consider in the coming years in order to make a more effective contribution. This chapter argues that while Canada has a modest but useful track record to date, more could be done to address the problems of fragmentation, imbalanced and ineffective research partnerships, and the "know-do gap."

## LOOKING BACK

Dating back many centuries, Africa has a historic record of achievements in the sciences, including mathematics, astronomy, agriculture, medicine and other fields. During the colonial period, however, the indigenous momentum in science and technology largely stopped. Health research during this time was concerned primarily with conditions that affected expatriates, with research activities based in disease-specific research centres, and conducted mostly by expatriates.

The relatively new and emerging field of global health research[1] can significantly be attributed to a flagship 1990 report, *Health Research: Essential Link to Equity in Development,* prepared by the independent international Commission on Health Research for Development (Commission on Health Research for Development, 1990). This group was supported by a diverse group of 16 donors, including Canada's International Development Research Centre (IDRC), and chaired by a Canadian, Dr. John Evans. The report's (1990) key finding was a gross mismatch between the global burden of illness located overwhelmingly in low- and middle-income countries (LMICs) and the global investment in health research, a large portion of which — more than 90 percent — was focussed on the problems of societies in high-income countries. This situation came to be called "the 10/90 gap" (Global Forum for Health Research, 1999). The Commission (1990) made four recommendations: all countries should undertake "essential national health research" (ENHR); more effective "South-North" research partnerships were needed; larger and more sustained financial support with specific targets was recommended; and an international mechanism was proposed to monitor progress and promote further financial and technical support.

Ten years later, progress related to Africa was evident in that 22 countries had, to some degree, adopted the principles of ENHR and had created an African ENHR network for mutual support (Council on Health Research for Development [COHRED], 2000). Overall, however, the African report was discouraging. Local financial investments in health were very low, with investments in health research even smaller. In fact, some countries had no budget line for health research. Virtually all health research funding came from outside of Africa. Consequently, research productivity was very low in terms of scientific publications and patents. Poor coordination led to considerable fragmentation of the health research efforts. Mechanisms for using research (that is, knowledge translation [KT]), particularly for evidence-based policy making, were weak. Partnership arrangements, both within Africa and with northern collaborators, were unbalanced and generally failed to build longer term capacities for health research.

Nevertheless, there were some important Canadian contributions to health research in Africa during this era (pre-2000). An example is the Tanzania

Essential Health Intervention Project (TEHIP) supported by the Canadian International Development Agency (CIDA) and IDRC. In collaboration with the Tanzanian Ministry of Health, the project involved testing a complex intervention in two districts, with two other districts serving as comparison sites. The key intervention was the training of district health teams to make accurate estimates of the district burden of illness, and use this information in planning and implementation of health services for the district. This work led to the development of several tools, such as tools to profile the district burden of illness, to account how funds are spent, to map how health services are used and to capture the "community voice." Some very modest additional funds (over and above the usual health financing) were made available if needed.

The results were remarkable. Within less than two years in one of the districts, infant deaths per 1,000 live births decreased from 100 to 46 — a decline of 40 percent (de Savigny et al., 2004). The deaths of children under five years per 1,000 live births declined from 131 to 74 (ibid.). The overall package was judged to be highly cost-effective, delivered at an increment of only 80 cents per person per year added to the annual national health investment of $6 per person (ibid.). Subsequently, the Tanzanian government has "rolled out" the tools and strategies to other districts, and across the whole country. Recently a nation wide study demonstrated that child mortality in Tanzania has continued to fall, to the point where it may be an example of a low-income country that will achieve the Millennium Development Goal (MDG) for child health (Masanja et al., 2008). To some extent, this achievement can be attributed to the scaling-up of the "TEHIP model" and its adaptation and use throughout Tanzania. In fact, the TEHIP example has influenced health-system strengthening efforts throughout Africa and beyond.

## RECENT AND CURRENT DEVELOPMENTS

In 2000, 10 years after the launch of the Commission report, a multi-component consultation, including an international Bangkok conference, was conducted to determine the extent to which the Commission's recommendations had been acted upon. Of the 800 participants at the conference, only a few were Canadians: several university-based health researchers, including the author, and the recently recruited leader of a new global health research program at IDRC. On returning to Canada, believing that this situation (that is, the insignificant Canadian presence at the conference) was unacceptable, this small group wrote editorials (Neufeld et al., 2001), conducted a national study of Canadian interest in global health research and met as an ad hoc "interim steering committee" to design and launch possible actions.

An early activity of this committee was an advocacy initiative made up of key "insiders" from four agencies: CIDA, IDRC, Health Canada and the then new Canadian Institutes of Health Research (CIHR). These credible individuals were able to influence policy makers within each agency to create this four-agency consortium. In June 2002, Canada hosted the Group of Eight (G8) summit in Kananaskis, Alberta. Led by then-Prime Minister Jean Chrétien, the discussions at this summit were focussed to a large extent on how the G8 countries could support the recently created New Partnership for Africa's Development. Working closely with Canada's Sherpa, the interim steering committee conducted a consultation that included several African health research leaders. The group then submitted a policy brief about health research in Africa that ultimately led to a statement included in the official G8 Africa Action Plan, under the heading "Improving Health and Confronting HIV/AIDS":

> Supporting health research on diseases prevalent in Africa, with a view to narrowing the health research gap, including by expanding health research networks to focus on African health issues, and by making more extensive use of research based in Africa. (G8 Africa Action Plan, 2002)

Another example of the steering committee's work was the creation of the Global Health Research Initiative (GHRI) that brought four federal agencies together to promote and increase support for global health research, through a formal memorandum of understanding (DiRuggiero et al., 2006). A GHRI secretariat was established in 2001 and, over the next few years, several innovative research programs were launched, such as the Teasdale-Corti Global Health Research Partnership Program (Stephen and Daibes, 2010).

To complement this grouping of federal government agencies, a non-governmental organization, the Canadian Coalition for Global Health Research (CCGHR), was launched in 2003 (Neufeld and Spiegel, 2006). CCGHR has become an influential Canada-based global network with more than 500 individual and 20 institutional members. It serves as a strategic

GHRI partner, focussing on advocacy, capacity building, policy influence and effective networking.

Around the time of CCGHR's launch, an important research program was derived from a major CIDA program — the Africa Health Systems Initiative (AHSI). Announced by the prime minister at the St. Petersburg G8 Summit in 2006, the Canadian government committed CDN$450 million in new funding over 10 years to support Africa-led efforts to strengthen health systems and make concrete progress toward achieving designated MDGs in Sub-Saharan Africa. Shortly after the launch of this initiative, the CCGHR was requested by CIDA to conduct a consultation to frame the research component of the AHSI, exploring the question: "What does a 21st century affordable, effective and sustainable health system in sub-Saharan Africa look like?"[2] The eventual result was a CDN$5 million fund to support a research partnership program that was managed by the GHRI. Over the past several years, the program has successfully supported Africa-Canada research teams working on three themes: human resources for health; equity in health systems development; and effective real-time monitoring of health outcomes.

A more recent Canadian story evolved from a federal government "Development Initiative Fund" that appeared in the 2009 federal budget. After a series of consultations, Canada's finance minister announced in March 2010 that Canada would invest CDN$225 million in an initiative that came to be called Grand Challenges Canada (GCC) (Daar and Singer, 2011). With a major emphasis on Africa, GCC has identified a series of "challenges." In the past two years, GCC has become a major player in the Canadian global health research scene, with the first round of projects funded and underway, and other programs at the application and selection stage.

A further important development, with some relation to Canada's contribution to health research in Africa, was the work of the Expert Panel on Canada's Strategic Role in Global Health. Sponsored by the Canadian Academy of Health Sciences (CAHS), the panel was convened in September 2010 and released its report in November 2011 (CAHS, 2011). The panel defined principles of a Canadian contribution to global health (equity, engagement and effectiveness); analyzed Canada's current role by reviewing strengths, barriers and opportunities; and identified five "strategic opportunities" for Canada in global health. These opportunities are: indigenous and circumpolar health research; population and public health; community-oriented primary health care; smart partnerships in education and research; and global health innovation (CAHS, 2011). The year 2012 has been designated by the panel as a "continued listening phase," encouraging the convening of global health leaders across all sectors to consider and comment on the findings of the panel's assessment.

## LOOKING AHEAD

In comparison to health research initiatives in Africa emanating from other high-income countries, most notably the United States and some European countries, Canada's profile is relatively small. It can be argued that this is all the more reason for the Canadian health research community to think about how its contributions can be most effective, and perhaps even distinctive. What follows are several challenges that represent opportunities for the Canadian health research community to consider tackling.

### Alignment and Harmonization

In 2005, Canada was one of many countries that signed an agreement known as the Paris Declaration on Aid Effectiveness. Among various identified concerns, the declaration recognized that "donors tended to use aid projects to 'show their flags' rather than coordinate their efforts or allow host countries or populations the chance to own and sustain the projects" (Organisation for Economic Co-operation and Development [OECD], 2005). The agreement stated five principles for countries and organizations to follow as they implemented this agreement including: alignment — aid programs must be aligned with countries' strategies, systems and procedures; and harmonization — donor actions must be coordinated.

In relation to health research in Africa, in 2008 COHRED conducted a study on "Alignment and Harmonization in Health Research" that examined the degree to which these two Paris Declaration principles were demonstrated by eight donor countries (including Canada) and five African countries (Burkina Faso, Cameroon, Mozambique, Uganda and Tanzania). Among the findings of this study was the view from the African countries that "donors do not align with the research priorities at country level and that financing channels favor Northern institutions as primary recipients" (COHRED, 2009). Among the study recommendations for donor countries were the following:

- support the strengthening of national health research systems, including the development of national health research priorities; and
- develop a good recording system for all research funded by a donor country.

Canada followed through on these recommendations, as illustrated in the following two examples.

Like several countries in Africa, Zambia has not had its own national health research organization. In 2009, the Zambian Ministry of Health invited the CCGHR to provide technical services for a consultation process to address the challenge of strengthening its national health research system. With financial support from IDRC, a comprehensive process was launched that addressed three concurrent activity streams: developing a legislative framework; creating an institution capable of providing coordination, management and guidance to the system; and focussing on networking among institutions to harmonize and strengthen the overall capacities of the research community. A specific outcome was the creation of a new national health research authority of Zambia (Chanda-Kapata, Campbell and Zarowsky, 2012).

More recently, a standing committee on research ethics of the CIHR indicated a need for comprehensive information about who was doing what and where with Canadian-funded research. With CIHR funding support, the CCGHR has launched a "harmonization" project to identify individuals and institutions conducting health research projects in several (pilot) African countries: Cameroon, Ethiopia, Tanzania, Uganda and Zambia. The project has demonstrated that several Canadian university research groups are active in a given country, often without knowledge of each other's work. The goal of this initiative is not only communication (information sharing), but also coordination (to avoid duplication and promote efficiency) and, ultimately, collaboration on shared ventures.

These stories represent examples where Canada can contribute more effectively to aligning health research investments with the national priorities and systems, and develop more coordinated "team Canada" arrangements in partner African countries.

## Effective Partnerships

The potential benefits of productive research partnerships between researchers in the South and North are well recognized. But there are also risks that involve asymmetries that can become obstacles to productive research collaboration. Included are disparities in access by LMIC partners to information, training and funding opportunities, as well as the disproportionate influence of high-income country partners in priority setting, project administration and budget management. Several agencies have published models and principles of partnership (Swiss Commission for Research Partnership with Developing Countries, 2011). In order to capture the "southern voice" in understanding "South-North" health research partnerships, an IDRC-supported series of consultations was conducted, including an Africa regional consultation. An outcome of this work was a partnership assessment tool, consisting of a series of questions related to four phases of a research project or program: inception, implementation, dissemination and "good endings and new beginnings."[3] It has been used in the context of training events and programs throughout Canada, and represents a potentially useful Canadian contribution to effective, respectful and sustainable research partnerships in Africa.

## Addressing the "Know-Do Gap"

Over the past 10 years, there has been a growing recognition that valid and relevant knowledge to address pressing global health problems is available, but for a variety of reasons is not used. To describe this problem, the term "know-do gap" was first used in a report by the World Health Organization (WHO) in preparation for a Ministerial Summit on Health Research, held in Mexico City in 2004 (WHO, 2004). Canada is internationally recognized as having special expertise in this relatively new field of KT, particularly in the health research sector, as outlined in the following examples:

- From its beginnings in 2001, CIHR has had the mandate in its official government charter, not only to create new knowledge, but also to translate that new knowledge into health benefits for Canadians and individuals around the world.
- The IDRC has also taken up a special interest in KT, for example, producing several editions of a "KT handbook."

- The Canadian Health Services Research Foundation (recently renamed as the Canadian Foundation for Healthcare Improvement) has been a pioneer in training Canadian health services managers to use timely and relevant evidence in their work.
- Several universities have created entities that specialize in research into the KT process, and are pioneering initiatives that link researchers with "knowledge users," including policy makers and program managers. An example is the McMaster Health Forum, now a WHO Collaborating Centre for evidence-informed policy.[4] This unit also maintains a repository of continuously updated syntheses of research evidence about health systems.[5] Several African health researchers are currently completing doctoral studies at the centre, in preparation for assuming leadership roles in their own countries.

To some extent, this Canadian expertise has been engaged in strengthening KT (evidence to policy) initiatives in Africa. An example is Canada's role (funded by IDRC and CIHR) in supporting the work of the WHO's Evidence-Informed Policy Network (EVIPNet) in Africa.[6] More could be done to involve Canadian expertise in this important area of KT in the African context.

The areas described above are consistent with global trends in the field of global health research, and to some extent are already reflected in the policies and programs of the GHRI.

There are features of Canada's experience and expertise that are distinctive and that could contribute to strengthening health research in Africa in the coming years.

- The IDRC: this institution is now the only remaining tax payer-supported organization in the world that has the specific mandate to support research in LMICs. It represents an important element of Canada's foreign policy and deserves the continuing support of citizens and organizations who believe its mandate and resources are relevant and critically important in the years ahead, including future support for health research in Africa.
- Canada's bilingual policy represents an important advantage that we have. The expertise and resources particularly of the Canadian francophone health research community have been invaluable in

the development of health research in francophone West Africa. This is a resource that needs to be supported and strengthened.

## CONCLUSION

To summarize, as the health research for development movement has evolved over the past 25 years, Canada has made important contributions to this field in Africa. But important challenges remain to be addressed. The fragmented efforts by the many players involved require clearer alignment with local priorities and more effective harmonization. Too often, health research arrangements between partners from the North and South are excessively influenced by researchers from high-income countries. Beyond the production of relevant new knowledge, more attention is needed to the process of synthesizing available knowledge and using it for effective policy making, program management and professional practice. Canada can play a stronger role in this endeavour, particularly through effective, respectful and sustainable partnerships with African collaborators.

## ENDNOTES

1   "Global health research" is a relatively recent term. It implies both the production and use of knowledge that prioritizes equity and includes trans-national issues. Still more recently, the concept of "research for health" has been introduced to indicate that multi-disciplinary research collaboration is needed to address the broad social and economic determinants of health.

2   This question is from the consultation exercise.

3   This tool is available (in several languages) as a self-study module at www.ccghr.ca.

4   See: www.mcmasterhealthforum.org.

5   See: www.healthsystemsevidence.org.

6   See: hwww.evipnet.org.

## WORKS CITED

CAHS (2011). "Canadians Making a Difference: the Expert Panel on Canada's Strategic Role in Global Health." Available at: www.cahs-acss.ca/canadians-making-a-difference-the-expert-panel-on-canadas-strategic-role-in-global-health/.

Chanda-Kapata, P., S. Campbell and C. Zarowsky (2012). "Developing a National Health Research System: Participatory Approaches to Legislative, Institutional and Networking Dimensions in Zambia." *Health Research Policy and Systems* 10: 17–28.

COHRED (2009). *Synthesis Report: Alignment and Harmonization in Health Research.* Geneva.

Commission on Health Research for Development (1990). *Health Research: Essential Tool for Equity in Development.* New York and London: Oxford University Press.

Daar, A. and P. Singer (2011). *The Grandest Challenge: Taking Life-saving Science from Lab to Village.* Toronto: Doubleday Canada.

de Savigny, D. et al. (2004). *Fixing Health Systems.* Ottawa, Canada: IDRC.

DiRuggiero, E. et al. (2006). "Coordinating Canada's Research Responses to Global Health Challenges: The Global Health Research Initiative." *Canadian Journal of Public Health* 97: 29–31.

G8 Africa Action Plan (2002). "G8 Africa Action Plan: Kananaskis, June 27, 2002." Available at: www.g8.utoronto.ca/summit/2002kananaskis/africaplan.html.

Global Forum for Health Research (1999). *The 10/90 Report on Health Research 1999. Global Forum for Health Research.* Geneva, Switzerland.

Masanja, H. et al. (2008). "Child Survival Gains in Tanzania: Analysis of Data from Demographic and Health Surveys." *Lancet* 371: 1276–1283.

Neufeld, V. R. et al., (2001). "The Rich-Poor Gap in Health Research: Challenges for Canada." *Canadian Medical Association Journal* 164: 1158-1159.

Neufeld, V. R. and J. Spiegel (2006). "Canada and Global Health Research: 2005 Update." *Canadian Journal of Public Health* 97: 39–41.

OECD (2005). *The Paris Declaration on Aid Effectiveness and the Accra Agenda for Action.* Available at: www.oecd.org/development/ effectiveness/34428351.pdf.

Stephen, Craig and Ibrahim Daibes (2010). "Defining Features of the Practice of Global Health Research: An Examination of 14 Global Health Research Teams." *Global Health Action* 3: 5118–5127.

Swiss Commission for Research Partnership with Developing Countries (2011). *Guidelines for Research in Partnership with Developing Countries: 11 Principles.* Available at: www.kfpe.ch/key_activities/ publications/guidelines/guidelines_e.php.

WHO (2004). *World Report on Knowledge for Better Health.* Geneva, Switzerland: WHO.

# Part Five:
# Research Capacity
· · · · · · · · · · · · · · · · · · · · · · · · · ·

## THE ORIGINS OF CANADA'S SOCIO-ECONOMIC RESEARCH CAPACITY SUPPORT FOR FRANCOPHONE AFRICA

In the highly divided world of the 1960s — marked by the Cold War between East and West, the armed liberation struggles in Portugal's former African colonies and in South Africa, peaceful demands for independence resisted by colonial powers and the Yalta proxy wars waged in Congo Kinshasa (currently the Democratic Republic of Congo), Namibia and Angola — Canada designed and implemented a strategy for development support that was bold and unprecedented. It enacted a policy of support for developing countries that cast them as partners who, to a large extent, set the agenda, unlike many European countries that sought to retain their colonial empires and prey on the very natural resources that countries from the south hoped to use to bolster their development. Canada's priorities, as we shall see later in detail, were an accurate reflection of the areas of social advancement that it had pursued for itself during the Pearson years. According to this view, newly independent countries in Africa, Asia and the Western Hemisphere deserved to attain social progress like any other part of the developed world. This strategy applied to the entire developing world and knew no significant boundary based on geography, ideology or Canadian economic interests. It was based on the postulate, still espoused today, that knowledge liberates.

Canada's development support over the past half century has, in many ways, played a path-breaking role in Africa in general, and francophone Africa in particular. Canada's bilingualism and the strong engagement of Quebec's academic and development communities give Canada a special role to play in francophone Africa. In spite of France's strong presence in its former African colonies and tendency to monopolize the academic and scientific agendas in these countries, Canada has initiated or provided support to a number of large educational and youth empowerment programs, such as the Ecole polytechnique de Thiès in Senegal, which it fully funded — construction, equipment, teaching staff and other current expenditures — for the training of engineers, as well as grants for francophone African students for tertiary studies in Canada and the program Jeunesse Canada Monde initiated by non-governmental organizations (NGOs) to facilitate exchanges between Canadian and francophone African youth.

It is important to stress that Canada's engagement cannot be explained by significant commercial interests in the region, which represent less than one percent of its foreign trade (Therrien, 1994). It stems more from the role of aid in Canada's overall foreign policy and a more specific desire on the part of the federal government to compete with Quebec's growing foreign policy independence, which began with the Quiet Revolution and was largely expressed through strong engagement in La Francophonie. The Organisation international de la Francophonie, often called La Francophonie, is an international organization of countries that use the French language or have a proximity with French culture. It is headquartered in Paris and has 56 member states, three associate members and 20 observers. Quebec is, to this day, one of the five core donors for the Agence universitaire de la Francophonie, which was founded in 1961 in Montreal and still has its headquarters there. Furthermore, roughly 50 percent of Quebec's current budget for "international solidarity programs" goes to francophone African countries (Government of Quebec, 2012).

## CANADA'S ARCHITECTURE FOR DEVELOPMENT RESEARCH SUPPORT IN FRANCOPHONE AFRICA

Is Canada's institutional system of development research support for francophone Africa complete and consistent? To answer this question, we analyze in turn the actors and then the objectives and strategies adopted. The key actors are the International Development Research Centre (IDRC), the Canadian International Development Agency (CIDA) and the Canadian Council for International Co-operation (CCIC).

The IDRC is Canada's primary tool for building research and policy capacity in francophone Africa, the third-largest source of development research funding in the world[1] and quite possibly the principal source in francophone Africa. Guided by the conviction that local researchers are best able to lead research on issues that concern their countries, the IDRC was created in 1970 to foster research and development research capacity at both the individual and institutional levels. Africa features strongly in the IDRC's activities, receiving roughly 40 percent of its CDN$171 million budget in 2010-2011, for example. From the beginning, it was recognized that — in addition to supporting pure scientific research on issues such as agricultural and information/communication technologies — policy analysis and policy debate between researchers and policy stakeholders in recipient countries must be encouraged. This effort has not always been easy in francophone African countries, given the long history of autocratic rule that afflicted many of them and discouraged healthy public policy debate, the weak tradition of scientific research in the university system, the fact that research was the purview of government-controlled institutes and the major financial difficulties faced by universities in the wake of the Structural Adjustment Programs (SAPs). But the research-policy debate has been improving gradually and, as a result, the role of the IDRC is becoming increasingly effective and appreciated because there is growing demand for research input in policy formulation.[2] It is also noteworthy that the IDRC's status as a Crown corporation gives it some independence from domestic political and government influence, although like CIDA, it is ultimately accountable to Canada's Parliament.

CIDA has a budget that is more than 20 times that of the IDRC. While capacity building in research and policy is not a major focus of its activities, Africa, which received roughly half of its total budget in 2011-2012, is. It is noteworthy, however, that only seven of CIDA's 20 current focus countries — "chosen based on their real needs, their capacity to benefit from aid, and their alignment with Canadian foreign policy priorities" (CIDA, 2011) — are African, of which only two —Mali and Senegal — are francophone. Unlike the IDRC, CIDA is a direct foreign policy tool for Canada.[3] CIDA has established a long-lasting and productive dialogue with African policy makers and other stakeholders. The priorities of national governments play a major part in CIDA's appropriations (CIDA, 2012) and there is a clear and continuous line of communication between African capitals and CIDA's headquarters, mediated by the national or regional offices of the agencies and bureaus for cooperation and support. CIDA's massive databases and monitoring instruments are useful in supplementing recipient countries' data collection efforts and provide a rich source of information for research and policy analysis. The latest policy move on the part of the federal government is to merge CIDA into the Department of Foreign Affairs and International Trade, seemingly to create more consistency between aid, trade and Canada's foreign direct investment. There is no doubt that this decision will raise questions about the altruistic motive of Canada's aid in Africa and elsewhere.

The CCIC is a coalition of Canadian NGOs that contributes to Canada's development support by conducting development research and publishing in areas of relevance to developing regions. It provides opportunities for North-South scientific collaboration and organizes many fora on development to which francophone researchers and policy stakeholders are convened. It can be argued that the CCIC maintains the scientific debate on development between Canada and its foreign partners.

In conclusion, it appears that Canada's architecture for development research support for francophone Africa is exhaustive and serves its stated goals well. But can we say as much for the objectives and strategies that it adopts?

## CANADA'S SUPPORT FOR ECONOMIC DEVELOPMENT POLICY IN FRANCOPHONE AFRICA

Given its predominant role in Canada's effort to build research and policy capacity in francophone Africa, the strategy adopted by IDRC, sometimes with the support of CIDA, will be our primary focus.

Canada's strategy for policy development support has consistently centred on empowerment and capacity building, which underscores its significant funding for educational initiatives and locally initiated research endeavours in francophone Africa. In the IDRC's own words: "In response to the worsening of sub-Saharan African economies during the 1980s, the Centre sought to expand its work in this part of Africa. In particular it focused on improving research capacity — skills that would strengthen the hand of African officials negotiating with the World Bank and the International Monetary Fund" (IDRC, 2010: 13-14).

Grant funding has historically been favoured over consultancy services to ensure that the selection of the topic, methodology and research team are the purview of the African side. The first sizable institutional grants in francophone Africa were given by the IDRC in the early 1990s to research centres such as the Centre ivoirien de recherchés économiques et sociales in Côte d'Ivoire, the Centre d'études, documentation et de recherche économiques et sociales in Burkina Faso and the Centre de recherche en économie appliquée in Senegal. This attempt at empowering francophone African institutions included the facilitation of joint meetings of researchers and policy makers aimed at encouraging dialogue between development stakeholders. The IDRC's collaboration with the commission of the Union économique et monétaire ouest-africaine on the regional integration agenda is an illustration of this policy.

In its effort to support development policy research, Canada signalled a strong desire for recipient countries to achieve social progress in the same areas that it pursued at home, although arguably, not to the same degree. The key research issues most supported by Canada in francophone Africa were health, education, youth and the fight against poverty. Two major projects, one focussing on research on the social welfare of households — Micro Impacts of Macro and Adjustment Policies (MIMAP) and its successor the Partnership for Economic Policy (PEP) — and the other on post-graduate economics training — Programme de troisième cycle interuniversitaire (PTCI), now called the Nouveau PTCI (NPTCI) — illustrate this point. MIMAP was initiated to examine how major economic reforms, such as the SAPs of the 1980s and 1990s, affected the daily lives of households in developing countries, first in Asia, and later (in the mid-1990s) extended to francophone Africa.

The successor to MIMAP — PEP — institutionalized and fostered a global partnership of development policy analysts straddling Africa, Asia and Latin America, with support from international experts from the South and North. Since 2002, PEP has quickly grown into an independent, multi-donor (including the IDRC and CIDA, as well as various international donors including the Australia Agency for International Development, DFID and the United Nations Development Programme) initiative to competitively fund policy-engaged and -relevant research on poverty and development issues throughout the developing world, and with a strong presence in francophone Africa. PEP is pushing beyond traditional capacity building in several ways. Much of this research has both been influenced by, and had influence on, policy makers and other stakeholders through a focus on building not only research capacities, but also skills in policy engagement.[4] Furthermore, PEP has been instrumental in assisting researchers to go beyond capacity building to effectively promote their participation in local and international policy debates and research initiatives, ensuring the attainment of a stronger voice for local researchers. MIMAP and PEP have been pioneers — in francophone Africa and the developing world as a whole — in generating and adapting innovative development policy analysis tools including community-based monitoring systems, locally led program/policy impact evaluations (notably a series of randomized control trials throughout Africa), multi-dimensional poverty measurement and macro-micro policy simulations.

Canadian support also featured the recognition of a need to increase the pool of researchers with modern and rigorous graduate training in economic policy analysis in francophone Africa. This challenged the long-held view, promoted by key donor organizations, that only primary education was important and should be the target of government funding over higher education. Scholarship programs allowed developing country researchers to pursue graduate studies in Canada. Foremost among these is CIDA's Canadian Francophonie Scholarship Program (CFSP), which was launched in 1986 at the first summit meeting of La Francophonie in Paris. This program has funded more than 2,000 researchers from eligible francophone countries, the vast majority of which are located in Africa. At the same time, the IDRC played a crucial role in helping create and promote an Africa-wide master's program in economics that raised and harmonized academic standards throughout francophone Africa.

Along with the graduate training programs fostered by the IDRC-initiated African Economic Research Consortium (AERC) from Nairobi — which services francophone African researchers to some degree — the NPTCI was designed and implemented, since 1992, to respond specifically to the advanced state of decay of francophone African universities that resulted from prolonged budgetary neglect during the SAP years. Based on the increasingly higher recruitment of the program's graduates by governments and regional organizations at professional and senior levels, the academic results were deemed very satisfactory and contributed to the significant enhancement of francophone African training in economics, including the inception of a Ph.D. program in economics for the most promising graduates. After 20 years of operation and more than 1,500 graduates, the NPTCI can be considered one of the best collective achievements of francophone universities in Africa.[5] However, Canadian universities did not seek to emulate US and South African universities, which have undertaken a new mode of academic collaboration with African countries that consists of organizing local degree-granting programs and sometimes offering African students the opportunity to receive part of their training abroad. Many US and South African institutions have opened campuses in various African countries over the last 20 years. This seems to indicate that the interests of Canadian authorities were misaligned with those of Canadian universities in francophone Africa. Indeed, while Canadian authorities have always valued direct intervention and partnership with local actors, Canadian universities, unlike their South African and US counterparts, did not establish a physical presence in Africa or specifically target francophone countries as potential partners.

One of the most innovative development support strategies, initiated in Africa by a number of donors including Canada, is the establishment of networks of developing country researchers, such as the AERC, MIMAP, PEP, NPTCI and Réseau de recherche sur les politiques industrielles (RPI) in the field of social sciences in francophone countries and the rest of Africa. The network configuration has been instrumental in helping francophone researchers escape the isolation of their own countries to interact with peers in other francophone Africa countries and, perhaps even more importantly, with peers in non-francophone Africa (AERC) and globally (PEP), with support from international experts from both the South and North.

In the same vein, the IDRC has been a pioneer in encouraging pooling of financial resources, in the form of a consortium or secretariat, on behalf of a specific project or organization: for example, the RPI and NPTCI in francophone Africa and the AERC, African Capacity Building Foundation (ACBF) and TrustAfrica for Africa as a whole. The secretariat format was embodied in Africa by the Secretariat for Institutional Support for Economic Research in Africa and the Think Tank Initiative. The secretariat formula has several desirable features. First, it ensures stable and closely monitored governance, but also a highly flexible and more ambitious program content and free entry/exit for donors. Second, it arouses a stronger sense of ownership for recipients, which is a positive trait for francophone researchers, who often feel left behind, even by their English-speaking African counterparts. Finally, its autonomy prepares it well for in-depth collaboration with other local organizations, a quality that needs to be further exploited in francophone Africa, where there is a high degree of fragmentation among researchers as well as research centres.

Canada's geographical coverage has capitalized on three synergistic features. First, the IDRC federated all francophone countries across Africa through support for the RPI, a network of francophone researchers that focussed on industrial policy, the Conférence des institutions d'enseignement et de recherchés économiques en Afrique and the NPTCI, the latter two comprising all the departments of economics in francophone Africa.

Canada's support for knowledge institutions also helped create the first scientific regional integration initiative with the inception of the West African Economic Association, a professional research network that grouped francophone and English-speaking West African economists. The same can be said for two other Pan-African research institutions, the AERC — which has made steady efforts to foster participation from francophone Africa — and the Council for the Development of Social Science Research in Africa. Through the ACBF, Canada provides funding to a wide array of African research institutions, many of them located in francophone countries.

Third, the IDRC's regional office in Dakar, Senegal, was, for over a generation, the only donor-funded, research-supporting facility based in a francophone African country, thus providing a valuable scientific bridge to the rest of the world and the benefits of the magnet for other donors that the IDRC constitutes on the international scene. In this context, its recent closure is cause for concern and the IDRC's commitment to the region requires careful monitoring. In other words, rethinking this decision of major institutional and political consequences would be a welcome development.

## CONCLUDING COMMENTS AND RECOMMENDATIONS

For quite some time, Canada's egalitarian approach to development support was spread too thinly across too many countries, which reduced its effectiveness. The current global financial crisis and budgetary restrictions at home should lead to a greater focus on a few worthy recipients, who would receive more funding support and, ultimately, serve as role models in their respective sub-regions.

The level of partnership between Canadian and francophone African institutions is too low to create proper synergy for development research. For example, CIDA's competition for grants given jointly to Canadian and knowledge institutions based in developing countries does not favour francophone institutions, considering their lack of international competitiveness.

So far, the IDRC and CIDA have displayed remarkable congruence in their support policies in the developing world in terms of geographical presence and budgetary appropriations. Arguably, while the IDRC, as a Crown corporation, has more independence than CIDA, especially with its recent integration into the Department of Foreign Affairs and International Trade, one can only hope that francophone Africa will continue to be a priority recipient region so that earlier gains can be safeguarded for both sides. If not, one may wonder whether Quebec, currently led by the separatist Parti Québécois, may take advantage of the void to become more engaged — especially in economic and social policy debates and research capacity development — as a way to affirm its nationalist ambitions and foreign policy independence.

Finally, Canada's strategy of leveraged funding through the inception of secretariats and other multi-donor initiatives has resulted in insufficient resource mobilization and could be enhanced, especially in the context of the current economic crisis that may force many donors to reduce their overseas development aid. In spite of all these achievements, the overriding context in francophone Africa is characterized by a weak tradition of research that is neither competitive internationally nor adequate for the training of young scholars and researchers. This leads to a vicious circle of training of future generations by poorly trained staff and research output that is inadequate — in quantity and quality — to serve as policy input. It also makes us question whether Canada is doing enough to encourage African national governments to value the role of research in policy formulation.

In light of the foregoing analysis, the search for improvements will not focus on how to do things better, but on what actions could help achieve Canada's long-term goals in development research support. The following recommendations naturally spring from Canada's decades-old aid paradigm on the one hand, and the current and future needs and aspirations that arise from francophone Africa's quest for development on the other hand.

The first recommendation is that Canada's previous unique contributions should galvanize its renewed commitment to building socio-economic policy research capacity in francophone Africa. This policy could take many forms and, perhaps, for the sake of efficiency, involve a broad-based dialogue with potential recipient countries and make use of fora such as La Francophonie.

The second recommendation is that in these efforts to support the emergence of local policy research capacity, Canada should continue to build on, and carry forward, past successes in creating and supporting tertiary education institutions in francophone Africa, possibly upscaling these to the sub-regional level, extending graduate scholarship programs, such as the CFSP, with widespread involvement of Canadian universities and directly fostering local socio-economic policy research and research capacity through more policy-engaged and scientifically supported research grant and networking activities.

Third, Canada's investment in local socio-economic policy research capacity is founded on the belief that enabled local researchers and research institutions can provide innovative and context-relevant solutions to development issues. This belief should carry over more to CIDA's program and policy work, both through more systematic integration of local expertise — supported through IDRC programs — in designing and implementing CIDA programs in the field, and through the promotion of greater use of local expertise by national governments and other bilaterals/multilaterals in national and international debates on development issues. Such a policy could contribute more effectively to a sea change in the design and evaluation of development policies and programs.

## Acknowledgements

We gratefully acknowledge research assistance from Stéphanie Maltais and comments from Elias Ayuk, Yiagadeesen Samy, Rohinton Medhora and participants at the Canada Among Nations authors' workshop, December 5-6, 2012, at CIGI, Waterloo, Canada.

## ENDNOTES

[1]  It is preceded by the Bill and Melinda Gates Foundation and the United Kingdom's Department for International Development (DFID). See Luc Mougeot (2012), speech given at the Le virage de l'aide publique canadienne au développement conference, November 15, Université Laval, Canada.

[2]  For example, in an external review, Tracy Tuplin (2003: 16) concluded that IDRC's support in Senegal contributed to "an internationally

recognized poverty reduction strategy that was owned by the Senegalese and revered by their neighbours."

3   "Canada's official development assistance advances Canada's foreign policy objectives: 1) increasing economic opportunity through international engagement; 2) mitigating security risks; and 3) promoting Canadian principles and values" (Government of Canada, 2012: 1).

4   See PEP (2013), *PEP Internal Monitoring and Evaluation Report.* February, available at: www.pep-net.org/fileadmin/medias/pdf/PEP_official_documents/M_E_report_Feb2013.final.pdf.

5   For further discussion of Canada's academic partnership with Africa, see the chapter by Jeffrey C. Fine and Peter Szyszlo.

## WORKS CITED

CIDA (2011). "Countries of Focus." Available at: www.acdi-cida.gc.ca/acdi-cida/ACDI-CIDA.nsf/eng/JUD-51895926-JEP.

———— (2012). "Aid Effectiveness Agenda." Available at: www.acdi-cida. gc.ca/acdi-cida/ACDI-CIDA.nsf/eng/FRA-825105226-KFT.

Government of Canada (2012). *Report to Parliament on the Government of Canada's Official Development Assistance 2011-2012.* Available at: www.acdi-cida.gc.ca/INET/IMAGES.NSF/vLUImages/Reports/$file/odaaa-2011-2012_eng.pdf.

Government of Quebec (2012). "Francophone Africa." Ministère des Relations internationales, de la Francophonie et du Commerce extérieur. Available at: www.mrifce.gouv.qc.ca/en/Solidarite-internationale/quebec-dans-le-monde/afrique-francophone.

IDRC (2010). *IDRC at 40: A Brief History.*

Therrien, Jean-Philippe (1994). Le Canada et l'Afrique francophone : jeu d'une puissance à la périphérie, *Présence africaine,* no 53: 145. Available at: www.politique-africaine.com/numeros/pdf/053143.pdf.

Tuplin, Tracy (2003). "The Influence of Research on Policy: The Case of MIMAP Senegal." December. Available at: http://web.idrc.ca/uploads/user-S/10799870931MIMAP_Senegal_FINAL_2004.doc.

# Academic Links between Canada and Africa

Jeffrey C. Fine and Peter Szyszlo

• • • • • • • • • • • • • • • • • • •

## INTRODUCTION

The nature and content of academic links between Canada and Africa are changing because of trends in higher education taking place globally, including both regions. The chapter begins by commenting briefly on three links: doctoral education; research; and institutional capacity building. However, our subsequent discussion focusses only on the first two because of their significance for the future development of strong academic links between Canada and Africa. Then we look at trends in higher education, first in Sub-Saharan Africa and secondly in Canada, to consider how they are affecting these academic links. Based on our observations, we propose, in the final section, a different strategic approach, which will be, in our view, required to sustain them over the coming decade.

## ACADEMIC LINKS BETWEEN CANADA AND AFRICA

Expanded access to high quality doctoral education is critical to the future of higher education in Sub-Saharan Africa. There is a severe shortage of qualified academics, worsened by the rapid expansion of undergraduate education. While explanations for this shortage have frequently cited conflicts in many countries, continuing "brain drain" and the ravages of HIV/AIDS, the principal cause has been insufficient investment to replace those academics trained between the 1960s and 1980s, let alone supply the increasing numbers required for current expanding demand.[1] A separate, but equally critical challenge is the quality of doctoral education, in particular, the need to move from what Professor Johann Mouton (2011) has termed the traditional "thin" doctoral program, focussing on thesis research, to the "thick" degree, comprising coursework and thesis, which has gained near global acceptance elsewhere.

**Figure 1: African University Head Count Enrollments, 2001 versus 2007**

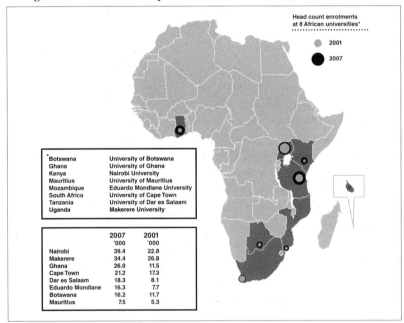

Source: Centre for Higher Education Transformation (CHET), 2013.

Looking beyond possible engagement in coursework, collaboration in thesis research is more likely to sustain academic links because of its mutual attraction to scholars in both Africa and Canada. Such research often takes place at the cutting edge of a discipline, forges lifelong ties (personal and intellectual) and, where properly supported and managed, can sustain longer-term shared inquiry into challenging problems. Such circumstances, of course, do not apply solely to partnerships between Canada and Africa. In the African case, however, they do signal a switch from more conventional modalities, notably formal doctoral scholarship programs based in Canadian institutions and funded principally from Canadian external assistance, if only for reasons of cost and numbers.[2]

Beyond research conducted as part of a doctoral program, there is a need to look afresh at other areas. In this regard, Africa must compete for the attention of Canadian institutions and academics that are attracted to compelling opportunities elsewhere, often with fewer constraints in terms of resources and access. Research in such areas as epidemiology, climate change and biodiversity remains globally important. The principal challenges lie in design and financing such research, because of the continuing reliance on financing from non-African sources. Without detracting from the support that has been provided by agencies, such as IDRC, future collaboration between African and Canadian researchers may be better assured by shifting support from external assistance, where support for research is typically a corollary of other development objectives toward mainstreaming it through those federal and provincial government programs that finance it directly. A proposal to this effect is set out in the concluding section of this chapter.

In order to complete this overview of partnerships, we briefly acknowledge links arising from projects designed to build institutional capacity. In practice, the majority are based on contractual arrangements, financed principally by development assistance and foundations, or by paying clients; one such example is support provided to the Botswana International University of Science and Technology by the Association of Universities and Colleges of Canada and the World University Service of Canada (Dutkiewicz, Fine and Nightingale, 2008). Undoubtedly, Canadian universities will continue to compete actively for such contracts, both in Africa and elsewhere. In this chapter, however, we focus on the first two, namely doctoral education and research, since they ultimately depend on shared intellectual, rather than commercial, motives. We first investigate whether there are converging interests in both areas between Africa and Canada. To answer this question, the next two sections examine some broad trends shaping higher education in each. In the final section, we posit the need for a new approach that can promote productive collaboration by taking advantage of shared intellectual and academic motivations.

## TRENDS AND INTERESTS: AFRICA

Africa is witnessing very rapid expansion in undergraduate education, an inevitable corollary of attempts to achieve universal primary education for a rapidly growing population, with ensuing unavoidable expansion of secondary education. Much of this growth is taking place within new, private for- and not-for-profit institutions. Furthermore, measured in real terms, government support for its own institutions has not kept pace with enrollment, leading to a decline in real support per student. Expanding entry of private providers has not been guided, in most countries, by a strategy based on longer-term policy objectives for higher education. Those graduates fortunate enough, because of their marks in school exams, to obtain one of the limited number of public scholarships, are often not free to select their own preferred university as opposed to a public one designated by the government educational authority. Private providers often confront an imposed ceiling on fees. At first glance, this practice would appear to protect students with intellectual potential but limited resources. In practice, it motivates providers to offer large classes in cheap disciplines, with underpaid instructors. More perniciously, it undercuts the motivation to innovate among a smaller number because of the predetermined amount available by way of fees (Mouton and Fine, 2011).

This market is also marked by other inconsistent practices. Non-government sponsors of universities must often conform to very detailed guidelines concerning institutional governance, internal administration and the provision of infrastructure.[3] Often, however, public authorities regulating higher education lack the resources, and in some cases mandate, to assess and enforce the quality of degree programs.

The most disturbing practice is pressure exerted on public universities to generate revenue through "parallel streams" of undergraduate students. The same course will be offered to two and sometimes three cadres, one being those receiving government support (in the form of scholarship students assigned to particular public universities), and others comprising "self-sponsored" (that is, fee paying students). Attempts by public universities to ring-fence their graduate programs and research by limiting undergraduate numbers are often thwarted by bureaucratic and political pressure to "expand access and revenue."[4] This practice is especially deleterious in light of the limited pool of qualified and underpaid staff. Teaching the same course two or three times, albeit with the added incentive of financial bonuses, leaves little energy for research and the supervision of graduate students.

The situation is not entirely bleak. In the face of these pressures and the absence of enlightened public policy and support, African academics have been able to innovate, typically but not always, with support from outsiders, in most instances foundations.[5] Two recent studies of African networks engaged in research and postgraduate education reveal an exciting range of activities across a gamut of disciplines and fields, and professional practice, including the pooling of scarce subject experts, experimentation in curriculum development, shared thesis supervision and the nurturing of research. Coverage is diverse: natural product chemistry, mathematics (applied and theoretical), human rights law, astrophysics, economics and agronomy, among others (Mouton and Fine, 2011; Fine and Szyszlo, 2008).

By and large, these efforts have been nurtured by the IDRC and various American foundations. For a decade, the latter coordinated their separate programs under the rubric of "The Partnership for Higher Education in Africa." Its operational weaknesses and, in the end, termination stem largely from the generic features of the differing ethos of the collaborating partners, the priority assigned by it to supporting both higher education and research in Africa, and the personalities heading it at a given time (Parker, 2010). Finally, its resources, even when pooled, are insufficient to address the needs of even a limited number of promising networks, and even less adequate because of the foundations' simultaneous need to respond to requests from major African universities.

Not surprisingly, the vast majority of these networks were either inspired by, or reliant upon, intellectual and administrative support of South African academics and institutions. While such capacities remain thinly drawn in relation to South Africa's own needs, this chapter notes the presence of some key features of the system, which will likely not appear in other African countries for decades to come. These include: significant and strategically determined support for higher education, as well as research within and outside academia; a network of research centres and institutes, within and outside universities; a robust, albeit small, pool of academics with strong links to Africa and beyond; motivation to conduct research, not least in terms of professional advancement and financial betterment; and a commitment to sound management (which is not always realized in practice).[6] Also important, for lack of a better term, is "intellectual entrepreneurship," articulated in a desire to form partnerships and initiate collaborative activities.[7] Of particular importance for the future of African higher education is the African Doctoral Academy's doctoral program, based at Stellenbosch University, which attempts to raise the quality and relevance of doctoral degree programs in South Africa and elsewhere.[8]

Such efforts, inadequate as they may be, offer a dramatic contrast to the lack of innovation in the official aid community. Those donors still engaged in higher education remain fixated on establishing, but typically not supporting operationally, centres of excellence, presumably in the hope of exploiting scalar economies and avoiding the normally high transactions costs entailed in launching aid projects. The fact that the African landscape is littered with the moribund products of earlier efforts has not inhibited some from contemplating a new effort, namely the Pan-Africa University, sponsored by the African Union.[9] Its political assignment of "hydrology and water management," at first to Libya and then with Colonel Gaddafi's demise, to Algeria, or of the proposed centre for social science to the University of Yaoundé, hardly a standout among African universities, should, but thus far has not, instill caution.[10] At the same time, the very sober recommendation of the African Ministerial Council on Science and Technology (AMCOST) initiative, to structure its research support along the lines of Networks of Centres of Excellence of Canada, has gone unnoticed.[11] One obvious explanation is the political priorities of donors. Another mundane, but perhaps more significant, cause is the difficulty that external actors, in particular the World Bank and European Union (as well as some bilateral donors), confront in actually mounting regional programs. Based on the authors' own experience, the alternative of supporting viable regional networks still remains a bridge too far.[12]

## CANADIAN TRENDS RELEVANT TO AFRICA

Higher education and research in Canada are actively responding to global trends. One manifestation is the proactive approach by most Canadian universities to "internationalize" through intense competition for foreign students, student and faculty exchanges, and global research networking. It is also recognized by the major federal agencies supporting research, which specifically provide for the inclusion of foreign students and scientists in Canadian-based initiatives.[13] There is strong interest in establishing partnerships in China, India and, to a lesser degree, Latin America, because of growing academic diasporas in Canadian institutions, intellectually stimulating collaborators and growing public support for research within these countries, from Canadian public sources and, in some fields, from the private sector. In this context, Canada-Africa collaboration, which once featured prominently in the international outreach of Canadian universities, has become far less significant. Indeed, it may soon be confined solely to the realm of "aid" given to worthy scholars, graduate scholarships in selected fields relevant to development, research supported through IDRC programs, attempts by the Canadian International Development Agency (CIDA) to engage Canadian universities in development, and to impressive, but under supported voluntary initiatives, such as Academics Without Borders Canada.[14] These efforts are worthy, but they lie far from the principal interests of Canadian universities and most leading academics. Consequently, ties with Africa are being marginalized by Canadian institutions and academics, not solely due to the lack of funds, but also the attraction being exerted by the newly emerging, as well as more "traditional," external destinations for academic partnerships and exchanges.

## FORGING STRONG ACADEMIC LINKS BETWEEN AFRICA AND CANADA: THE NEED FOR A NEW APPROACH

Responding to the danger of growing marginalization is not simply a question of more resources, although these are always welcomed by academics, Canadians and Africans alike. What is required is a new approach. Its premise is that linkages need to be recast, not as "development assistance," but rather toward the mainstreaming of links with Africans within higher education and, more specifically, research. Partnerships cannot be sustained where there is an absence of intellectual symmetry and a dearth of mutually attractive problems. The case for links between Canada and Africa can be advanced on its own academic merits: interesting and important research issues; good people to work with; solid contributions to global and regional knowledge; and the existence of a strong portal, namely South African institutions and research centres with their own networks and ties elsewhere in the subcontinent. This latter consideration is important in terms of avoiding the high transaction costs entailed in identifying counterpart scholars and conducting research in difficult settings. Another advantage is the IDRC — a unique Canadian organization with a research mandate, a high reputation across the region and with proven mechanisms for facilitating research and collaboration.

We propose that the major federal funders of research, including the Natural Sciences and Engineering Research Council of Canada, the Canadian Institutes of Health Research and the Social Sciences and Humanities Research Council, add what may be called a "global bonus" to their current grant programs. In addition to responding to requests for proposals by these bodies, applicants would have the option of submitting a second proposal for a global bonus grant. The latter would only be opened and reviewed if the institution's principal submission won the grant in question on its own merits. The global bonus proposal would be directly linked to the proposed research, but could expand upon it in one or more of the following ways:

- geographical extension and/or elaboration of the principal research directions;
- links to regional networks;
- student and staff exchanges; and
- doctoral fellowships.

An additional possibility could be linkages, within research supported by the principal grant, with Canadian firms actively partnering with the Canadian research community.[15] Such links are totally undeveloped in Africa (outside South Africa) and many other poor countries. Practical exposure by African scholars may eventually result in a more proactive and entrepreneurial approach by their own institutions.

The cost of global bonus grant supplements could be partially defrayed from funds currently allocated to CIDA's university cooperation program, which has generally proven cumbersome and ineffectual, especially since excellence in research and higher education is not an organizational priority for CIDA. A small proportion of these funds would also be better spent on such dynamic, grassroots initiatives as Academics without Borders or MBAs

Without Borders. Rollout of activities financed from the global bonus could be facilitated in various ways by the IDRC, including the identification of promising researchers and institutions, logistics, collaboration with parallel efforts and clearances for research. Finally, the global bonus grants supplement should not be confined to Africa, but extended to what may be classified as "underprovided regions," according to criteria that measure capacities for research and doctoral education.[16]

This new approach, based on placing support for research and post-doctoral education within the mainstream of Canada's own support for these activities, will help preserve and nurture mutually productive links between Africa and Canada over the coming decades.

## ENDNOTES

[1] See William S. Saint (1992), "Universities in Africa: Strategies for Stabilization and Revitalization," Technical Paper No. 194, The World Bank, for an insightful prediction anticipation of the pending crisis in African Higher Education. See also Figure 1 for growth of eight major African universities.

[2] For example, the International Development Research Centre's (IDRC's) Canadian partnership branch confines its support for African postgraduate students to African universities.

[3] The National Universities Commission of Nigeria, for example, sets out very detailed guidelines for the layout of a "university farm" for learning and research. The Uganda Higher Education Act specifies the positions and job descriptions of senior university staff for private as well as public institutions.

[4] Personal exchanges with then-Vice Chancellors of the University of Ghana, University of Ibadan and University of Dar Es Salaam, March/ April, 2010.

[5] We would characterize IDRC as a Canadian public foundation in this regard.

[6] For example, the University Science, Humanities and Engineering Partnerships in Africa network, comprising eight universities in eastern and southern Africa, has still not been able to devolve significant thesis supervision and coursework from the University of Cape Town to the

other seven (non-South African) members. For a mid-term analysis of the associated issues and constraints, see J.C. Fine and N. Warner (2004), *External Evaluation of the University Science Humanities and Engineering Partnerships in Africa Program.*

[7]  Partnership offices in major South African universities are much better resourced and managed than those in other parts of Sub-Saharan Africa.

[8]  See: http://sun025.sun.ac.za/portal/page/portal/Arts/ADA.

[9]  See: www.pau-au.org/home.jsp.

[10]  See World University News (2011), December 18, Issue No. 87.

[11]  AMCOST, which is serviced by the African Union, is responsible for implementing the Africa's Science And Technology Consolidated Plan Of Action (drafted by the New Partnership for Africa's Development in 2005).

[12]  The case for supporting such regional networks is set out in J.C. Fine and J. Mouton (2011), *World Bank Support for Regional Post-Graduate Education and Research Networks: A Project Concept Note.* One exception to the absence of donor engagement is economics where there has been strong continuing support for the African Economic Research Consortium as well as the Partnership for Economic Policy network (see the chapter by John Cocburn and Diéry Seck for a description of this). However, both efforts remain totally dependent on external support — in the case of the IDRC for more than two decades.

[13]  For example, the Social Sciences and Humanities Research Council whose grants provide for the inclusion of non-Canadian scholars.

[14]  See: www.awbc-usfc.org.

[15]  One example has been the attempt by the University of Toronto's MaRS program to promote commercial exploitation of products resulting from health research in Rwanda. See K. Simiyu et al. (2010). "Science-Based Health Innovation In Rwanda: Unlocking The Potential Of A Late Bloomer BMC," *International Health and Human Rights* Vol. 10: Suppl 1.

[16]  Such criteria can be developed from metrics used by the IDRC/Hewlett Think Tank Initiative to select research institutes for longer-term support. The Initiative's purview could be extended to cover university departments.

# WORKS CITED

CHET (2013). "African Higher Education: Open Data." Available at: http://chet.org.za/data/african-he-opendata.

Dutkiewicz, P., J. Fine and M. Nightingale (2008). *Academic Programming and Structure Report for the Botswana International University of Science and Technology.* August.

Fine, J. and P. Szyszlo (2008). *The Partnership For Higher Education In Africa: Network Study.*

Mouton, Johann (2011). "The State of Post-graduate Training in Sub-Saharan Africa: Challenges and Approaches." PowerPoint presentation, February.

Mouton, J. and J. Fine (2011). *World Bank Support for Regional Post-Graduate Education and Research Initiatives and Networks In Sub-Saharan Africa.* Report. June 25.

Parker, Susan (2010). *Lessons From a Ten-Year Funder Collaborative: A Case Study of the Partnership for Higher Education in Africa.* New York: Clear Thinking Communications Report for the Partnership for Higher Education in Africa. Available at: www.foundation-partnership.org/pubs/pdf/phea_case_study.pdf.

# Conclusion

## Gerald Helleiner

● ● ● ● ● ● ● ● ● ● ● ● ● ● ● ● ● ●

As rich and varied a collection of essays as those in this volume is obviously difficult to summarize. The different foci and perspectives they display can certainly elicit enormous admiration and respect; but they also bring to mind the Indian folk tale of the blind man and the elephant. Each author's conclusion is inevitably influenced by the particular part of the Africa-Canada "anatomy" subjected to his or her touch. Depending upon the specific area of analysis, Canada-Africa relationships, past and future, can legitimately be seen in a variety of ways. Yet, despite many differences, there are some common themes or directions that seem to run persistently, however frequent the diversions, throughout this volume. They also featured in lively discussion among the authors when they met.

First, an underlying, but recurrent, element both in this volume and, even more, in the authors' interactions among themselves, has been the expression of the continuing need for informed and objective analysis of Africa-Canada relationships in all of their dimensions, and availability of such analysis to the public and to policy makers both in Canada and in Africa. No doubt calls for objective analysis are fairly common themes among academics; they frequently conclude their papers and conferences with appeals for further research. In this instance, however, the concern expressed is different — more broadly based, more concerned about the prospect and more serious in its implications. The call for the continuation of independent policy-relevant analysis comes not only from academia but also, tellingly, from representatives of civil society and business, and even from erstwhile public servants. In Africa, the scarcity of such informed and independent analyses is chronic but, given the continent's skill shortages, understandable. In Canada there can be no such excuses. Under the present Government of Canada, a relative "chill" on critical analysis has developed. Independent evidence-based analysis of the federal government's policies has not always been encouraged. On the contrary, whether within public institutions or civil society, many informed analysts are now reluctant, as rarely before, to express critical views publicly. Threats of reduced governmental funding and/or elimination of tax benefits for civil society organizations, and a clampdown upon public servants' reporting of potentially inconvenient research results or views, have had a deleterious effect on the potential for informed public discussion of controversial policy issues. Many of the contributions in this volume are quite critical of Canadian governmental policies, present and past. It is important in any free society that such open criticism be encouraged and welcomed. Critical voices, not least in this instance, African voices and those of their Canadian partners, must continue to be heard. On this, all the authors agree.

Before turning to some of the substantive themes in this volume's analyses of Canada-Africa relationships, it is important to emphasize the enormous diversity of African experience. As is wearily and repeatedly expressed by Africans themselves, facing unfortunately too-frequent limitations in Canadians' knowledge, "Africa is not a country." At last count, Sub-Saharan Africa, with which this volume is primarily concerned, contained 51 national political units (countries) and a wide range of regional bodies. These countries' resources, cultures, histories and more recent experiences are highly varied. There are some very large countries, for example, Nigeria, and many more tiny ones, such as The Gambia. Their economic prospects differ markedly. There are unique concerns in a number of landlocked countries. And so it goes. It follows that any generalizations about Africa or Africa-Canada relations need to be offered, if at all, only with great care and appropriate caveats.

## CHANGING AFRICA

The most important theme, reflected in this volume's title, is the incredible extent of change which has taken place on the African continent over the past

50 years, and perhaps most dramatically within the most recent decade. Still prevalent in much of the media and the Canadian (and other Northern) public consciousness is the image of a "dark continent," mired in deep poverty, civil strife and political disarray. Yet, whether or not such a depiction was ever fair, it has been very far from reality in most of Africa for many decades. There have been incredible social achievements in Africa in the post-independence period — probably unprecedented in their dimensions and pace in human history — as measured, for instance, by infant and child mortality, life expectancy, literacy, numeracy and higher educational attainments. Political democracy and a free press are developing and strengthening in many African countries. An urban educated middle class is emerging and looks set to grow; some of its members now reside in a growing diaspora in Canada. These and other positive changes, not least higher commodity prices in recent years, have at long last generated rapid economic growth in a large number of African countries. Foreign investment has been flowing into Africa, particularly in the resource sector, in increased volume. Demographic prospects are potentially highly favourable, as expected declines in the birth rate generate significantly reduced dependency rates (higher proportions of the population of working age). Technological improvements, both "catching up" and on the frontier, bid fair to generate further positive effects. Far from the widespread "Afro-pessimism" of the 1980s there is a new, sometimes almost euphoric sense, both within Africa and abroad, of an "Africa rising." A recent Organisation for Economic Co-operation and Development (OECD) conference, for instance, was entirely devoted to the topic of "ascending Africa."

True, there are still problems enough — HIV/AIDS, corruption, civil wars, imperfect leadership, weak institutions, inadequate infrastructure and continuing poverty — and many have been addressed in this volume. Moreover, much of the recent accelerated growth is unfortunately unaccompanied by real structural change or poverty reduction. Nor is there any guarantee that rapid economic growth can be sustained. Some of the recent near-euphoria about the African future is undoubtedly overdone. A lot can still go wrong, and even if the overall trends are positive there are bound to continue to be many glitches and setbacks. Climate change is expected to deliver serious negative consequences for African agriculture and public health, and there are serious unaddressed environmental concerns surrounding Africa's current growth path. African exports remain highly vulnerable to global economic circumstances and commodity prices may not be sustained. If opportunities for productive employment do not materialize, notably in smallholder agriculture and the rural economy, the potential dividend from demographic change can instead generate massive youth unemployment and underemployment in Africa's urban areas, with its serious by-products of social malaise and political discontent. Ethnic division, civil strife and state fragility are bound to continue to be serious impediments to progress in many corners of the continent. Yet, when all is said and done, there is indeed a new Africa emerging, and Canada will have to respond to it.

## CHANGE IN CANADA-AFRICA RELATIONSHIPS

The new and emerging Africa — with its rich natural resources, improved skill base, more self-confident political institutions and, above all, its more solid economic prospects — is real, and must imply a change in the nature of its relationships with the rest of the world...and with Canada. For better or worse, Canadians will be paying more attention to Africa. Recent and forthcoming change in Canada-Africa relationships is a second major theme of these papers.

Relationships with Africa in the immediate post-independence period were motivated, on the Canadian side, primarily by charitable impulses — a desire to help in a remote and needy part of the world — reflecting traditional Canadian values. Political and commercial objectives were never completely absent from Canadian governmental policy making, but the principal concerns at that time were to assist newly independent countries with their development and "nation building" — attempting to reduce poverty, investing in education and health, strengthening economies, peacekeeping, and promoting democracy and human rights. The principal policy instrument was official (government-to-government) development assistance, and civil society organizations were both active and influential in the provision of this Canadian assistance. Canada's relatively modest international presence, and its lack of a colonial past seemed to render its aid less suspect and more welcome than that of the former colonial or stronger powers. In these respects, Canada shared some of the attributes of the so-called "like-minded" in Scandinavia and the Netherlands. Moreover, Canada's bilingualism provided entrée to a wider range of African countries than most other Western countries enjoyed, and was especially valued in pan-African institutions.

The first, and probably most important, policy-related message of this volume's authors is that this past approach has begun noticeably to change, and indeed must in future change further. With independent African governments and people more self-confident and assertive, and as African economies further strengthen, the aid-based and implicitly patronizing relationships of the past cannot remain dominant. The enormous changes in Africa require new Canadian approaches, and probably new policy and institutional instruments in every sphere of Canada-Africa relationships. In particular, commercial opportunities, potentially of mutual benefit to Canada and Africans, are now far more prominent, indeed probably already dominant, in overall Canada-Africa relationships. These will require new policies to ensure that this potential is maximized, or at least not squandered or damaged by unnecessary international disagreements and dispute.

In the extractive industry sector, in which Africa is rich in resources and Canadian mining companies are particularly prominent, it is essential that rules and practices are developed both by private firms and by governments to generate positive developmental effects from their investments and reduce the prospect of further examples of a "resource curse." As the details of such agreements are negotiated on a case-by-case basis, there will be a high premium on analytical, bargaining, monitoring and contract enforcement capacities in African governments; unfortunately, such capacities remain weak or absent in many instances. Corporate social responsibility is admirable, but in the face of responsibility to shareholders can only go so far. A clear responsibility, therefore, rests with the Government of Canada to ensure such aspects of these arrangements as complete transparency of Canadian firms' contracts and payments, full protection of African human and economic rights, fair shares of revenues accruing to the host African countries, and implementation of other measures needed to promote local development and protect the local environment. Failure of Canadian companies and concomitant Canadian governmental passivity in these spheres can poison relationships for decades to come. There probably exists no more important potential source of Canada-Africa misunderstanding, disagreement and interest conflict. It will be critically important to the future of Canada-Africa relationships to get these rules and arrangements right, and to implement them to mutual benefit.

Canadian civil society organizations will also have to adapt, as many already have done, so as to meet the changed needs and sensitivities of their African partners. The growing African diaspora in Canada will be seeking an enhanced role as well, and the new opportunities for fruitful collaboration it creates will offer fresh challenges for Canadian partnerships in Africa. Aid relationships are also changing; as will be seen below, some of the elements of the appropriate direction for change therein will continue to be contested.

## TENSION WITHIN THE CANADIAN RESPONSE

The papers in this volume reveal significant tension within the Canadian body politic as to how best to respond to the new Africa and its growing opportunities for Canadian commercial gain. This tension is most obvious in the struggle over the policies of the Canadian International Development Agency (CIDA), now rolled into the new Department of Foreign Affairs, Trade and Development (DFATD). At its baldest, the question is: in the potential conflict between the interests of Canada's African partners and Canadian interests, whose are to be assigned priority? This is by no means a new issue. Nor is it a purely Canadian one. It is a third common theme of this volume.

China, Brazil and other new Southern suppliers of development assistance have made much of the mutual benefits in their activities on the African continent, which they contrast with more patronizing Western approaches to Africa. But the mutual interest rationale has also long been found in traditional aid sources. It should go without saying that there is a profound longer-term global (and Canadian) interest in the development of poor countries in Africa (and elsewhere). Reduced poverty and improved institutions abroad will contribute to a more politically and economically stable, more sustainable and healthier planet. This has long been motivation enough for the post-World War II international development project. This mutual interest argument for Northern assistance for Southern development has a long history, extending back at least to the Pearson report of 1969 and, later, emphasized in the Brandt Commission report of 1980. Properly understood, then, assistance to African progress is, and always has been, broadly in Canada's self-interest.

When it comes to the specifics of official development assistance and other Canadian governmental relationships with Africa, however, there are choices to be made. Political and commercial objectives have always played some role in CIDA's African aid practice, but, as already noted, they have not dominated them. As the commercial opportunities for Canadian business in Africa continue to expand, so do the political pressures upon the Government of Canada's overseas development programs to assist with their realization. Canadian companies are particularly active in Africa's extractive industries, and the current government has clearly (and controversially) been responsive to their concerns. Under an act of Parliament, CIDA was required to seek the reduction of poverty as its primary goal. Can and should the mandate for Canadian development assistance increasingly now extend, as the current aid minister has proclaimed, to the pursuit of Canadian business interests? This is controversial and politically contested ground.

As both developing countries and Northern aid agencies gained more experience with their interrelationships, and as Southern policy makers gained new confidence and capacity, aid relationships began to change. At a series of meetings over the past decade in Rome, Paris, Accra and Busan, commitments were made by OECD members, including Canada, not only to recognize but also to promote African "ownership" of their own development programs. Among other reforms, they also committed themselves to align more effectively their aid contributions to local programs and priorities. These and other promises to reform aid practices, although not as yet very effectively delivered, were designed to make their inputs more supportive of Africans' own development objectives. Clearly, these commitments are inconsistent with a new emphasis on commercial objectives in Canadian official development assistance.

The Canadian private sector can be an important contributor to Africans' pursuit of development objectives, with or without cooperation from official development assistance (such as recently recommended by a Conservative-majority House of Commons report as well as the relevant minister). The consensus among authors in this volume is that while Canadian companies may often work with the government in pursuit of its objectives, now interpreted as more coincident with African ones, it is best for Canadian commercial objectives to be pursued via governmental institutions and policy instruments other than those providing poverty-oriented development assistance. Otherwise, confusion and dispute over aid policy is bound to ensue. In general, it is a well-established theoretical policy principle that when there are two policy objectives, efficiency requires that there be two policy instruments to pursue them. A recent study of these very issues, done for the Norwegian Parliament, states the matter most clearly:

> The primary objective of Norwegian development policy is to assist developing countries to pursue policies that will promote their economic and social development. Norway's policies in other areas are chiefly aimed at promoting interests of importance for our own development. In the interface between these two objectives, conflicts of interests will arise: initiatives that serve Norwegian interests may have adverse effects on developing countries and vice versa...
>
> Making Norwegian policy more coherent for development means, first of all, acknowledging the problems involved and increasing awareness of conflicts of interest. Secondly, it means striving to ensure that Norwegian and international policies promote development in poor countries, also outside the framework of development cooperation, as long as this does not clash unduly with the interests that Norway's policies are primarily intended to safeguard. (Norwegian Ministry of Foreign Affairs, 2011)

It is a similar clarity that our authors seek for Canada. Current Canadian aid policies are inconsistent and confused. Perhaps an independent study of these issues as they pertain to Canadian development cooperation programs, and Africa in particular, could be helpful in achieving it.

## THE NEED FOR COHERENT STRATEGY IN CANADIAN POLICY TOWARDS AFRICA

A related further theme in this volume relates to Canadian policy toward Africa more generally. Over the post-independence years, authors regretfully agreed that the Canadian government's overall approaches — political-diplomatic, economic, immigration, military — have typically been episodic, uncoordinated, ad hoc and directed at relatively short-run problems and results. At the official level, there has been little sign or sense of longer-term commitment to Africa, and certainly no coherent strategy for Canadian relations with Africa. African governments and peoples, therefore, have little basis for their expectations, if any, of a Canadian role or relationship in their future, let alone for any trust in them. They now have more external sources of finance and expertise than ever before. Canada is not one of the most prominent players in the international arena, and Africans have no compelling reason for interacting with such a middle-sized power. Why should they choose Canadian companies, civil society organizations or DFATD with which to build relationships?

This official incoherence and inconsistency is undesirable and unnecessary. Indeed, this volume's authors record several examples of exactly the kind of enduring and productive Africa-Canada relationship that is so lacking at higher levels. The Canadian institutions involved have demonstrated the patience, humility and specificity implicit in any trusting and mutually beneficial long-term relationship. They have not been fixated, as too many current would-be "fixers" still are, on immediate or short-term results. To borrow others' phraseology, they have sought to "grow oak trees not sunflowers." Among the examples of such successes cited in these pages are those in university-led health research, a variety of church and other civil society organizations, the Kimberley Process for "conflict diamonds" (which also demonstrated the potential for effective collaboration among business, civil society and government) and, of course, the many African activities of the International Development Research Centre.

Consensus among the authors at their meeting, and reflected in this volume, is that Canada-Africa relations and diplomacy would benefit from the development of a coherent, consistent and transparent framework for future interaction — a longer-term strategy for relations with Africa — on the part of the Government of Canada. (Arguably, this could be useful in other areas of Canadian foreign policy as well. But the authors' consensus is that the need is particularly urgent in the previously relatively neglected African case at this time of significant change.) Nuanced and textured to reflect the variety on the African continent, and reflective both of African and Canadian long-term interests and perspectives, it could both generate greater mutual gains and contribute to the building of greater mutual trust. It should incorporate assessments, intentions and principles governing cooperation in such spheres as trade in goods and services, investment, cultural exchange, illicit capital flows, migration, migrant remittances, official development assistance, peacekeeping, security and peace building, and diplomatic relations in general. In some spheres, there could usefully be added, either within the strategy statement or in separate model agreements, the specifics necessary to translate general policies and principles into actual practice. (This could be especially valuable in the controversial and often tortured area of bilateral investment treaties, where far more than traditional investor rights and "protection" are likely in future to be at issue.) A comprehensive strategy should also address intentions and principles governing Canada's continuing utilization of multilateral institutions, notably the United Nations, World Bank and African Development Bank, as vehicles for engagement and the pursuit of its strategic objectives in Africa. However difficult it may at present seem to achieve it, continuity and credibility of any such officially promulgated strategy would obviously demand bipartisan political support. Particularly, could such a strategy be valuable now that Canada is no longer able to rest on its Pearsonian reputation and its behaviour has become much less predictable. Only with a transparent and predictable road map for future relations may Africans begin to understand, and even trust, Canadian intentions.

## Acknowledgement

I am very grateful for the contributors' comments and suggestions on the preliminary ramblings I offered at the conclusion of the authors' meeting. They have greatly improved the product.

## WORK CITED

Norwegian Ministry of Foreign Affairs (2011). *Report to the Storting (the Norwegian Parliament) on Policy Coherence for Development 2011.* Available at: www.regjeringen.no/upload/UD/Vedlegg/Utvikling/0412_report_policy_coherence_for_development.pdf.

# Contributors

• • • • • • • • • • • • • • • • • • • • • • • •

**Edward Ansah Akuffo** (edward.akuffo@ufv.ca) teaches international relations in the Department of Political Science at the University of the Fraser Valley, in British Columbia. He holds a Ph.D. in international relations from the University of Alberta, an M.A. in international relations from Brock University and a B.A. in political science from the University of Ghana, Legon. His research focusses on Canada's foreign and security policy in Africa, inter-regional security cooperation, human security and humanitarian law in Africa, and emerging economies-Canada relations. He is the author of the recent book, *Canadian Foreign Policy in Africa: Regional Approaches to Peace, Security, and Development* (2012), and he was a fellow of the Canadian Consortium on Human Security.

**Hany Besada** (hbesada@nsi-ins.ca) is theme leader and senior researcher of the Governance of Natural Resources Program at the North-South Institute in Ottawa. In November 2012, he was seconded to the United Nations in New York, where he joined an international team of researchers on the High-level Panel Secretariat to advise on the global development agenda beyond 2015. Previously, he was program leader and senior researcher at The Centre for International Governance Innovation (CIGI) in Waterloo. He is currently pursuing a Ph.D. at the University of Warwick in the United Kingdom.

**David R. Black** (david.black@dal.ca) is Lester B. Pearson Professor of International Development Studies, professor of political science and director of the Centre for Foreign Policy Studies at Dalhousie University. He has published widely on Canada's involvement in Sub-Saharan Africa, including issues of development assistance, human security, human rights, diplomacy and extractive industry investment.

**Chris Brown** (chris_brown@carleton.ca) is associate professor of political science at Carleton University in the field of comparative politics, with a specialization in the politics of southern Africa. He was one of the founding members of the Institute of African Studies at Carleton and will serve as its director in 2013-2014. He has worked for several years as a development planner in Botswana and on regional relations in southern Africa. He is currently working on a book on the institutionalization of democracy in Botswana, which is funded by a research grant from the Social Sciences and Humanities Research Council.

**Stephen Brown** (brown@uottawa.ca) is associate professor of political science at the University of Ottawa. He is the editor of *Struggling for Effectiveness: CIDA and Canadian Foreign Aid* (2012) and the author of numerous publications on foreign aid, democratization, political violence, peace building and transitional justice, mainly in relation to Sub-Saharan Africa. In 2013, he was a senior fellow at the Centre for Global Cooperation Research, University of Duisburg-Essen, Germany.

**David Carment** (david_carment@carleton.ca) is full professor of international affairs at the Norman Paterson School of International Affairs (NPSIA), Carleton University; fellow of the Canadian Defence and Foreign Affairs Institute; and research associate at the University of Otago's National Centre for Peace and Conflict Studies.

**John Cockburn** (jcoc@ecn.ulaval.ca) is the executive director of the Partnership for Economic Policy and professor at Laval University in Québec since 2002. He holds a Ph.D. in economics from Oxford University (Nuffield College and the Centre for the Study of African Economies). His areas of specialization include child welfare, policy modelling and trade policy analysis. He has been involved in training and technical support to developing country researchers throughout the developing world since 1990. He is associate editor of the *International Journal of Microsimulation*.

**Dacia Douhaibi** (douhaibi@yorku.ca) is currently a Ph.D. student at York University studying transnational migration in the Department of Geography. Most recently, she attended NPSIA at Carleton University.

**David C. Elder** (david.elder@queensu.ca) is an adjunct professor and fellow in the School of Policy Studies of Queen's University, where he teaches in the Master of Public Administration program. He worked in the Privy Council Office for more than 10 years and has served as Assistant Secretary to the Cabinet, Machinery of Government. In the 25 years he served in the Department of Foreign Affairs and International Trade, he was the Department's senior assistant to the minister and director of international economic relations, and had foreign assignments in the Canadian Embassy in Dakar, Sénégal, the Canadian High Commission in Harare, Zimbabwe, and as Deputy Permanent Representative of Canada to the Organisation for Economic Co-operation and Development (OECD). He is now also a consultant on public policy and public administration reform.

**Jeffrey C. Fine** (jcfine@telepraxis.com), a professional economist, has worked on different aspects of African development for more than four decades. He has consulted to various multilateral and bilateral agencies, and foundations on education projects and strategic reviews in southern, eastern and francophone Africa. His engagement in higher education and research has included design and rollout of the African Economic Research Consortium and the Collaborative Regional Masters in Agricultural and Applied Economics, surveys of regional academic networks for the Partnership for Higher Education in Africa and the World Bank (with Peter Szyszlo and Johann Mouton), and most recently, technical support to the Partnership for African Social Governance and Research.

**Gerald Helleiner** (ghellein@sympatico.ca) is professor emeritus, economics and distinguished research fellow, Munk School of Global Affairs, University of Toronto. He has written widely on international trade, finance and development, particularly with reference to Africa. His work in Africa has included posts in the Universities of Ibadan and Dar es Salaam; responsibilities in the African Economic Research Consortium, African Capacity Building Foundation and Partnership for African Social and Governance Research; service on the UN Secretary-General's expert groups on African debt and commodity problems; and numerous consultancies. In Canada, he has served on the boards of the North-South Institute, International Development Research Centre (IDRC), and International Lawyers and Economists Against Poverty.

**Paul Hitschfeld** (paulfeld@sympatico.ca) has worked in international development since 1970. He started as a science teacher in the Democratic Republic of Congo, and since then has also lived in Tanzania and Ethiopia.

Mr. Hitschfeld worked for the Canadian International Development Agency (CIDA). He has managed programs in Asia, Central America, the Caribbean, Africa, the Middle East and Eastern Europe. He has been on mission to over 40 countries, including 30 countries in Africa. Since his retirement from CIDA, Mr. Hitschfeld now teaches a course on international development issues at Carleton University and works closely with two non-governmental organizations (NGOs), the Trade Facilitation Office of Canada and the Africa Study Group.

**Evan Hoffman** (ehoffman@ciian.org) is the executive director of the Canadian International Institute of Applied Negotiation located in Ottawa, Canada. He has published numerous articles on the themes of conflict prevention and resolution, peace building and mediation, and he has provided consulting services on these topics to the Carter Center, the United Nations, the European Union, the Ottawa Police Service, St. Lawrence College (Cornwall), the Vietnamese Ministry of Justice and others.

**David J. Hornsby** (david.hornsby@wits.ac.za) is a lecturer in international relations at the University of the Witwatersrand, Johannesburg. He maintains research interests in Canada-South Africa relations, the international political economy of trade conflict, middle powers and large class pedagogy. In May 2012, he hosted a colloquium on the Canada-South Africa relationship. Mr. Hornsby is the recipient of the 2013 Faculty of Humanities Teaching and Learning Award, lead editor of *Large Class Pedagogy: Interdisciplinary Perspectives for Quality Education* (forthcoming 2013), and sole author of *Risk, Science and Interests in Transatlantic Trade* (forthcoming 2013).

**Philip Martin** (philmartin54@gmail.com) is a program support officer with Norwegian People's Aid, and formerly a research assistant for the North-South Institute's Governance of Natural Resources Program. He has previously worked for the Canadian Department of Foreign Affairs and International Trade, CANADEM and the Canadian International Council. He received his M.A. from NPSIA, Carleton University, and is beginning doctoral studies in political science at the Massachusetts Institute of Technology (MIT).

**The Right Honourable Paul Martin** entered the Canadian government in 1993 as minister of finance, becoming prime minister in 2003. In these positions he dealt extensively with the question of the debt of the Heavily Indebted Poor Countries, elementary school education in Africa emphasizing the education of girls and gender equality, and the humanitarian tragedy of Darfur. On leaving government, he co-chaired the High Level Panel for the African Development Bank (AfDB) on the future role of the AfDB, and today chairs the Congo Basin Forest Fund, which focusses on poverty alleviation and the protection of the second-largest tropical forest in the world. He is one of two non-Africans on the board of the Coalition for Dialogue on Africa, a think tank sponsored by the African Union, the ADB and the United Nations Economic Commission for Africa.

**Rohinton Medhora** (rmedhora@cigionline.org) joined CIGI as president in 2012 after having served on CIGI's International Board of Governors since 2009. Previously, he was vice president of programs at IDRC. He received his doctorate in economics in 1988 from the University of Toronto, where he also subsequently taught for a number of years. Mr. Medhora's fields of expertise are monetary and trade policy, international economic relations and aid effectiveness. He has published extensively on these issues, and in addition to his association with the Canada Among Nations series, is currently co-editing (with Bruce Currie-Alder, Ravi Kanbur and David Malone) a history of development thought and practice to be published in early 2014.

**Bruce Montador** (bruce.montador@gmail.com) is a senior fellow at the Graduate School of Public and International Affairs at the University of Ottawa. From 2007 to 2011, he was executive director for Canada (as well as China, Korea and Kuwait) at the African Development Bank. Prior to that, he was vice-president, Multilateral Programs Branch, CIDA. From 1997 to 2002, he was general director, International Trade and Finance at the Department of Finance, Ottawa. Most of his earlier career was spent with the Bank of Canada (where his last post was chief, Financial Markets Department) and the OECD. He did graduate work in economics at Queen's University after a Ph.D. in mathematics at the Université de Montréal and undergraduate education at the University of British Columbia.

**Bill Morton** (billomorton@gmail.com) has previously worked for Oxfam Australia, most recently as international development policy analyst, and previously as coordinator of their Horn of Africa Program. He worked for six years with The North-South Institute as senior researcher, Development Cooperation, where he led the Institute's work on international aid policy and aid effectiveness, and on strengthening Canada's aid program. His main areas of interest are how developing countries can more strongly influence the global development agenda, innovative approaches to aid and development effectiveness, and the role of research in influencing policy. He is currently an independent research consultant.

**Dr. Victor Neufeld** (vrneufeld@gmail.com) is a physician, educator and international consultant based in Hamilton, Ontario, where he is professor emeritus of health sciences at McMaster University, and where he held various academic leadership positions over a period of more than 25 years. He has served as a consultant and adviser to many international agencies, organizations and institutions. He is currently the national coordinator of the Canadian Coalition for Global Health Research.

**Milana Nikolko** (Milana_Nikolko@carleton.ca) is adjunct research professor at Carleton University, and associate professor of political science (Docent) at V. Vernadsky Taurida National University, Ukraine. She is also a director of the NGO, Institute for Social Anthropology, Ukraine. She was a visiting scholar at the University of Ottawa and visiting professor at Valdosta State University (Georgia, United States) in 2008-2009. She has more than 30 publications in the field of diaspora research, methodology of political science and processes of national identity transformation.

**Betty Plewes** (bplewes@sympatico.ca) is a member of the McLeod Group and a former CEO of the Canadian Council for International Cooperation.

**Robert I. Rotberg** (robert_rotberg@hks.harvard.edu) is the Fulbright Research Chair in Political Development at the Balsillie School of International Affairs and Visiting Fulbright Scholar at CIGI. He is the founding director of Harvard Kennedy School's Program on Intrastate Conflict and president emeritus of the World Peace Foundation. He is a fellow of the American Academy of Arts and Sciences. He taught for many years at MIT and then at the Kennedy School. His latest books are *Transformative Political Leadership: Making a Difference in the Developing World* (2012) and *Africa Emerges: Consummate Challenges, Abundant Opportunities* (2013).

**Dane Rowlands** (dane_rowlands@carleton.ca) received his Ph.D. in economics from the University of Toronto, and has since been teaching at NPSIA, Carleton University, where he currently serves as director. His primary research interests are in multilateral financial institutions, official development assistance, economic development, migration and conflict intervention.

**Yiagadeesen Samy** (yiagadeesen_samy@carleton.ca) is associate professor and the associate director of the M.A. program at NPSIA, Carleton University, and a distinguished research associate with the North-South Institute, both in Ottawa, Canada. He is the author or co-author of a book on fragile states, as well as several peer-reviewed articles and book chapters in edited volumes on various issues, such as trade and labour standards, the political economy of foreign direct investment, state fragility and small island developing states.

**Victora Schorr** (victoria.schorr@gmail.com) is an independent researcher, writer, consultant and blogger with more than 10 years of experience regarding Sub-Saharan Africa. She is currently on the executive of the Africa Study Group and has worked for organizations ranging from grassroots capacity-building NGOs to the United Nations. She holds an M.Sc. in African politics from the School of Oriental and African Studies, and a B.A. in African studies from McGill University. Her areas of specialization include international relations, political economy, policy, Afro-pessimism and perceptions, business, trade, investment and development.

**Diéry Seck** (dieryseck@hotmail.com) has been director of the Center for Research on Political Economy since January 2009. Past positions include director of the United Nations African Institute for Economic Development and Planning in Dakar, Senegal, executive director of the Secretariat for Institutional Support for Economic Research in Africa of IDRC, associate professor of finance at the University of Windsor, Canada, and economist at the World Bank in Washington, DC. He has co-edited several books and authored numerous articles in academic journals and chapters in books on financial economics and modelling of economic development issues.

**Ian Smillie** (ismillie@magma.ca) has been an international development practitioner, consultant, teacher and writer for many years. He is the author of several books, including *Freedom From Want* (2008) and *Blood on the Stone: Greed, Corruption and War in the Global Diamond Trade* (2010). He served on a UN Security Council Expert Panel examining the relationship between diamonds and weapons in West Africa, and he helped develop the 70-government "Kimberley Process," a global certification system to halt the traffic in conflict diamonds. He was the first witness at Charles Taylor's war crimes trial in The Hague, he chairs the Diamond Development Initiative and he co-chairs the Advisory Panel of the Office of Canada's Extractive Sector Corporate Social Responsibility Counsellor.

**Peter Szyszlo** (pszyszlo@uOttawa.ca) is an international partnership adviser at the University of Ottawa. In addition to his advisory role to the associate vice-president international, his portfolio includes the development of strategic initiatives and research on new and emerging developments in international higher education. Recent projects include the design and implementation of AIMS-HeadStart, a program that supports students and graduates of the African Institute for Mathematical Sciences — Next Einstein Initiative, and a recently completed training series on academic governance and management of tertiary institutions in Haiti. Prior to joining the University of Ottawa, he provided technical support on a major survey of African academic networks commissioned by the Partnership for Higher Education in Africa (with Jeffrey C. Fine). Other international assignments include a visiting faculty fellowship with the Soros Foundation and a consultative role to the United Nations Development Programme in Belarus.

**Brian Tomlinson** (brian.t.tomlinson@gmail.com) is the executive director of AidWatch Canada and former senior policy analyst for the Canadian Council for International Cooperation.

*by Derek Walcott*

POETRY

*In a Green Night*

*Selected Poems*

*The Castaway*

*The Gulf*

PLAYS

*Dream on Monkey Mountain*

*The Sea at Dauphin*

*Malcochon*

*Ti-Jean and His Brothers*

*The Gulf*

*Poems by*

# DEREK
# WALCOTT

~~~~~~~~~~~~~~~~~~~~~~~~~~~~~~~~~~~~~~~~~~~~~~~~~~~~~~~~~~~~

~~~~~~~~~~~~~~~~~~~~~~~~~~~~~~~~~~~~~~~~~~~~~~~~~~~~~~~~~~~~

*Farrar, Straus and Giroux*

N E W   Y O R K

m

# THE GULF

# Note

Although this volume goes by the over-all title of *The Gulf*, it includes not only the whole of that book (published by Jonathan Cape, 1969), but selections from *The Castaway* (Cape, 1965), in which I have made minor changes. Acknowledgments are due to the editors of the *London Magazine, The Bulletin* (Australia), the Chicago *Tribune, The Times* (London), *Art and Man* (Trinidad) and *Fifteen Poems for William Shakespeare* (The Arts Council, England).

D.W.

# Contents

*ix*

*x*

from *The Castaway*

TO JOHN HEARNE

## The Flock

The grip of winter tightening, its thinned
volleys of blue-wing teal and mallard fly
from the longbows of reeds bent by the wind,
arrows of yearning for our different sky.
A season's revolution hones their sense,
whose target is our tropic light, while I
awoke this sunrise to a violence
of images migrating from the mind.
Skeletal forest, a sepulchral knight
riding in silence at a black tarn's edge
hooves cannonading snow
in the white funeral of the year,
ant-like across the forehead of an alp
in iron contradiction crouched
against those gusts that urge the mallards south.
Vizor'd with blind defiance of his quest,
its yearly divination of the spring.
I travel through such silence, making dark
symbols with this pen's print across snow,
measuring winter's augury by words
settling the branched mind like migrating birds,
and never question when they come or go.

The style, tension of motion and the dark,
inflexible direction of the world
as it revolves upon its centuries
with change of language, climate, customs, light,
with our own prepossession day by day

year after year with images of flight,
survive our condemnation and the sun's
exultant larks.
            The dark impartial Arctic
whose glaciers encased the mastodon,
froze giant minds in marble attitudes,
revolves with tireless, determined grace
upon an iron axle, though the seals
howl with inhuman cries across its ice
and pages of torn birds are blown across
whitening tundras like engulfing snow.
Till its annihilation may the mind
reflect his fixity through winter, tropic,
until that equinox when the clear eye
clouds, like a mirror, without contradiction,
greet the black wings that cross it as a blessing
like the high, whirring flock that flew across
the cold sky of this page when I began
this journey by the wintry flare of dawn,
flying by instinct to their secret places
both for their need and for my sense of season.

# A Village Life

[FOR JOHN ROBERTSON]

I

Through the wide, grey loft window,
I watched that winter morning, my first snow
crusting the sill, puzzle the black,
nuzzling tom. Behind my back
a rime of crud glazed my cracked coffee-cup,
a snowfall of torn poems piling up
heaped by a rhyming spade.
Starved, on the prowl,
I was a frightened cat in that grey city.
I floated, a cat's shadow, through the black wool
sweaters, leotards and parkas of the fire-haired,
snow-shouldered Greenwich Village mädchen,
homesick, my desire
crawled across snow
like smoke, for its lost fire.

All that winter I haunted
your house on Hudson Street, a tiring friend,
demanding to be taken in, drunk, and fed.
I thought winter would never end.

I cannot imagine you dead.

But that stare, frozen,
a frosted pane in sunlight,
gives nothing back by letting nothing in,

your kindness or my pity.
No self-reflection lies
within those silent, ice-blue irises,
whose image is some snow-locked mountain lake
in numb Montana.

And since that winter I have learnt to gaze
on life indifferently as through a pane of glass.


I I

Your image rattled on the subway glass
is my own death-mask in an overcoat;
under New York, the subterranean freight
of human souls, locked in an iron cell,
station to station cowed with swaying calm,
thunders to its end, each in its private hell,
each plumped, prime bulk still swinging by its arm
upon a hook. You're two years dead. And yet
I watch that silence spreading through our souls:
that horn-rimmed midget who consoles
his own deformity with Sartre on Genet.
Terror still eats the nerves, the Word
is gibberish, the plot Absurd.
The turnstile slots, like addicts, still consume
obols and aspirin, Charon in his grilled cell
grows vague about our crime, our destination.
Not all are silent, or endure

the enormity of silence; at one station,
somewhere off 33rd and Lexington,
a fur-wrapped matron screamed above the roar
of rattling iron. Nobody took her on,
we looked away. Such scenes
rattle our trust in nerves tuned like machines.
All drives as you remember it, the pace
of walking, running the rat race,
locked in a system, ridden by its rail,
within a life where no one dares to fail.
I watch your smile breaking across my skull,
the hollows of your face below my face
sliding across it like a pane of glass.
Nothing endures. Even in his cities
man's life is grass.
Times Square. We sigh and let off steam,
who should screech with the braking wheels, scream
like our subway-Cassandra, heaven-sent
to howl for Troy, emerge
blind from the blast of daylight, whirled
apart like papers from a vent.

III

Going away, through Queens we pass
a cemetery of miniature skyscrapers. The verge
blazes its rust, its taxi-yellow leaves. It's fall.
I stare through glass,

my own reflection there, at
empty avenues, lawns, spires, quiet
stones, where the curb's rim
wheels westward, westward, where thy bones  .  .  .

Montana, Minnesota, your real
America, lost in tall grass, serene idyll.

# Goats and Monkeys

. . . even now, an old black ram
is tupping your white ewe.
OTHELLO

The owl's torches gutter. Chaos clouds the globe.
Shriek, augury! His earthen bulk
buries her bosom in its slow eclipse.
His smoky hand has charred
that marble throat. Bent to her lips,
he is Africa, a vast sidling shadow
that halves your world with doubt.
'Put out the light,' and God's light is put out.

That flame extinct, she contemplates her dream
of him as huge as night, as bodiless,
as starred with medals, like the moon
a fable of blind stone.
Dazzled by that bull's bulk against the sun
of Cyprus, couldn't she have known
like Pasiphaë, poor girl, she'd breed horned monsters?
That like Eurydice, her flesh a flare
travelling the hellish labyrinth of his mind
his soul would swallow hers?

Her white flesh rhymes with night. She climbs, secure.

Virgin and ape, maid and malevolent Moor,
their immortal coupling still halves our world.
He is your sacrificial beast, bellowing, goaded,

9

a black bull snarled in ribbons of its blood.
And yet, whatever fury girded
on that saffron-sunset turban, moon-shaped sword
was not his racial, panther-black revenge
pulsing her chamber with raw musk, its sweat,
but horror of the moon's change,
of the corruption of an absolute,
like a white fruit
pulped ripe by fondling but doubly sweet.

And so he barbarously arraigns the moon
for all she has beheld since time began
for his own night-long lechery, ambition,
while barren innocence whimpers for pardon.
And it is still the moon, she silvers love,
limns lechery and stares at our disgrace.
Only annihilation can resolve
the pure corruption in her dreaming face.

A bestial, comic agony. We harden
with mockery at this blackamoor
who turns his back on her, who kills
her element, night; his grief
farcically knotted in a handkerchief
a sibyl's
prophetically stitched remembrancer
webbed and embroidered with the zodiac,
this mythical, horned beast who's no more
monstrous for being black.

## The Prince

Genderers of furies, crouching, slavering beasts
those paps that gave me suck! His dragonish scales
are velvet-sheathed, even at those feasts
of coiling tongues. Lust has not soured
that milky stomach. Something more than love
my father lacked which God will not approve:

a savage, sundering sword, vile to the touch
breeding fidelity by its debauch.
Calm, she reclines on her maternal couch,
knitting revenge and lechery in my head.
I ease the sword, and, like her victim, quaking,
I, in my father, stalk my father's dread.

# Laventille

[ FOR V. S. NAIPAUL ]

To find the Western Path
Through the Gates of Wrath—
BLAKE

It huddled there
steel tinkling its blue painted metal air,
tempered in violence, like Rio's favelas,

with snaking, perilous streets whose edges fell as
its episcopal turkey-buzzards fall
from its miraculous hilltop

shrine,
down the impossible drop
to Belmont, Woodbrook, Maraval, St. Clair

that shine
like peddlers' tin trinkets in the sun.
From a harsh

shower, its gutters growled and gargled wash
past the Youth Centre, past the water catchment,
a rigid children's carousel of cement;

we climbed where lank electric
lines and tension cables linked its raw brick
hovels like a complex feud,

where the inheritors of the middle passage stewed
five to a room, still clamped below their hatch,
breeding like felonies,

whose lives revolve round prison, graveyard, church.
Below bent breadfruit trees
in the flat, coloured city, class

escalated into structures still,
merchant, middleman, magistrate, knight. To go downhill
from here was to ascend.

The middle passage never guessed its end.
This is the height of poverty
for the desperate and black;

climbing, we could look back
with widening memory
on the hot, corrugated iron sea
whose horrors we all

shared. The salt blood knew it well,
you, me, Samuel's daughter, Samuel,
and those ancestors clamped below its grate.

And climbing steeply past the wild
gutters, it shrilled
in the blood, for those who suffered, who were killed,

and who survive.
What other gift was there to give
as the godparents of his unnamed child?

Yet outside the brown annexe of the church, the
stifling odour of bay rum and talc, the particular,
neat sweetness of the crowd distressed

that sense. The black, fawning verger
his bow tie akimbo, grinning, the clown-gloved
fashionable wear of those I deeply loved

once, made me look on with hopelessness and rage
at their new, apish habits, their excess
and fear, the possessed, the self-possessed;

their perfume shrivelled to a childhood fear
of Sabbath graveyards, christenings, marriages,
that muggy, steaming, self-assuring air

of tropical Sabbath afternoons. And in
the church, eyes prickling with rage,
the children rescued from original sin

by their Godfather since the middle passage,
the supercilious brown curate, who intones,

healing the guilt in these rachitic bones,
twisting my love within me like a knife:
'across the troubled waters of this life . . .'

Which of us cares to walk
even if God wished
those retching waters where our souls were fished

for this new world? Afterwards, we talk
in whispers, close to death
among these stones planted on alien earth.

Afterwards,
the ceremony, the careful photograph
moved out of range before the patient tombs,

we dare a laugh,
ritual, desperate words,
born like these children from habitual wombs,

from lives fixed in the unalterable groove
of grinding poverty. I stand out on a balcony
and watch the sun pave its flat, golden path

across the roofs, the aerials, cranes, the tops
of fruit trees crawling downward to the city.
Something inside is laid wide like a wound,

some open passage that has cleft the brain,
some deep, amnesiac blow. We left
somewhere a life we never found,

customs and gods that are not born again,
some crib, some grill of light
clanged shut on us in bondage, and withheld

us from that world below us and beyond,
and in its swaddling cerements we're still bound.

## The Almond Trees

There's nothing here
this early;
cold sand
cold churning ocean, the Atlantic,
no visible history,

except this stand
of twisted, coppery, sea-almond trees
their shining postures surely
bent as metal, and one

foam-haired, salt-grizzled fisherman,
his mongrel growling, whirling on the stick
he pitches him; its spinning rays
'no visible history'
until their lengthened shapes amaze the sun.

By noon,
this further shore of Africa is strewn
with the forked limbs of girls toasting their flesh
in scarves, sunglasses, Pompeian bikinis,
brown daphnes, laurels, they'll all have
like their originals, their sacred grove:
this frieze
of twisted, coppery, sea-almond trees.

The fierce acetylene air
has singed

their writhing trunks with rust, the same
hues as a foundered, peeling barge.
It'll sear a pale skin copper with its flame.

The sand's white-hot ash underheel,
but their aged limbs have got their brazen sheen
from fire. Their bodies fiercely shine!
They're cured,
they endured their furnace.

Aged trees and oiled limbs share a common colour!

Welded in one flame,
huddling naked, stripped of their name,
for Greek or Roman tags, they were lashed
raw by wind, washed
out with salt and fire-dried,
bitterly nourished where their branches died,

their leaves' broad dialect a coarse,
enduring sound
they shared together.

Not as some running hamadryad's cries
rooted, broke slowly into leaf
her nipples peaking to smooth, wooden boles

their grief
howls seaward through charred, ravaged holes.

One sunburnt body now acknowledges
that past and its own metamorphosis
as, moving from the sun, she kneels to spread
her wrap within the bent arms of this grove
that grieves in silence, like parental love.

# *Veranda*

[FOR RONALD BRYDEN]

Grey apparitions at veranda ends
like smoke, divisible, but one
your age is ashes, its coherence gone,

Planters whose tears were marketable gum, whose voices
scratch the twilight like dried fronds
edged with reflection,

Colonels, hard as the commonwealth's greenheart,
middlemen, usurers whose art
kept an empire in the red,

Upholders of Victoria's china seas
lapping embossed around a drinking mug,
bully-boy roarers of the Empire club,

To the taran-tara of the bugler, the sunset furled
round the last post,
the 'flamingo colours' of a fading world,

A ghost steps from you, my grandfather's ghost!
Uprooted from some rainy English shire,
you sought your Roman

End in suicide by fire.
Your mixed son gathered your charred blackened bones,
in a child's coffin.

And buried them himself on a strange coast.
Sire,
why do I raise you up? Because

Your house has voices, your burnt house,
shrills with unguessed, lovely inheritors,
your genealogical roof tree, fallen, survives,
like seasoned timber through green, little lives.

I ripen towards your twilight, sir, that dream
where I am singed in that sea-crossing, steam
towards that vaporous world, whose souls,

Like pressured trees brought diamonds out of coals.
The sparks pitched from your burning house are stars.
I am the man my father loved and was.

I climb the stair
and stretch a darkening hand to greet those friends
who share with you the last inheritance
of earth, our shrine and pardoner,

grey, ghostly loungers at veranda ends.

# God Rest Ye Merry, Gentlemen

Splitting from Jack Delaney's, Sheridan Square,
that winter night, stewed, seasoned in Bourbon,
my body kindled by the whistling air
snowing the Village that Christ was reborn,
I lurched like any lush by his own glow
across towards Sixth, and froze before the tracks
of footprints bleeding on the virgin snow.
I tracked them where they led across the street
to the bright side, entering the wax-
sealed smell of neon, human heat,
some all-night diner with its wise-guy cook
his stub thumb in my bowl of stew and one
man's pulped and beaten face, its look
acknowledging all that, white-dark outside,
was possible: some beast prowling the block,
something fur-clotted, running wild
beyond the boundary of will. Outside,
more snow had fallen. My heart charred.
I longed for darkness, evil that was warm.
Walking, I'd stop and turn. What had I heard,
wheezing behind my heel with whitening breath?
Nothing. Sixth Avenue yawned wet and wide.
The night was white. There was nowhere to hide.

# Lines in New England

*The cruel lie of caste refute,*
*Old forms remould, and substitute*
*For Slavery's lash the freeman's will,*
*For blind routine, wise-handed skill;*
*A school-house plant on every hill,*
*Stretching in radiate nerve-lines thence*
*The quick wires of intelligence;*
*Till North and South together brought*
*Shall own the same electric thought,*
*In peace a common flag salute,*
*And, side by side in labour's free*
*And unresentful rivalry,*
*Harvest the fields, wherein they fought!*
WHITTIER, *Snowbound*


Geese creaking south, a raucous
chain unlocking winter's cavernous
barn, cross me
going the other way.
Why am I so far north,
who dread these stripped trees' polar
iron, and fear fall,
cinders and brimstone of
the pilgrim's prophecy? I look
from arrowing train lines at the track
this crabbed hand makes, at every trick
of its shot trade. It runs, cramped
from itself with loathing: the pumped
detonation under sulphurous
sheets, the white, treacherous

hands it has been gripped by;
a crab wallowing in the water of
a salt, warm, drifting eye;
the breasts it's held in love,
in hollow love. The ruled lie
it follows. Yet not once has this hand
sought to strike home. Outside,
an Indian summer whose trees radiate
like veins, a salt-blue pond,
where I imagine a crazed, single, deer-
skinned quarry drinking, the last
Mohican. Redcoat, redman, their thirst-
ing, autumn battle-ground,
its savage lacerations healed
by salt white spire and green field.
I watch from my side of the glass
the lantern slides clicking across
the window glazed by ocean air.
Mine, or another history there?
A civilization with its dreams
of guilt; the trails drive grittily,
their power clamps the jaw
tight with abhorrence and with love;
these parallels, that seem to move
to blue infinity, laid down the law
of separate but equal love.

## November Sun

In our treacherous
seasonless climate's
dry heat or muggy heat or rain
I'm measuring winter by this November sun's
diagonals shafting the window pane,
by my crouched shadow's
embryo on the morning study-floor. Once

I wallowed in ignorance
of change, of windfall, snowfall,
skull-cracking heat, sea-threshing hurricane.
Now I'd prefer to know.
We age desiring
these icy intuitions
seasons bring.

Look, they'll be pierced with knowledge
as with light! One boy, nine years in age
who vaults and tumbles, squirrelling
in his perpetual spring,
that ten-month, cautious totterer
my daughter.
I rarely let them in.

This is a sort of
death cell
where knowledge of our fatality is hidden.
I trace here, like a bent astronomer

the circle of the year,
nurturing its inner seasons'
mulch, drench, fire, ash.
In my son's
restless gaze
I am time-ridden,
the sedentary dial of his days.
Our shadows point one way,
even their brief shadows on the cropped morning grass.

I am pierced with this. I cannot look away.
Ah Christ, how cruelly the needles race!

# Crusoe's Journal

I looked now upon the world as a thing remote, which I
had nothing to do with, no expectation from, and, indeed
no desires about. In a word, I had nothing indeed
to do with it, nor was ever like to have; so I thought
it looked as we may perhaps look upon it hereafter,
viz., as a place I had lived in but was come out
of it; and well might I say, as Father Abraham
to Dives, 'Between me and thee is a great gulf fixed.'
ROBINSON CRUSOE


Once we have driven past Mundo Nuevo trace
      safely to this beach house
perched betwen ocean and green, churning forest
      the intellect appraises
objects surely, even the bare necessities
      of style are turned to use,
like those plain iron tools he salvages
      from shipwreck, hewing a prose
as odorous as raw wood to the adze;
      out of such timbers
came our first book, our profane Genesis
      whose Adam speaks that prose
which, blessing some sea-rock, startles itself
      with poetry's surprise,
in a green world, one without metaphors;
      like Christofer he bears
in speech mnemonic as a missionary's
      the Word to savages,
its shape an earthen, water-bearing vessel's

whose sprinkling alters us
into good Fridays who recite His praise,
    parroting our master's
style and voice, we make his language ours,
    converted cannibals
we learn with him to eat the flesh of Christ.

All shapes, all objects multiplied from his,
    our ocean's Proteus;
in childhood, his derelict's old age
    was like a god's. ( Now pass
in memory, in serene parenthesis,
    the cliff-deep leeward coast
of my own island filing past the noise
    of stuttering canvas,
some noon-struck village, Choiseul, Canaries,
    crouched crocodile canoes,
a savage settlement from Henty's novels,
    Marryat or R.L.S.,
with one boy signalling at the sea's edge,
    though what he cried is lost.)
So time that makes us objects, multiplies
    our natural loneliness.

For the hermetic skill, that from earth's clays
    shapes something without use,
and separate from itself, lives somewhere else,
    sharing with every beach

a longing for those gulls that cloud the cays
          with raw, mimetic cries,
never surrenders wholly for it knows
          it needs another's praise
like hoar, half-cracked Ben Gunn, until it cries
          at last, 'O happy desert!'
and learns again the self-creating peace
          of islands. So from this house
that faces nothing but the sea, his journals
          assume a household use;
we learn to shape from them, where nothing was
          the language of a race,
and since the intellect demands its mask
          that sun-cracked, bearded face
provides us with the wish to dramatize
          ourselves at nature's cost,
to attempt a beard, to squint through the sea-haze,
          posing as naturalists,
drunks, castaways, beachcombers, all of us
          yearn for those fantasies
of innocence, for our faith's arrested phase
          when the clear voice
startled itself saying 'water, heaven, Christ,'
          hoarding such heresies as
God's loneliness moves in His smallest creatures.

# *Lampfall*

Closest at lampfall
Like children, like the moth-flame metaphor,
The Coleman's humming jet at the sea's edge
A tuning fork for our still family choir
Like Joseph Wright of Derby's astrological lecture
Casts rings of benediction round the aged.
I never tire of ocean's quarrelling,
Its silence, its raw voice,
Nor of these half-lit windy leaves, gesticulating higher
'Rejoice, rejoice . . .'

But there's an old fish, a monster
Of primal fiction that drives barrelling
Undersea, too old to make a splash,
To which I'm hooked!
Through daydream, through nightmare trolling
Me so deep that no lights flash
There but the plankton's drifting, phosphorescent stars.

I see with its aged eyes,
Its dead green, glaucous gaze,
And I'm elsewhere, far as
I shall ever be from you whom I behold now
Dear family, dear friends, by this still glow,
The lantern's ring that the sea's
Never extinguished.
Your voices curl in the shell of my ear.

All day you've watched
The sea-rock like a loom
Shuttling its white wool, sheer Penelope!
The coals lit, the sky glows, an oven.
Heart into heart carefully laid
Like bread.
This is the fire that draws us by our dread
Of loss, the furnace door of heaven.

At night we have heard
The forest, an ocean of leaves, drowning her children,
Still, we belong here. There's Venus. We are not yet lost.

Like you, I preferred
The firefly's starlike little
Lamp, mining, a question,
To the highway's brightly multiplying beetles.

## Codicil

Schizophrenic, wrenched by two styles,
one a hack's hired prose, I earn
my exile. I trudge this sickle, moonlit beach for miles,

tan, burn
to slough off
this love of ocean that's self-love.

To change your language you must change your life.

I cannot right old wrongs.
Waves tire of horizon and return.
Gulls screech with rusty tongues

Above the beached, rotting pirogues,
they were a venomous beaked cloud at Charlotteville.

Once I thought love of country was enough,
now, even I chose, there's no room at the trough.

I watch the best minds root like dogs
for scraps of favour.
I am nearing middle-

age, burnt skin
peels from my hand like paper, onion-thin,
like Peer Gynt's riddle.

At heart there's nothing, not the dread
of death. I know too many dead.
They're all familiar, all in character,

even how they died. On fire,
the flesh no longer fears that furnace mouth
of earth,

that kiln or ashpit of the sun,
nor this clouding, unclouding sickle moon
whitening this beach again like a blank page.

All its indifference is a different rage.

# The Gulf

TO MARGARET

# Ebb

Year round, year round, we'll ride
this treadmill whose frayed tide
fretted with mud,

leaves our suburban shoreline littered
with rainbow muck, the afterbirth
of industry, past scurf-

streaked bungalows
and pioneer factory;
but, blessedly, it narrows

through a dark aisle
of fountaining, gold coconuts, an oasis
marked for the yellow Caterpillar tractor.

We'll watch this shovelled too, but as we file
through its swift-wickered shade there always is
some island schooner netted in its weave

like a lamed heron
an oil-crippled gull;
a few more yards upshore

and it heaves free,
it races the horizon
with us, railed to one law,

ruled, like the washed-up moon
to circle her lost zone,
her radiance thinned.

The palm fronds signal wildly in the wind,
but we are bound elsewhere,
from the last sacred wood.

The schooner's out too far,
too far that boyhood.
Sometimes I turn to see

the schooner, crippled, try to tread the air,
the moon break in sere sail,
but without envy.

For safety, each sunfall,
the wildest of us all
mortgages life to fear.

And why not? From this car
there's terror enough in the habitual,
miracle enough in the familiar. Sure . . .

## The Corn Goddess

Silence asphalts the highway, our tires hiss
like serpents, of God's touching weariness;
His toil unfinished, while in endless rows
the cabbage fields, like lilies, spin in air;
his flags rot, and the monkey god's nerves rattle
lances in rage. Human rags tend cattle
more venal every year, and chrome-tooled cars
lathered like estate horses nose the shallows.
At dusk the Presbyterian cattle-bell
collects lean, charcoal-brittle elders,
stalled in their vision of a second hell,
as every crossroad crucifies its sect
of bell-voiced, bell-robed sisters, god-gelders
baying for self-respect. But, over braziers
of roasting corn while their shucked souls
evenly char, the sibyl glows. Her seal's skin
shines like drizzled asphalt, in that grin
all knowledges burnt out. Jeer, but their souls
catch an elation fiercer than your desolate
envy; from their fanned, twisting coals
their shrieks crackle and fly. The sparks
are sorrowing upward though they die.

# *Metamorphoses*

## 1 / MOON

Resisting poetry I am becoming a poem.
O lolling Orphic head silently howling,
my own head rises from its surf of cloud.

Slowly my body grows a single sound,
slowly I become
a bell,
an oval, disembodied vowel,
I grow, an owl,
an aureole, white fire.

I watch the moonstruck image of the moon burn,
a candle mesmerised by its own aura,
and turn
my hot, congealing face, towards that forked mountain
which wedges the drowned singer.

That frozen glare,
that morsured, classic petrifaction.
Haven't you sworn off such poems for this year,
and no more on the moon?

Why are you gripped by demons of inaction?
Whose silence shrieks so soon?

## II / S E R P E N T

Behind this porous skull, cold as this star,
below membranous veins the serpent drowses.
The quartz eyes glint from its adze-heavy head.

Leisurely as evil, rehearsing vice,
conducting its self-seducing sibilance,
the only creature without hands, it broods upon

the obese split and coupling of time
when its forked tongue rhymed all,
crotch, apple, breath, and you, forked fool, approaching

this coral oracle to hear how it once sung
of lust, of wisdom from God's sorrow wrung,
who step back, stung.

## III / CAT

As carefully as
old Carlos Williams's cat's foot
forks the air,
and the curled tines, sheathing, back
from some pneumatic
nothing,

my nerves feeler each crack
in that blue sky.
It is going to pieces.
There is a stain
there, from the brain,
on that blue plaster.
Spell it, it spells
disaster. I'll

hoard, I'll huddle, I'll
contain myself.
Between this bed and mirror is
a mould I must inhabit.
It itches, it is ill.
To be a bridge, they said,
all you need do is keep still,

to surrender the ill-
usion that mirrors crouch, clothes

wait from their gibbet.
The green eyes socket
every action like a pinball.
She coils around some quiet
which is inward.

Finely she ovals
her fine, ringing teeth.
Their silent yowl.
The green eyes swallow yours,
they gulp, replete.
Waking, each hair is stirred.
I feel my body walking,
silent, furred.
Those feet.
Whose are those feet?

# IV / HAWK

[FOR OLIVER JACKMAN]

Leaves shudder the drizzle's shine
like a treng-ka-treng from the cuatros,
beads fly from the tension line.
Gavilán, ay, gavilán,
high shadow, pitiless!
The old men without teeth,
rum-guzzlers, country fiddlers,
their rum-heads golden lakes
of a fabulous Yucatán,
Gavilán, ay, gavilán!

Caribs, like toothless tigers;
talons raking, a flash,
arrows like twanging wires,
catgut and ocelot,
merciless, that is man,
Gavilán, eh, gavilán?
Arima to Sangre Grande,
your wings like extended hands,
a grandee waltzing alone,
alone, to the old parang.

Gavilán, ay, gavilán,
the Negroes, bastards, mestizos,

proud of their Spanish blood,
of the flesh, dripping like wires,
praising your hook, gavilán.
Above their slack mouths the hawk
floats tautly out of the cedars,
leaves the limbs shaking.

Slaves yearn for their master's talons,
the spur and the cold, gold eyes,
for the whips, whistling like wires,
time for our turn, gavilán!
But this hawk above Rampanalgas
rasps the sea with raw cries.
Hawks have no music.

## Junta

The sun's brass clamp electrifies a skull
kept shone since he won Individual
of the Year, their first year on the road,
as Vercingetorix and His Barbarous Horde;
lurching from lounge to air-conditioned lounge
with the crazed soldier ant's logistic skill
of pause as capture, he stirs again to plunge,
his brain's antennae on fire through the black ants
milling and mulling through each city fissure;
banlon-cool limers, shopgirls, Civil Servants.
"Caesar," the hecklers siegheil, "Julius Seizure!"
He fakes an epileptic, clenched salute,
taking their tone, is no use getting vex,
some day those brains will squelch below his boot
as sheaves of swords hoist Vercingetorix!

So that day bursts to bugling cocks, the sun's gong
clangs the coup, a church, a bank explodes,
and, bullet-headed with his cow-horned gang
of marabunta hordes he hits the road.
Dust powders the white dead in Woodford Square;
his black, khaki canaille, panting for orders,
surge round the kiosk, then divide to hear
him clomp up silence louder than the roars
of rapine. Silence. Dust. A microphone
crackles the tinfoil quiet. On its paws
the beast mills, basilisk-eyed, for its one
voice. He clears his gorge and feels the bile

of rhetoric rising. Enraged, that every clause
"por la patria, la muerte!" resounds
the same, he fakes a frothing fit and shows his wounds,
while, as the steel sheaves heighten, his eyes fix
on one black, bush-haired convict's widening smile.

47

## Mass Man

Through a great lion's head clouded by mange
a black clerk growls.
Next, a gold-wired peacock withholds a man,
a fan, flaunting its oval, jewelled eyes;
What metaphors!
What coruscating, mincing fantasies!

Hector Mannix, water-works clerk, San Juan, has entered a
    lion,
Boysie, two golden mangoes bobbing for breastplates, barges
like Cleopatra down her river, making style.
"Join us," they shout, "O God, child, you can't dance?"
But somewhere in that whirlwind's radiance
a child, rigged like a bat, collapses, sobbing.

But I am dancing, look, from an old gibbet
my bull-whipped body swings, a metronome!
Like a fruit-bat dropped in the silk-cotton's shade,
my mania, my mania is a terrible calm.

Upon your penitential morning,
some skull must rub its memory with ashes,
some mind must squat down howling in your dust,
some hand must crawl and recollect your rubbish,
someone must write your poems.

## Miramar

There'll be no miracle tonight; by the third drink
you can tell. The nerves deaden from steel
or a hollow sax. I look through the window:
a bus goes by like an empty hospital,
and turn. The stripper's spinning, pink
tits, falsies in a false light, her crotch's
mechanical lurch is her own rut, and think
of the night I almost burned my balls
off with some abrasive, powdery chemical
and in the next ward of the teaching hospital
would listen all night to the clenched, stuck
howl of a child dying of lockjaw. Clench, hold
on to what you have. After a while, this whole,
slow grinding circus doesn't give a fuck.
There is nowhere to go. You'd better go.

## Exile

Wind-haired, mufflered
against dawn, you watched the herd
of migrants ring the deck
from steerage. Only the funnel
bellowing, the gulls who peck
waste from the ploughed channel
knew that you had not come
to England; you were home.

Even her wretched weather
was poetry. Your scarred leather
suitcase held that first
indenture, to her Word,
but, among cattle docking, that rehearsed
calm meant to mark you from the herd
shook, calf-like, in her cold.

Never to go home again,
for this was home! The windows
leafed through history to the beat
of a school ballad, but the train
soon changed its poetry to the prose
of narrowing, pinched eyes you could not enter,
to the gas-ring, the ringing Students' Centre,
to the soiled, icy sheet.

One night, near rheum-eyed windows
your memory kept pace with winter's

pages, piled in drifts,
till Spring, which slowly lifts
the heart, broke into prose
and suns you had forgotten
blazoned from barrows.

And earth began to look
as you remembered her,
herons, like sea-gulls flock-
ed to the salted furrow,
the bellowing, smoky bullock
churned its cane sea,
a world began to pass
through your pen's eye,
between bent grasses and one word
for the bent rice.

And now, some phrase
caught in the parenthesis
of highway quietly states
its title, and an ochre trace
of flags and carat huts opens
at Chapter One,
the bullock's strenuous ease is mirrored
in a clear page of prose,
a forest is compressed in a blue coal,
or burns in graphite fire,
invisibly your ink nourishes

leaf after leaf the furrowed villages
where the smoke flutes
and the brittle pages
of the Ramayana stoke the mulch fires,

the arrowing, metal
highways head nowhere,
the tabla and the sitar amplified,
the Path unrolling like a dirty bandage,
the cinema-hoardings leer
in language half the country cannot read.

Yet, when dry winds rattle
the flags whose bamboo lances bend
to Hanuman, when, like chattel
folded in a cloth-knot, the debased
brasses are tremblingly placed
on flaking temple lintels,
when the god stamps his bells
and smoke writhes its blue arms
for your lost India,

the old men, threshing rice,
rheum-eyed, pause,
their brown gaze flecked with chaff,
their loss chafed by the raw
whine of the cinema-van calling the countryside
to its own dark devotions,

summoning the drowned from oceans
of deep cane. The hymn
to Mother India whores its lie.
Your memory walks by its soft-spoken
path, as flickering, broken,
Saturday jerks past like a cheap film.

## The Train

On one hand, harrowed England,
iron, an airfield's mire,
on the other, fire-
gutted trees, a hand
raking the carriage windows.

Where was my randy white grandsire from?
He left here a century ago
to found his 'farm,'
and, like a thousand others,
drunkenly seed their archipelago.
Through dirty glass
his landscape fills my face.

Black with despair
he set his flesh on fire,
blackening, a tree of flame.
That's hell enough for here.
His blood burns through me as this engine races,
my skin sears like a hairshirt with his name.

On the bleak Sunday platform
the guiltless, staring faces
divide like tracks before me as I come.
Like you, grandfather, I cannot change places,
I am half-home.

## Homage to Edward Thomas

Formal, informal, by a country's cast
topography delineates its verse,
erects the classic bulk, for rigid contrast
of sonnet, rectory or this manor-house
dourly timbered against these sinuous
Downs, defines the formal and informal prose
of Edward Thomas's poems which make this garden
return its subtle scent of Edward Thomas
in everything here hedged or loosely grown.
Lines which you once dismissed as tenuous
because they would not howl or overwhelm,
as crookedly grave-bent, or cuckoo-dreaming,
seeming dissoluble as this Sussex down
harden in their indifference, like this elm.

## A Change of Skin

[FOR LAURENCE GOLDSTRAW]

The fog, a sheepdog circling, bared
its teeth from slavering hedges
at the dark, sheepskin-collared

stranger; then coldly it grew clear
as those green, lucent panes
of England that his fear

of history was its lack. Pins
of fine rain prickled his skin's
horror of that cold, and the bone

shuddered from deep-tutored
awe of arrogant stone,
as when dark tribes ground to his tread,

mulch-black and brown leaves seethed
nourishing England. In an air
cold as iron, he freely breathed

the exhilaration of pure hatred;
now on grey mornings, when like hair
prickling the scalp, the trees stir

memory of their irresolute temperature
now kind, now cold, he waits,
knowing its fire purifies with sweat,

for the unsubtle, unequivocal sun,
for heat that shapes his shadow surely like the blow from glare to sudden

shade, from fear to fondness of a fever
shed, like history cured of hatred,
like life of literature.

# The Gulf

[FOR JACK AND BARBARA HARRISON]

I

The airport coffee tastes less of America.
Sour, unshaven, dreading the exertion
of tightening, racked nerves fuelled with liquor,

some smoky, resinous Bourbon,
the body, buckling at its casket hole,
a roar like last night's blast racing its engines,

watches the fumes of the exhausted soul
as the trans-Texas jet, screeching, begins
its flight and friends diminish. So, to be aware

of the divine union the soul detaches
itself from created things. 'We're in the air,'
the Texan near me grins. All things: these matches

from LBJ's campaign hotel, this rose
given me at dawn in Austin by a child,
this book of fables by Borges, its prose

a stalking, moonlit tiger. What was willed
on innocent, sun-streaked Dallas, the beast's claw
curled round that hairspring rifle is revealed

on every page as lunacy or feral law;

circling that wound we leave Love Field.
Fondled, these objects conjure hotels,

quarrels, new friendships, brown limbs
nakedly moulded as these autumn hills
memory penetrates as the jet climbs

the new clouds over Texas; their home means
an island suburb, forest, mountain water;
they are the simple properties for scenes

whose joy exhausts like grief, scenes where we learn,
exchanging the least gifts, this rose, this napkin,
that those we love are objects we return,

that this lens on the desert's wrinkled skin
has priced our flesh, all that we love in pawn
to that brass ball, that the gifts, multiplying

clutter and choke the heart, and that I shall
watch love reclaim its things as I lie dying.
My very flesh and blood! Each seems a petal

shrivelling from its core. I watch them burn,
by the nerves' flare I catch their skeletal
candour! Best never to be born

the great dead cry. Their works shine on our shelves,
by twilight tour their gilded gravestone spines,
and read until the lamplit page revolves

to a white stasis whose detachment shines
like a propeller's rainbowed radiance.
Circling like us; no comfort for their loves!

I I

The cold glass darkens. Elizabeth wrote once
that we make glass the image of our pain;
I watch clouds boil past the cold, sweating pane

above the Gulf. All styles yearn to be plain
as life. The face of the loved object under glass
is plainer still. Yet, somehow, at this height,

above this cauldron boiling with its wars,
our old earth, breaking to familiar light,
that cloud-bound mummy with self-healing scars

peeled of her cerements again looks new;
some cratered valley heals itself with sage,
through that grey, fading massacre a blue

light-hearted creek flutes of some siege
to the amnesia of drumming water.

Their cause is crystalline: the divine union

of these detached, divided States, whose slaughter
darkens each summer now, as one by one,
the smoke of bursting ghettos clouds the glass

down every coast where filling-station signs
proclaim the Gulf, an air, heavy with gas,
sickens the state, from Newark to New Orleans.

III

Yet the South felt like home. Wrought balconies,
the sluggish river with its tidal drawl,
the tropic air charged with the extremities

of patience, a heat heavy with oil,
canebrakes, that legendary jazz. But fear
thickened my voice, that strange, familiar soil

prickled and barbed the texture of my hair,
my status as a secondary soul.
The Gulf, your gulf, is daily widening,

each blood-red rose warns of that coming night
when there's no rock cleft to go hidin' in
and all the rocks catch fire, when that black might,

their stalking, moonless panthers turn from Him
whose voice they can no more believe, when the black X's
mark their passover with slain seraphim.

I V

The Gulf shines, dull as lead. The coast of Texas
glints like a metal rim. I have no home
as long as summer bubbling to its head

boils for that day when in the Lord God's name
the coals of fire are heaped upon the head
of all whose gospel is the whip and flame,

age after age, the uninstructing dead.

# Elegy

Our hammock swung between Americas,
we miss you, Liberty. Che's
bullet-riddled body falls,
and those who cried the Republic must first die
to be reborn are dead,
the freeborn citizen's ballot in the head.
Still, everybody wants to go to bed
with Miss America. And, if there's no bread,
let them eat cherry pie.

But the old choice of running, howling, wounded
wolf-deep in her woods,
while the white papers snow on
genocide is gone;
no face can hide
its public, private pain,
wincing, already statued.

Some splintered arrowhead lodged in her brain
sets the black singer howling in his bear trap,
shines young eyes with the brightness of the mad,
tires the old with her residual sadness;
and yearly lilacs in her dooryards bloom,
and the cherry orchard's surf
blinds Washington and whispers
to the assassin in his furnished room
of an ideal America, whose flickering screens
show, in slow herds, the ghosts of the Cheyennes

scuffling across the staked and wired plains
with whispering, rag-bound feet,

while the farm couple framed in their Gothic door
like Calvin's saints, waspish, pragmatic, poor,
gripping the devil's pitchfork
stare rigidly towards the immortal wheat.

*6 June 1968*

## Postcards

. . . the chilling blast
of a vault opening,
the iron light deflected from a shield,
the ringing reticence of marble boulevards,
the cool of autumn's air-conditioning.

The earnest, tilted face of President Johnson
wincing with concern,
and only blocks away, addresses me
directly from the console TV,
lined, habituated to crisis:
problems of space,
our child's wish for the moon,

while bombs of sumac burst below my window
and the live oaks catch fire,
and saffron beeches, gay
as a Buddhist's robes,
charred,
drop their rags, naked.

## II / MAYARO

here, the season's dead;
the bleached beach-huts, the summer bungalows boarded,
their eyes sealed from devilish sand,
their deck chairs mired in dunes.
Almond leaves rake the dead terrace.

THE ATLANTIS BEACH HOTEL
hoards two lost souls,
its population vanished without trace

except where its fabled shore
is littered with the puffed, violet
prophylactics of Portuguese-man-o'-war.

## Blues

Those five or six young guys
hunched on the stoop
that oven-hot summer night
whistled me over. Nice
and friendly. So, I stop.
MacDougal or Christopher
Street in chains of light.

A summer festival. Or some
saint's. I wasn't too far from
home, but not too bright
for a nigger, and not too dark.
I figured we were all
one, wop, nigger, jew,
besides, this wasn't Central Park.
I'm coming on too strong? You figure
right! They beat this yellow nigger
black and blue.

Yeah. During all this, scared
in case one used a knife,
I hung my olive-green, just bought
sports coat on a fire-plug.
I did nothing. They fought
each other, really. Life
gives them a few kicks,
that's all. The spades, the spicks.

My face smashed in, my bloody mug
pouring, my olive-branch jacket saved
from cuts and tears,
I crawled four flights upstairs.
Sprawled in the gutter, I
remember a few watchers waved
loudly, and one kid's mother shouting
like 'Jackie' or 'Terry,'
'Now that's enough!'
It's nothing really.
They don't get enough love.

You know they wouldn't kill
you. Just playing rough,
like young America will.
Still, it taught me something
about love. If it's so tough,
forget it.

# *Air*

The unheard, omnivorous
jaws of this rain forest
not merely devour all,
but allow nothing vain;
they never rest,
grinding their disavowal
of human pain.

Long, long before us,
those hot jaws like an oven
steaming, were open
to genocide; they devoured
two minor yellow races, and
half of a black;
in the word made flesh of God
all entered that gross, un-
discriminating stomach;

the forest is unconverted,
because that shell-like noise
which roars like silence, or
ocean's surpliced choirs

entering its nave, to a censer
of swung mist, is not
the rustling of prayer
but nothing; milling air,
a faith, infested cannibal,
which eats gods, which devoured
the god-refusing Carib, petal
by golden petal, then forgot,
and the Arawak
who leaves not the lightest fern-trace
of his fossil to be cultured
by black rock,

but only the rusting cries
of a rainbird, like a hoarse
warrior summoning his race
from vaporous air
between this mountain ridge
and the vague sea
where the lost exodus
of corials sunk without trace—

there is too much nothing here.

## Guyana

**I**

The surveyor straightens from his theodolite.
'Spirit-level,' he scrawls, and instantly
the ciphers staggering down their columns
are soldier ants, their panic radiating in the shadow
of a new god arriving over Aztec anthills.

The sun has sucked his brain pith-dry.
His vision whirls with dervishes, he is dust.
Like an archaic photographer, hooded in shade,
he crouches, screwing a continent to his eye.

The vault that balances on a grass blade,
the nerve-cracked ground too close for the word 'measureless,'
for the lost concept, 'man,'
revolve too slowly for the fob-watch of his world,
for the tidal markings of the five-year plan.

Ant-sized to God, god to an ant's eyes,
shouldering science he begins to tread
himself, a world that must be measured in three days.

The frothing shallows of the river,
the forest so distant that it tires of blue,
the merciless idiocy of green, green . . .

a shape dilates towards him through the haze.

## II / THE BUSH

Together they walked through a thickness pinned with birds
silent as rags, grackles and flycatchers mostly,
shaking words from their heads.

their beaks aimed at one target, the clotting sun.
Tight, with the tension of arrows.

Dark climbed their knees until their heads were dark,
The wind, wave-muscled, kept its steady mowing.
Thoughts fell from him like leaves.

He followed, that was all,
his mind, one step behind,
pacing the poem, going where it was going.

## III / THE WHITE TOWN

'Man, all the men in that damned country mad!'
There was the joke on W. and Mayakovsky.
There was the charred bush of a man found in the morning,
there was the burgher's glare of whitewashed houses
outstaring guilt,
                    there was the anthropologist
dropping on soft pads from the thorn branches
to the first stance hearing the vowels
fur in his throat the hoarse
pebbles of consonants rattling his parched gullet,
there was the poet howling in vines of syntax
and the surveyor
dumbstruck by a stone;
                        at noon, the ferment
of white air, lilies and canal water
heavy as bush rum, then amber
saddening twilights without ice.
A fist should smash the glare of skylight open.
In the asylum the prisoners slept like snakes,
their eyes wide open.
                    They wait.

All of us wait.

## IV / THE FALLS

Their barrelling roar would open like a white oven
for him,
who was a spirit now, who could not burn or drown.

Surely in that 'smoke that thundered' there was a door—
but the noise boiled to the traffic of a white town
of bicycles, pigeons, bells, smoke, trains at the rush hour

revolving to this roar.
He was a flower,
weightless. He would float down.

## v / A MAP OF THE CONTINENT

The lexicographer in his cell records the life and death
        of books;
the naked buck waits at the edge of the world.

One hefts a pen, the other a bone spear;
between them curls a map,
between them curl the vigorous, rotting leaves,

shelves forested with titles, trunks that wait for names—
it pierces knowledge, the spear-flash!
the fish thrashing green air
on a pen's hook,

above the falls reciting its single flower.

The lexicographer's lizard eyes are curled
in sleep. The Amazonian Indian enters them.

Between the Rupununi and Borges,
between the fallen pen-tip and the spearhead
thunders, thickens and shimmers the one age of the world.

75

## VI/A GEORGETOWN JOURNAL

Begun, with its own impulse of destruction,
this elegy that chokes its canals
like the idle, rotting lilies of this frontier,
its lines that rust, however shiningly they thrust forward,
    like the elementary railway
besieging the whitewashed city
that reminds the poet on his balcony of thunder.

Begun, with a brown heron,
like the one I named for an actor,
its emblem answering a question with a question:
"What bird is that,
whose is that woman,
what will become of their country?"

If the neck of the heron is condemned to its question,
if the woman is silent,
and if, at the most appropriate hour
of a rose-scrim twilight budding with onion domes
like the gaze of clerkish guerrillas hazed by an epoch,
if nothing comes,
if no one ever escapes,
if the shoreline longs sadly for spires,
there is nothing left for us
but to make these coarse lilies lotuses,
for filth to contemplate its own reflection.

Cycle bells startle the pigeons.
The air has been cleared of hawks,
and the bourgeois gurgling like canals
reminisce over carrion.

Spires walk the sea-wall.

The wind unwraps them to wires.
They recede, skeletal, skeletal,
the streets have grown ordinary as heroes.

And the prose of polemics grows, spreading lianas of syntax
for the rootless surveyor,
the thunderous falls have been measured,
the thickening girth of the continent has been buttoned
till a man knows his weight to the stone,
his worth to the inch,
yet imagines he hears in his hair
the rain horses crossing savannahs
and his pores prickle like water.

The towns are clogged at their edges,
a glutinous dialect chokes the slum's canals,
and the white, finical houses
lift their lace skirts, stepping over the creeks.

Hawsers have lifted the country on delicate ankles.

The dead face of an orator revolves by lamplight,
the glazed scar itches for blood.

The girl waits in the wings, heron-still;
she will rise to the roar of the playhouse
its applauding cataract,

and the train rusts, travelling to a few sad sparks,
and the muck, and the tins, and the sogged placards choke
the sad, motionless green of the canals.

*ii*

So, safest, I had unimagined time;
thus we forget our element
like a fish that gasps with surprise on the nib of a hook.

There was always death,
but that came in the cheapest pricklings,
in old songs, in the amazed fading of letters,
in the change in one's penmanship:
how an l wavers like a single lily shaken
by a stone, how an r reaches rightly, to touch
some vertical end,

and at startling moments, the rattle of a kite
on a pluperfect sky.
Now words like 'azure,' for instance, suddenly touch,

such homilies as 'infinite' momentarily burn,
and for these lined eyes to widen
the heart, when to have written 'heart'
was to know a particular spasm—
how an old rock could spout such crystalline gibberish
amuses me, like the exact dancing of machines.

Nothing could turn my head, not the night moth,
like a nun beating her prison, but now pain comes
where I least expect it:
in the hissing of bicycle tires on drizzled asphalt,
in the ambush of little infinities
as supple with longing as the word 'horizon.'
Sad is the felon's love for the scratched wall,
beautiful the exhaustion of old towels,
and the patience of dented saucepans
seems mortally comic.

All these predictions do not disappoint but bring us nearer.
They uphold history like a glass of water.
If the poem begins to shrivel
I no longer distend my heart,
for I know how profound is the folding of a napkin
by a woman whose hair will go white,
age, that says more than an ocean,
I know how final is the straightening of a sheet
between lovers who have never lain, the heart-breaking curve

of a woman, her back bent, concerned
with the finical precisions of farewell.

*iii*

And there I entered your green, sibilant Russias,
those canes that like wheat must blacken after harvest,
and I honoured your dead, those few
arranged in postures for your great elegies,
who are what they were, not heroes, merely men.

The age will know its own name when it comes,
as love will find its breath softly expelling
"was I like this?"
with the same care, the precise exhilaration
with which the heron's foot pronounces 'earth.'

What if impulsive, delicate bird,
one instinct made you rise
out of this life, into another's,
then from another's, circling to your own?
You are folded in my eyes,
whose irises will open
to a white sky with bird and woman gone.

## Che

In this dark-grained news-photograph, whose glare
is rigidly composed as Caravaggio's,
the corpse glows candle-white on its cold altar—

its stone Bolivian Indian butcher's slab-
stare till its waxen flesh begins to harden
to marble, to veined, white Andean iron;
from your own fear, *cabrón*, its pallor grows;

it stumbled from your doubt, and for your pardon
burnt in brown trash, far from the embalming snows.

## Negatives

A newsclip; the invasion of Biafra:
black corpses wrapped in sunlight
sprawled on the white glare entering what's its name—
the central city?
                Someone who's white
illuminates the news behind the news,
his eyes flash with, perhaps, pity:
"The Ibos, you see, are like the Jews,
very much the situation in Hitler's Germany,
I mean the Hausas' resentment." I try to see.

I never knew you Christopher Okigbo,
I saw you when an actor screamed "The tribes!
The tribes!" I catch
the guttering, flare-lit
faces of Ibos,
stuttering, bug-eyed
prisoners of some drumhead tribunal.

The soldiers' helmeted shadows
could have been white, and yours
one of those sun-wrapped bodies on the white road
entering . . . the tribes, the tribes, their shame—
that central city, Christ, what is its name?

# Landfall, Grenada

[FOR ROBERT HEAD, MARINER]

Where you are rigidly anchored,
the groundswell of blue foothills, the blown canes
surging to cumuli cannot be heard;
like the slow, seamless ocean,
one motion folds the grass where you were lowered,
and the tiered sea
whose grandeurs you detested
climbs out of sound.

Its moods held no mythology
for you, it was a working-place
of tonnage and ruled stars;
you chose your landfall with a mariner's
casual certainty,
calm as that race
into whose heart you harboured;
your death was a log's entry,
your suffering held the strenuous
reticence of those
whose rites are never public,
hating to impose, to offend.
Deep friend, teach me to learn
such ease, such landfall going,
such mocking tolerance of those
neat, gravestone elegies
that rhyme our end.

# Homecoming: Anse La Raye

[FOR GARTH ST. OMER]

Whatever else we learned
at school, like solemn Afro-Greeks eager for grades,
of Helen and the shades
of borrowed ancestors,
there are no rites
for those who have returned,
only, when her looms fade,
drilled in our skulls, the doom-
surge-haunted nights,
only this well-known passage

under the coconuts' salt-rusted
swords, these rotted
leathery sea-grape leaves,
the seacrabs' brittle helmets, and
this barbecue of branches, like the ribs
of sacrificial oxen on scorched sand;
only this fish-gut reeking beach
whose frigates tack like buzzards overhead,
whose spindly, sugar-headed children race
pelting up from the shallows
because your clothes,
your posture
seem a tourist's.
They swarm like flies
round your heart's sore.

Suffer them to come,

entering your needle's eye,
knowing whether they live or die,
what others make of life will pass them by
like that far silvery freighter
threading the horizon like a toy;
for once, like them,
you wanted no career
but this sheer light, this clear,
infinite, boring, paradisal sea,
but hoped it would mean something to declare
today, I am your poet, yours,
all this you knew,
but never guessed you'd come
to know there are homecomings without home.

You give them nothing.
Their curses melt in air.
The black cliffs scowl,
the ocean sucks its teeth,
like that dugout canoe
a drifting petal fallen in a cup,
with nothing but its image,
you sway, reflecting nothing.
The freighter's silvery ghost
is gone, the children gone.
Dazed by the sun
you trudge back to the village
past the white, salty esplanade

under whose palms, dead
fishermen move their draughts in shade,
crossing, eating their islands,
and one, with a politician's
ignorant, sweet smile, nods,
as if all fate
swayed in his lifted hand.

# D'Aubaignan

[FOR GRACE AUGUSTIN]

Here, cries the child, the river's mirror drowned me!
Smiling at first, it went
too fast, viciously cold.
It is so with rivers and friends.
I was a hand stroking a burnished serpent.
Ten or eleven; heaven
was nearer; the yellowing, old estate house crumbled like cake
stencilled with fern-prints, veiled in mosquito nets;
after the virgin lamp's light paled
there were moths dead by morning and moths
staggering through the breaking gauze
of vapour, water-logged as the souls
of schoolboys climbing from old water-holes.
His thin ghost, doubtless, coils
from the mist where he would gaze
the last time on his lack of sin,
the worst: to outlast his father
to live till he could write
lines finer than his own.
Burdened with both worlds' weight
he should have sunk like a stone.

Now, such ambition thins
like mist, but not my terror,
my knowledge of rivers and friends;
no heaven is ruled as neat
as those blue copybooks in which he wrote
those lines which never held

him, as he yelled,
"Father, Father, I'll drown!"
I am used to those cries,
I have watched him go down
coldly, a smiling coward,
envying him what is called the 'easiest death,'
in coiling glass that steams when I have showered,
I watch his father with a drowned child's eyes.

## The River

was one, once;
reduced by circumstance
the Council tends it. Once

it could roar through town,
foul-mouthed, brown-muscled, brazenly
drunk, a raucous country-bookie,

but lately it has grown
too footloose for this settlement
of shacks, rechristened a city;

its strength wasted on gutters,
it never understood the age,
what progress meant,

so its clear, brown integument
shrivelled, its tongue stutters
through the official language,

it surrenders its gutturals
to the stern, stone Victorian bridge;
reclaimed, it dies a little

daily, it crawls towards a sea
curdled with oil-slick, its force
thins like the peasantry,

it idles like those resinous
wrinkled woodsmen, the country
reek still on them, hoarse

with municipal argument,
who, falling suddenly silent
on wire-bright afternoons, reflect

on mornings when a torrent
roared down their gorges, and
no one gave a damn what the words meant.

## To the Hotel Saint Antoine

At dawn, dead-tired from dancing in the streets,
we fell on its white, wooden rooms to rest
till the next day's parades;

indigo darkness thinned, the north-east trades,
wind I'd forgotten, like a beast,
foraged its thicket.

I tracked its trough downhill by the leaves churn,
the power it embodied visible
as I, who had returned, a voluble ghost,

as that dead friend, or the first love I lost,
but whether in grief or rage its branches tossed,
joy next day shook the wretched, flag-girt town.

Now, back in our own house, stirred by that noise,
which while you slept, pawed at our hotel windows,
I watch how, from your trunk, our daughter grows

within that casual mimicry of death,
of Margaret branching to Elizabeth,
and envy the wind's power to rejoice

that all are wrapped within earth's winding sheet,
sailing with her, in these cloud-coloured shrouds;
that the air is at war, that every prism

of nothing renews its Thermopylae,
the caged inch netted with furies. Nothing consumes.
A fistful of home earth fumes

with the rose of a girl, the grass is
the hair of some skull, a razor
opens the grave's wrist.

Dead and dreaming exchange pities.
Huddled, till dawn in wooden, echoing rooms,
they share their different and indifferent cities.

## Goodnight Ladies,
## Goodnight Sweet Ladies . . .

Even there the chasm yawns, between twin bed
and boredom; like lilies her mind drifts
backwards, oh, towards some lost romance; his
careers rakehell through red, flickering stews
through every brothel of imagination
where lewd, insatiable harlots are spread
white, or a black, tangled harem dances.
This is the last of nature's wedding gifts.
Celibates may rise in righteous indignation;
only to newlyweds will this be news.

## The Cell

Woman, wasp-waisted, then wasp-tongued,
hissing to enemies how much I wronged
you, how just you were! We would secrete
in every cell, each separate room
the stink and stigma of my name,
and nothing, not the bedside flame
charring in coils by the child's net
could calm your virulent regret
or my last effort, lust. You cried
against the poison charged inside
his flesh and yours, I prayed we'd clasp
each other fierce as coupling wasps,
as bitter-sweet it seemed to flesh
to die in self-stung martyrdom,
for mind and body bitten black
with shame to take its poison back,
to build, even in hate, a home,
in that hexagonal lace mesh
shuddering, exchanging venom.

# Saturday Morning at the Flying Club

Jets like smoke-bleeding dragons scarved the air
on the sun's flashing lance-point, but for us,
crossing that breezy headland,
the small planes purred like pigeons in a square,
one strutted waddling almost to my hand;
at every roar
the sky shut trundling its iron door,
but we were free,
locked in each other's hands,
freer than lovers with their wives and husbands.

Now memory circles there,
a pigeon homing on a detail, a hawk
wheeling to fasten on some phrase
gripping that field of flowers whose name you knew,
that whole harbour and headland
hazing from distance like your eyes,
grey, or grey-blue,
already, then, it knew
the lancings of this poem,
its lines, its outlines, they were there
in the tiered waves,
the scarves and scallops of their virginal elation,
their joy shot higher,
and that charged silhouette of golden hair
against its yellow field, St. Elmo's fire!

Joy balanced on its needle point of noon!

one needle stroke past twelve, it whirled
like the jets' roar
on its inflexible point of aerial law,
the pigeon homing, the hawk remarrying
the ringed wrist. O heart and sky
inflexible in their fidelity!
Ah, patience, tiring
of a pain's pin glint into memory.

## Star

If, in the light of things, you fade
real, yet wanly withdrawn
to our determined and appropriate
distance, like the moon left on
all night among the leaves, may
you invisibly delight this house,
O star, doubly compassionate, who came
too soon for twilight, too late
for dawn, may your pale flame
direct the worst in us
through chaos
with the passion of
plain day.

## Cold Spring Harbour

From feather-stuffed bolsters of cloud
falling on casual linen
the small shrieks soundlessly float.
The woods are lint-wreathed. Dawn
crackles like foil to the rake
of a field mouse nibbling, nibbling
its icing. The world is unwrapped
in cotton and you would tread wool
if you opened, quietly, whitely,
this door, like an old Christmas card
turned by a child's dark hand, did
he know it was dark then,
the magical brittle branches, the white house
collared in fur, the white world of men,
its bleeding gules and its berry drops?

Two prancing, immobile white ponies
no bigger than mice pulled a carriage
across soundless hillocks of cotton;
bells hasped to their necks didn't tinkle
though you begged God to touch them to life,
some white-haired old God who'd forgotten
or no longer trusted his miracles.
What urges you now towards this white,
snow-whipped woods is not memory
of that dark child's toys, not the card
of a season, forever foreign, that went
over its ridges like a silent

sleigh. That was a child's sorrow, this is
child's play, through which you cannot go,
dumbstruck at an open door,
stunned, fearing the strange violation
(because you are missing your children)
of perfect snow.

## In the Kitchen

She feels her eyelids narrowing
on one fierce, drifting speck
that splinters to a sorrowing
hymn of midges, or to mercurial
angels dancing on a pinhead,
she finds, week after week,
more friends among the dead;
they were not all angels; all
this is is the glittering note
of a tinpenny flute
of a houseboy in the kitchen,
with 'when the saints, the saints'
stuck in its throat.

And the phrase note by note,
and one by one the dead,
and the grass, blade by blade,
begins to be remembered;
each hair upon that head
mother, is numbered, numbered;
numbered the tan, charcoal kitten's
wisps of fur; the mirror hazes
as your own vision brightens,
as the saints, one by one,
take their accustomed places.

O their faint, golden congregations
mother! O their ballooning, zephyr-

bugling cheeks, their shining patience!
When I could really kneel,
not stew in the imagination's
drab adulteries. I wait
each week like you, my own breath
bated, my faith stuck in my throat,
for father to come down. Husband,
take up your young wife's hand,
embrace this woman who has waited
since her first death for this.

## Love in the Valley

The sun goes slowly blind.
It is this mountain, shrouding
the valley of the shadow,

widening like amnesia
evening dims the mind.
I shake my head in darkness,

it is a tree branched with cries,
a trash-can full of print.
Now, through the reddening squint

of leaves leaden as eyes,
a skein of drifting hair
like a twig, fallen on snow,

branches the blank pages.
I bring it close, and stare
in slow vertiginous darkness,

and now I drift elsewhere,
through hostile images
of white and black, and look,

like a thaw-sniffing stallion, the head
of Pasternak emerges with its forelock,
his sinewy wrist a fetlock

pawing the frozen spring,
till his own hand has frozen
on the white page, heavy.

I ride through a white childhood
whose pines glittered with bracelets,
when I heard wolves, feared the black wood,

every wrist-aching brook
and the ice maiden
in Hawthorne's fairy book.

The hair melts into dark,
a question mark that led
where the untethered mind

strayed from its first track;
now Hardy's sombre head
upon which hailstorms broke

looms, like a weeping rock,
like wind, the tresses drift
and their familiar trace

tingles across the face
with light lashes.
I knew the depth of whiteness,

I feared the numbing kiss
of those women of winter,
Bathsheba, Lara, Tess,

whose tragedy made less
of life, whose love was more
than love of literature.

# Gib Hall Revisited

[FOR WAYNE BROWN]

In those raft-planked bunkhouses christened Gibraltar
by World War II DPs, as if they knew
we'd drift like displaced persons too, but even further
from Europe than the homesick, homeless Jew
to that new world already tagged and named
what could we add but rhetoric, who had
less faith than the prophetically maimed?
A generation late, I sadden
that the brightest ones were sold
to a system, like those stars to Arabic,
that our first Christmas riots hid the sick
envy of Caliban for our master's gown
of ersatz ermine; fearing the fission
of red gown to black, of fire to ash, we moved
across dry campus grass in separate flames,
cold, unlit candles looking for one vision,
our red gowns wilted like poinsettia.
Now, in the black, processioned and approved,
old hands acknowledge us by our first names,
the red gowns mark the same betrayals down.

## Nearing Forty

[FOR JOHN FIGUEROA]

The irregular combination of fanciful invention may delight awhile by that novelty of which the common satiety
of life sends us all in quest. But the pleasures of sudden
wonder are soon exhausted and the mind can only repose
on the stability of truth . . .

SAMUEL JOHNSON

Insomniac since four, hearing this narrow,
rigidly-metred, early-rising rain
recounting, as its coolness numbs the marrow,
that I am nearing forty, nearer the weak
vision thickening to a frosted pane,
nearer the day when I may judge my work
by the bleak modesty of middle-age
as a false dawn, fireless and average,
which would be just, because your life bled for
the household truth, the style past metaphor
that finds its parallel however wretched
in simple, shining lines, in pages stretched
plain as a bleaching bedsheet under a guttering rainspout, glad for the sputter
of occasional insight; you who foresaw
ambition as a searing meteor
will fumble a damp match, and smiling, settle
for the dry wheezing of a dented kettle,
for vision narrower than a louvre's gap,
then watching your leaves thin, recall how deep
prodigious cynicism plants its seed,
gauges our seasons by this year's end rain

which, as greenhorns at school, we'd
call conventional for convectional;
or you will rise and set your lines to work
with sadder joy but steadier elation,
until the night when you can really sleep,
measuring how imagination
ebbs, conventional as any water-clerk
who weighs the force of lightly-falling rain,
which, as the new moon moves it, does its work
even when it seems to weep.

## The Walk

After hard rain the eaves repeat their beads,
those trees exhale your doubt like mantled tapers,
drop after drop, like a child's abacus
beads of cold sweat file from high tension wires,

pray for us, pray for this house, borrow your neighbour's
faith, pray for this brain that tires,
and loses faith in the great books it reads;
after a day spent prone, haemorrhaging poems,

each phrase peeled from the flesh in bandages,
arise, stroll on under a sky
sodden as kitchen laundry,

while the cats yawn behind their window frames,
lions in cages of their choice,
no further though, than your last neighbour's gates
figured with pearl. How terrible is your own

fidelity, O heart, O rose of iron!
When was your work more like a housemaid's novel,
some drenched soap-opera which gets
closer than yours to life? Only the pain,

the pain is real. Here's your life's end,
a clump of bamboos whose clenched
fist loosens its flowers, a track
that hisses through the rain-drenched

grove: abandon all, the work,
the pain of a short life. Startled, you move;
your house, a lion rising, paws you back.

## Hic Jacet

### I

They'll keep on asking, why did you remain?
Not for the applauding rain
of hoarse and hungry thousands at whose centre
the politician opens like a poisonous flower,
not for the homecoming lecturer
gripping his lectern like a witness, ready to explain
the root's fixation with earth,
nor for that new race of dung beetles, frock-coated, iridescent
crawling over the people.
Before the people became popular
he loved them.

Nor to spite some winter-bitten novelist
praised for his accuracy of phlegm,
but for something rooted, unwritten
that gave us its benediction,
its particular pain,
that may move its clouds from that mountain,
that is packing its bags on that fiction
of our greatness, which, like the homecoming rain,
veers to a newer sea.

### II

I loved them all, the names
of shingled, rusting towns, whose dawn

touches like metal,
I should have written poems on the Thames,
shivered through cities furred and cracked with ice,
spat, for their taste, in some barge-burdened river.

I I I

Convinced of the power of provincialism,
I yielded quietly my knowledge of the world
to a grey tub steaming with clouds of seraphim,
the angels and flags of the world,
and answer those who hiss, like steam, of exile,
this coarse soap-smelling truth:

I sought more power than you, more fame than yours,
I was more hermetic, I knew the commonweal,
I pretended subtly to lose myself in crowds
knowing my passage would alter their reflection,
I was that muscle shouldering the grass
through ordinary earth,
commoner than water I sank to lose my name,
this was my second birth.